Page deliberately left blank

SSAGE track

Authors!
Submit your article online with SAGE Track

SAGE Track is a web-based peer review and submission system powered by ScholarOne® Manuscripts

The entire process, from article submission to acceptance for publication is now handled online by the SAGE Track web site. 300 of our journals are now on SAGE Track, which has a graphical interface that will guide you through a simple and speedy submission with step-by-step prompts.

SAGE Track makes it easy to:

- Submit your articles online

- Submit revisions and resubmissions through automatic linking

- Track the progress of your article online

- Publish your research faster

SSAGE

VOLUME 666

JULY 2016

THE ANNALS

of The American Academy of Political
and Social Science

Undocumented Migration in a Global Economy

Special Editors:
KATHARINE M. DONATO
Vanderbilt University

DOUGLAS S. MASSEY
Princeton University

⑤SAGE

Los Angeles | London | New Delhi
Singapore | Washington DC | Melbourne

The American Academy of Political and Social Science

202 S. 36th Street, Annenberg School for Communication, University of Pennsylvania,
Philadelphia, PA 19104-3806; (215) 746-6500; (215) 573-2667 (fax); www.aapss.org

Origin and Purpose. The Academy was organized December 14, 1889, to promote the progress of political and social science, especially through publications and meetings. The Academy does not take sides in controverted questions, but seeks to gather and present reliable information to assist the public in forming an intelligent and accurate judgment.

Meetings. The Academy occasionally holds a meeting in the spring extending over two days.

Publications. THE ANNALS of The American Academy of Political and Social Science is the bimonthly publication of the Academy. Each issue contains articles on some prominent social or political problem, written at the invitation of the editors. These volumes constitute important reference works on the topics with which they deal, and they are extensively cited by authorities throughout the United States and abroad.

Subscriptions. THE ANNALS of The American Academy of Political and Social Science (ISSN 0002-7162) (J295) is published bimonthly—in January, March, May, July, September, and November—by SAGE Publications, 2455 Teller Road, Thousand Oaks, CA 91320. Periodicals postage paid at Thousand Oaks, California, and at additional mailing offices. POSTMASTER: Send address changes to The Annals of The American Academy of Political and Social Science, c/o SAGE Publications, 2455 Teller Road, Thousand Oaks, CA 91320. Institutions may subscribe to THE ANNALS at the annual rate: $1014 (clothbound, $1146). Individuals may subscribe to the ANNALS at the annual rate: $118 (clothbound, $175). Single issues of THE ANNALS may be obtained by individuals for $37 each (clothbound, $50). Single issues of THE ANNALS have proven to be excellent supplementary texts for classroom use. Direct inquiries regarding adoptions to THE ANNALS c/o SAGE Publications (address below).

All correspondence concerning membership in the Academy, dues renewals, inquiries about membership status, and/or purchase of single issues of THE ANNALS should be sent to THE ANNALS c/o SAGE Publications, 2455 Teller Road, Thousand Oaks, CA 91320. Telephone: (800) 818-SAGE (7243) and (805) 499-0721; Fax/Order line: (805) 375-1700; e-mail: journals@sagepub.com. *Please note that orders under $30 must be prepaid.* For all customers outside the Americas, please visit http://www.sagepub.co.uk/customerCare.nav for information.

THE ANNALS

Editorial Office: 202 S. 36th Street, Philadelphia, PA 19104-3806
For information about individual and institutional subscriptions address:
SAGE Publications
2455 Teller Road
Thousand Oaks, CA 91320

For SAGE Publications: Peter Geraghty (Production) and Mimi Nguyen (Marketing)

From India and South Asia, write to:	From Europe, the Middle East, and Africa, write to:
SAGE PUBLICATIONS INDIA Pvt Ltd	SAGE PUBLICATIONS LTD
B-42 Panchsheel Enclave, P.O. Box 4109	1 Oliver's Yard, 55 City Road
New Delhi 110 017	London EC1Y 1SP
INDIA	UNITED KINGDOM

International Standard Serial Number ISSN 0002-7162
ISBN 978-1-5063-6244-1 (Vol. 666, 2016) paper
ISBN 978-1-5063-6243-4 (Vol. 666, 2016) cloth
First printing, July 2016

Please visit http://ann.sagepub.com and under the "More about this journal" menu on the right-hand side, click on the Abstracting/Indexing link to view a full list of databases in which this journal is indexed.

Information about membership rates, institutional subscriptions, and back issue prices may be found on the facing page.

Advertising. Current rates and specifications may be obtained by writing to The Annals Advertising and Promotion Manager at the Thousand Oaks office (address above). Acceptance of advertising in this journal in no way implies endorsement of the advertised product or service by SAGE or the journal's affiliated society(ies) or the journal editor(s). No endorsement is intended or implied. SAGE reserves the right to reject any advertising it deems as inappropriate for this journal.

Claims. Claims for undelivered copies must be made no later than six months following month of publication. The publisher will supply replacement issues when losses have been sustained in transit and when the reserve stock will permit.

Change of Address. Six weeks' advance notice must be given when notifying of change of address. Please send the old address label along with the new address to the SAGE office address above to ensure proper identification. Please specify the name of the journal.

THE ANNALS

OF THE AMERICAN ACADEMY OF
POLITICAL AND SOCIAL SCIENCE

Volume 666   July 2016

IN THIS ISSUE:

Undocumented Migration in a Global Economy

Special Editors: KATHARINE M. DONATO and DOUGLAS S. MASSEY

Twenty-First-Century Globalization and
  Illegal Migration .... *Katharine M. Donato and Douglas S. Massey*   7

The Challenge of Studying Undocumented Migration

The Potential and Limitations of Cross-Context Comparative Research
  on Migration...................................... *Fernando Riosmena*   28

Social Capital in Polish-German Migration Decision-Making: Complementing
  the Ethnosurvey with a Prospective View...... *Frank Kalter and Gisela Will*   46

How Representative Are Snowball Samples? Using the Ethnosurvey to Study
  Guatemala-U.S. Migration .... *David P. Lindstrom*   64

Undocumented Latinos in the United States

Double Disadvantage: Unauthorized Mexicans in the U.S.
  Labor Market.......... *Jorge Durand, Douglas S. Massey, and Karen A. Pren*   78

The Precarious Position of Latino Immigrants in the United States: A Comparative
  Analysis of Ethnosurvey Data .... *Douglas S. Massey*
                                          Jorge Durand, and Karen A. Pren   91

Shadow Labor: Work and Wages among Immigrant Hispanic Women in
  Durham, North Carolina .... *Chenoa A. Flippen*   110

The Departed: Deportations and Out-Migration among Latino Immigrants
  in North Carolina after the Great Recession .... *Emilio A. Parrado*
                                          and Chenoa A. Flippen   131

Undocumented Others: Bangladeshis, Africans, and Chinese

The Effects of Legal Status on Employment and Health Outcomes among Low-Skilled Chinese Immigrants in New York City. . . . . . . *Zai Liang and Bo Zhou* 150

Legal Status, Gender, and Labor Market Participation of Senegalese Migrants in France, Italy, and Spain. . . . . . *Erik R. Vickstrom and Amparo González-Ferrer* 164

Different but the Same: How Legal Status Affects International Migration from Bangladesh . . . . *Katharine M. Donato, Amanda R. Carrico, Blake Sisk, and Bhumika Piya* 203

FORTHCOMING

Elections in America
Special Editor: LARRY M. BARTELS

Briefing to the President: Failed Middle Eastern States and Countering Violent Extremism
Special Editors: RICHARD A. CLARKE, RAND BEERS, EMILIAN PAPADOPOULOS, and PAUL SALEM

Twenty-First-Century Globalization and Illegal Migration

By

KATHARINE M. DONATO
and
DOUGLAS S. MASSEY

Also labeled undocumented, irregular, and unauthorized migration, illegal migration places immigrants in tenuous legal circumstances with limited rights and protections. We argue that illegal migration emerged as a structural feature of the second era of capitalist globalization, which emerged in the late twentieth century and was characterized by international market integration. Unlike the first era of capitalist globalization (1800 to 1929), the second era sees countries limiting and controlling international migration and creating a global economy in which all markets are globalized except for labor and human capital, giving rise to the relatively new phenomenon of illegal migration. Yet despite rampant inequalities in wealth and income between nations, only 3.1 percent of all people lived outside their country of birth in 2010. We expect this to change: threat evasion is replacing opportunity seeking as a motivation for international migration because of climate change and rising levels of civil violence in the world's poorer nations. The potential for illegal migration is thus greater now than in the past, and more nations will be forced to grapple with growing populations in liminal legal statuses.

Keywords: illegal migration; globalization; unauthorized migration; undocumented migration; climate change; violence

Migration is a fundamental means of human adaption, commonly used both to avoid risks and access opportunities. *Homo sapiens* emerged in East Africa about 150,000 years ago and through migration settled the entire globe within a very short span of geological time, reaching East Asia and Australia about 50,000 years ago, Northern Europe about 40,000 years ago, the Americas about 12,000 years ago, and

Katharine M. Donato is a professor of sociology at Vanderbilt University. Her recent work examines the effects of environmental stress on out-migration from villages in southwestern Bangladesh. In 2015, she published (with Donna Gabaccia) Gender and International Migration: From the Slavery Era to the Global Age (Russell Sage Foundation).

Correspondence: Katharine.donato@vanderbilt.edu

DOI: 10.1177/0002716216653563

the most distant Pacific islands about 2,000 years ago (Oppenheimer 2003). No other organism has moved through space and time so widely or quickly. Humans are a migratory species. It is hardly surprising, therefore, that migration is being widely used by people today to adapt to the unequal distribution of risks and opportunities that prevail in the contemporary world.

Modern times have witnessed three eras of mass human migration, each associated with a period of global economic change. The era from 1500 to 1800 was one of European colonial expansion during which European powers colonized the Americas, Africa, and Asia and created a global mercantile economy based on trade, resource extraction, and the production of valuable commodities. Although European administrators, entrepreneurs, and settlers migrated outward to manage the political and economic affairs of their mercantile empires, the total size of the outflow was not large. By far the largest movement of people during this period was the involuntary transport of some 10 million slaves out of Africa to provide forced labor for European-owned mines and plantations (Klein 1999).

The second stage of mass migration unfolded between 1800 and 1929 and was driven by industrialization in Europe and its spread to a small set of settler nations overseas (O'Rourke and Williamson 1999). This was also the first era of global capitalism, when nearly 50 million people emigrated from the densely populated industrializing nations of Europe to sparsely populated industrializing nations in the Americas and Oceania, with roughly 60 percent going to the United States and the rest scattered mainly among Canada, Argentina, Brazil, Australia, and New Zealand (Massey 1988). This period of mass migration in the first era of global capitalism came to an abrupt halt with the First World War in August 1914, which destroyed massive amounts of land, labor, and capital and left the international order in tatters. Although economic growth, trade, and immigration revived somewhat during the 1920s, they were brought to a definitive end by the market crash of 1929 (Kershaw 2015).

We are currently in the midst of a second era of capitalist globalization (Williamson 2004). Its foundations were laid in the ashes of the Second World War, when the great global powers joined together to create a new set of multilateral institutions that could maintain peace while promoting global trade and investment. The United Nations was created to defuse conflicts and prevent world war, the World Bank to finance economic development, the International Monetary Fund to guarantee international liquidity, and the General Agreement

Douglas S. Massey is the Henry G. Bryant Professor of Sociology and Public Affairs at Princeton University, where he directs the Office of Population Research in addition to serving as codirector of the Mexican Migration Project.

NOTE: The first author thanks the U.S. Office of Naval Research (grant N00014-11-1-0683) for its generous support of a project that examines environment and migration, and Vanderbilt University's College of Arts and Science for its support of "The Ethnosurvey in Global Context," a conference held at Vanderbilt in January 2015. The second author thanks the MacArthur Foundation (grant 12-102305-000-CFP) and the National Institute of Child Health and Human Development (grants R01 HD035643 and P2C HD047879-11) for support of research included in this volume.

on Tariffs and Trade (GATT) to lower barriers to cross-border commerce. Over the course of successive rounds of the GATT, negotiations gradually removed obstacles to trade and investment, culminating in the creation of the World Trade Organization in 1995 (Stiglitz 2002).

This current wave of globalization proceeded slowly at first, as the economies of Europe and Japan were rebuilt after the war; but the pace of change accelerated after 1970 when the digital revolution advanced to create a new, knowledge-based economy. With China's turn toward the market in 1979 and the collapse of the Soviet Union in 1991, a truly global economy finally emerged and was firmly established by the beginning of the new century. Unlike the first era of globalization, however, the current era is plagued by a fundamental contradiction.

The Paradox of Twenty-First-Century Globalization

Although human migration is hardly new, undocumented, unauthorized, or illegal migration is a recent phenomenon. The current system of passports and visas dates only to 1920, when the newly formed League of Nations convened an international conference to establish standards for passports and guidelines for their use (Lloyd 2003). Thus, the first era of capitalist globalization unfolded before the current regime of restrictive migration had been established, and it was characterized by the relatively free movement of people across international borders. This openness left markets free to equilibrate transnationally. In addition to the globalization of markets for capital, land, goods, services, and commodities, the labor market was also free to equilibrate globally (Hatton and Williamson 1998). Although qualitative restrictions on population movements were implemented in some countries during the nineteenth century, these were weakly enforced, and strong numerical limits on immigration were not imposed anywhere until the 1920s.

Today, of course, no nation permits the free entry of immigrants. Indeed, all nations impose both qualitative and quantitative restrictions on international migration, thus constraining the globalization of markets for labor and human capital. This is the fundamental contradiction of postindustrial globalism: nations today seek to create and participate in a global market in which only some factors of production are mobile. This paradox has forced policymakers throughout the world into a Faustian bargain: international factor mobility is encouraged and facilitated only to the extent that the factors in question lack agency. Under the terms of this bargain, immigration must be restricted because labor and human capital are attached to people and people have agency.

The essence of the dilemma is well captured by the Swiss playwright Max Frisch's celebrated remark: "We asked for workers. We got people instead." As beings with agency, people are problematic. They have needs, make demands, and ask questions. They seek out others for romance and sex, often producing babies. If people originate from a foreign country, these exigencies become especially problematic. In this case, those providing labor and human capital bear divergent cultures, speak unfamiliar languages, have different values, and generally look at the world in seemingly odd ways, thus increasing the likelihood of misunderstanding and raising the risk of conflict. Foreign workers, in particular, may behave in strange ways that policymakers and the public find perplexing and threatening. And the greater the difference from natives in terms of culture, sociality, and appearance, the more societies perceive immigrants as threatening and believe they must be restricted and controlled.

In today's global economy, we generally observe three levels of international mobility. A very high level of mobility is accorded financial and physical capital, consumer goods, knowledge, information, commodities, and natural resources. Moderate mobility is permitted but regulated for those people who embody forms of capital that are valued and in demand, be it human, social, or cultural capital. Cross-border mobility is limited and tightly controlled, however, for people who lack a valued form of capital, whose principal contribution to economic production is the power of their own labor. As a result, the entry of skilled and highly educated workers linked to investment, trade, and production is permitted and sometimes even encouraged, whereas the entry of mere workers is tightly restricted.

In the twentieth century, the earliest efforts to limit the status of immigrants to that of workers and prevent their recognition as people took the form of "guest worker" programs arranged through international agreements that specified the number of migrants, the length of visits, the conditions of employment, and the end date of any approved period of wage labor. In the United States during the 1950s and early 1960s, for example, the Bracero Program annually imported hundreds of thousands of seasonal workers from Mexico. From the 1950s through the mid-1970s, Western European nations negotiated a series of treaties with nations in Southern Europe, the Middle East, and North Africa that arranged for the temporary entry of many thousands of guest workers to sustain the postwar economic boom in Western Europe. In each case, however, when policymakers attempted to curtail the programs in response to domestic political pressures and economic belt tightening, they discovered that the workers were, in fact, people who often wished to stay, marry, raise families, and participate in their host society as citizens rather than as guests.

Among industrial countries, the United States was first to attempt to curtail its postwar guest worker program. At the end of 1964, the U.S. Congress acted unilaterally to terminate the Bracero Program despite objections from Mexico. Although migrant inflows from Mexico fell abruptly in the immediate aftermath of the program's demise, they quickly resumed without authorization and, by the end of the 1970s, had returned to the peak volumes observed prior to 1964 (Massey and Pren 2012). The rise of undocumented migration gave rise to a new Latino threat narrative in public discourse, since, as "illegal aliens," migrants were by definition "criminals" and "lawbreakers" who menaced American society and had to be stopped (Chavez 2001, 2008), leading to a new politics of immigration restriction and border control that after 1986 resulted in the militarization of the Mexico–U.S. border (Massey, Durand, and Pren 2014).

Through 1985, however, the unauthorized migration that emerged in response to the end of the Bracero Program was heavily circular, with 85 percent of all illegal entries offset by departures. Unfortunately, after 1986, the rising tide of border enforcement dramatically increased the costs and risks of border crossing, prompting migrants to cease circulating—not by remaining in Mexico but by remaining in the United States after absorbing the rising costs and risks at the border (Massey, Durand, and Pren 2015). In addition, the concentration of enforcement resources at the busiest crossing point in San Diego diverted flows away from California, through the Sonoran desert, into Arizona, and on to new destinations throughout the United States (Massey, Durand, and Malone 2002). Border militarization transformed what had been a circular flow of male workers going to three states into a settled population of immigrant families living in fifty states (Massey, Durand, and Pren 2016).

The Mexico–U.S. case exemplifies well the fundamental contradictions and paradoxes of the current era of globalization. In 1994, Mexico and the United States joined, with Canada, to sign the North American Free Trade Agreement (NAFTA), which lowered barriers for cross-border movements of capital, goods, services, and information in an effort to create an integrated North American economy. In that same year, however, the United States launched Operation Gatekeeper in San Diego, an all-out militarization of the busiest sector of the Mexico–U.S. border, in an effort to curtail undocumented migration. The build-up of enforcement resources along the border failed to achieve its stated goal and instead increased the net volume of unauthorized migration, accelerating undoc-umented population growth and spreading migrants more widely throughout the nation (Massey, Durand, and Malone 2002).

During the 1980s, the United States also intervened politically and militarily in Central America to contain Communism in the wake of the 1979 Sandinista Revolution in Nicaragua, yielding a period of intense civil violence, guerilla war-fare, and economic dislocation that displaced people throughout the region. Although those fleeing Nicaragua were welcomed in the United States as refu-gees from communist tyranny, refugees from El Salvador, Guatemala, and Honduras had the misfortune of fleeing right-wing regimes allied with the United States, leading to their label as "economic" rather than "political" migrants (Lundquist and Massey 2005; Massey, Durand, and Pren 2014). As a result, many Central Americans entered without authorization. From 1988 to 2008, the total number of unauthorized residents of the United States grew from 2 million to 12 million, the largest resident population lacking social, economic, and political rights since the end of slavery (Massey 2013). Of the approximately 12 million unauthorized residents, roughly 60 percent were Mexicans and 15 percent Central Americans.

Nations in Western Europe underwent a similar experience when they sought to end their guest worker programs in the wake of the 1973 economic recession. As in the United States, European nations had negotiated binational labor agree-ments with various source countries to fulfill what were seen as temporary worker shortages in certain industries (Martin 1980). Policymakers viewed tem-porary migrants as a flexible labor supply that could be imported during periods of high demand and sent home when demand faltered. Few efforts were made to integrate them into the host societies. Instead, they were separated from native populations and sequestered in poor neighborhoods or employer-provided barracks and initially granted little or no access to social welfare benefits, labor mobility, or family reunification privileges (Castles and Kosack 1973). By 1973, a total of 6.7 million foreigners were employed throughout Western Europe, where they composed about one-seventh of the total labor force (Berger and Mohr 1975).

When the oil boycott of 1973 brought on a worldwide economic recession, nations throughout Europe sought to end temporary worker recruitment and initiate the repatriation of their "guests." Although guest worker populations in Western Europe indeed fell by around 400,000 in 1974 and 200,000 in 1975, thereafter the number of foreign workers stabilized and the total number of foreign residents began to grow. Instead of returning home, guest workers dug in and stayed for fear of not being able to reenter. As their stays proceeded, they began to apply for the entry of family members from abroad. In West Germany, for example, the foreign workforce dropped by 500,000 persons between 1973 and 1975, but the total foreign population grew by 100,000 (Reichert and Massey 1982). Former guests began to demand the rights of citizens and took advantage of the legal resources of the liberal democracies to bring in dependents and other relatives. In response, immigration policies tightened and enforcement increased along the EU's external borders, giving rise to new inflows of undocumented migrants.

In the ensuing decades, foreign-born percentages rose throughout Europe, even as the EU expanded to incorporate nations in Southern and Eastern Europe and passage of the 1985 Schengen Agreement guaranteed free cross-border mobility within the EU itself. As various countries were incorporated into the EU, they shifted from the exportation to the importation of labor and became countries of immigration, inevitably producing illegal migrants and making undocumented migration a continent-wide phenomenon.

Table 1 draws on the Clandestino Project (2016) and presents estimates of national, foreign, and undocumented populations in selected EU countries. The figures were compiled on the eve of the Great Recession in 2008 and are estimated with varying degrees of reliability, so they should not necessarily be taken as accurate indicators. For our purposes, we picked the central (median) estimate with the highest quality available rating in the year specified. Given the surge of refugees into Europe between 2014 and 2016, these data are clearly outdated but are presented here to indicate the rough size of immigrant populations in nations that for centuries had been zones of emigration and to reveal the spread of undocumented migration across the European continent early in the twenty-first century.

Foreign populations are generally larger in Western than Eastern Europe, with notably large totals in Germany (6.7 million), Spain (5.5 million), France (3.5 million), Britain (3.4 million), and Italy (2.7 million). Whereas Germany, France, and Britain became labor-importing nations early in the postwar period, Italy and Spain began as labor exporters and only became countries of immigration as the EU consolidated and expanded (Durand and Massey 2010; Martin and Zucher 2008). In proportional terms, immigrants constitute the largest shares of the population in Spain (10 percent), followed by Austria (9.9 percent), Germany (8.2 percent), Greece (7.9 percent), Britain (5.7 percent), and France

TABLE 1

Estimates of National, Foreign, and Undocumented Populations
(in thousands) within Selected European Nations

	Total Population	Foreign Population	Foreign Percentage	Undocu-mented Population	Foreign Undocu-mented Percentage
Austria (2007)	8,299	826	9.9	43	5.2
Britain (2006)	60,393	3,425	5.7	618	18.0
Czech Republic (2006)	10,251	258	2.5	80	30.9
France (2006)	62,999	3,510	5.6	300	8.5
Germany (2007)	82,315	6,745	8.2	325	4.8
Greece (2006)	11,125	844	7.9	190	21.5
Hungary (2007)	10,066	168	1.7	40	23.8
Italy (2006)	58,752	2,671	4.5	650	24.3
Netherlands (2007)	16,358	682	4.1	88	12.9
Poland (2007)	38,125	55	0.1	50	91.1
Slovakia (2007)	5,394	32	0.6	15	46.7
Spain (2007)	44,475	5,474	10.0	305	6.6

SOURCE: Clandestino Project (2016).

(5.6 percent). Foreign populations are small in both absolute and relative terms in newer EU nations such as the Czech Republic, Greece, Hungary, Poland, and Slovakia. In all cases, however, the figures in Table 1 likely understate the size of the immigrant population, since the figures are based on tallies of foreign nationals rather than all persons born abroad, which is the standard means of defining immigrants in the United States.

Among European nations, former imperial powers generally receive the bulk of their immigrants from ex-colonies. Thus, immigrants to France hail from North Africa, sub-Saharan Africa, and Indochina; those to Britain from South Asia, Africa, and the Caribbean; those to the Netherlands from Indonesia and Suriname; and those to Spain from North Africa and Latin America. Having lost its colonies after the First World War, Germany recruited most of its migrants as guest workers from nations in the Middle East, especially Turkey, but also received immigrants from the Balkans and more recently from Eastern Europe. In the past several years, of course, Greece, Italy, Hungary, Austria, and Germany have emerged as major conduits and destinations for migrants fleeing civil violence, political turmoil, and economic dislocation in the Middle East and North Africa.

All the nations in Table 1 have come to house undocumented populations. Estimates show the greatest numbers in Italy (650,000), Britain (618,000), Germany (325,000), Spain (305,000), and France (300,000). Although they are probably much less reliable, the numbers are much smaller in Eastern Europe, but in some cases the percentage of undocumented among all foreigners appears to be quite large, as in Poland (91 percent), Slovakia (47 percent), the Czech Republic (31 percent), and Hungary (24 percent). Many unauthorized migrants in Eastern Europe come from former Soviet Republics such as Ukraine and Belarus. Even among larger foreign populations, however, undocumented migrants often account for substantial shares of the total, including 24 percent in Italy, 21 percent in Greece, and 18 percent in Britain. The percentage undocumented has likely been kept down in Spain through a series of regularization programs directed mainly at Latin Americans (Aysa-Lastra and Cachón 2015).

In both North America and Europe, therefore, the consolidation of markets and expansion of international commerce during the current era of globalization have been associated with rising immigration into core nations from the periphery and, inevitably, growing irregular migration. This duality arises from the natural tendency for people to move within integrated, globalizing markets, as clearly occurred during the first era of global capitalism when some 50 million people displaced by industrialization and urbanization in Europe were free to leave for rapidly expanding economies in nations such as the United States, Canada, and Argentina. Freedom of movement allowed transnational labor markets to emerge and equilibrate and, over time, wage differentials between the old and new worlds gradually diminished (Hatton and Williamson 1994).

During this earlier era of capitalist globalization, emigrants from Europe did not relocate randomly but followed avenues of trade, investment, and exchange. A common pattern was the alternation over time of capital flows and immigrant flows from Europe to the Americas (Thomas 1973). Today similar patterns prevail, and migrants continue to move along pathways well established by a shared colonial past; prior guest worker treaties; and ongoing relations of trade, investment, and exchange. The difference today is that immigrant flows are restricted and unable to equilibrate international labor markets because national leaders want to create a global economy with selective factor mobility, a core contradiction finessed by the imposition of ever more repressive controls on the international movement of people.

In a very real way, therefore, illegal migration is built into the structure of the contemporary global economy. Policymakers throughout the world have implemented treaties and trade agreements to integrate markets that ensure the free movement of economic inputs and outputs, with two notable exceptions: labor and human capital. The problem, of course, is that trade and the integration of other global markets create interpersonal connections among people and entail the construction, transportation, and communication networks to connect consumers, producers, and investors in different countries. Over time a social and physical infrastructure invariably arises to reduce the costs of movement between trading nations and increase the diffusion of information between them, leading to migrant flows that cannot be accommodated within today's restrictive immigration policy regimes. This situation inevitably produces various forms of irregular migration and growing populations that lack full legal status.

Although policymakers, members of the general public, and scholars all commonly treat legal status as a dichotomy, in reality it is more of a continuum extending from the total absence of rights within a host society to the conferral of the same rights as native citizens, with the number of categories in between varying across time and from nation to nation. In between legal and illegal typically lies a variety of categories characterized by what Menjívar (2006, 1004) calls liminal legality or "the gray areas between documented and undocumented." The restriction of immigrants' rights clearly has consequences for their well-being and integration into host societies. Therefore, labor market consequences for illegal migrants is the fundamental topic of this volume.

From Seeking Opportunity to Evading Threats

The bulk of the migration between developing and developed regions in the final decades of the twentieth century and the first decade of the twenty-first century consisted of people moving to take advantage of opportunities. Wages in the Global North were relatively high and employment demand was steady, and people from the Global South moved to increase earnings, diversify income sources, and accumulate savings as part of self-conscious strategies of social and economic mobility. Population movements often began under the auspices of negotiated guest worker arrangements and later continued under increasingly controlled regimes of international movement put in place over time, creating both documented and undocumented immigrants. These developments transpired not only in traditional countries of immigration such as the United States, Canada, Argentina, Australia, and New Zealand, but also in new immigrant-receiving nations such as Britain, Germany, Italy, and Spain (Massey et al. 1998).

Although Western Europe led the way among new immigrant-receiving nations, eventually all nations in the expanded EU switched from the export to import of labor. The rise in oil prices and revenues during the 1970s turned the Persian Gulf into a major importer of labor, and during the 1980s and 1990s the "Asian Tigers" of Japan, Hong Kong, Taiwan, Singapore, and South Korea successively became countries of immigration as their economies matured. As this shift progressed, immigrant populations became more gender balanced because global labor demand targeted both men and women for employment, and policymakers increasingly controlled immigrant entry by employing regulatory systems based on employment and/or marriage (Donato and Gabaccia 2015).

What is perhaps most remarkable about international migration during this period is not that people increasingly moved within a steadily more integrated global economy but that so few people actually left the lands of their birth. Out of 6.9 billion people alive worldwide in 2010, only 214 million were international migrants, composing just 3.1 percent of the earth's population (United Nations 2011). Therefore, given the pervasive inequalities in wealth and income that prevail between nations, what is most surprising is not how many people became international migrants as globalization spread during the early twenty-first century, but how few did.

There are signs, however, that this relatively benign state of affairs is shifting and that a growing share of migrants in the future will not be moving to access opportunities but to evade threats. Rather than moving to increase earnings, diversify sources of income, or accumulate savings, they will be seeking to escape immediate threats from civil violence, crime, warfare, family violence, natural disasters, political upheavals, and economic catastrophe—events that often produce a stream of out-migrants whose mobility is motivated by fear. Such people perceive a tangible risk and move rapidly to escape it, usually proceeding to the nearest and most accessible safe haven (Kunz 1973). If they remain within their home nation, they become internally displaced persons; and if they cross an international border, they become refugees or asylees.

Natural disasters, wars, and revolutions have occurred commonly throughout human history to displace people from their homelands and will no doubt continue to do so in the future. Moreover, the structural transformation of the economy during the shift from agrarian to industrial or postindustrial modes of production has long been known to displace people from traditional livelihoods and turn them into migrants (Massey 1988; Sassen 1988). In recent years, however, researchers have begun to pay closer attention to two potential drivers of migration that appear endemic to the twenty-first century: climate change and civil violence.

The term "environmental refugees" was introduced by El-Hinnawi (1985) to describe people forced to leave their place of origin, either temporarily or permanently, because of environmental disruptions triggered by human or natural events. Suhrke (1994) identified desertification, land degradation, deforestation, and rising sea levels as the most important forms of environmental change leading to out-migration; whereas Hugo (2008) lists environmental disasters, environmental degradation, climate change, and disruptions from large-scale human projects as the principal causes. Afifi and Warner (2008) indeed found a positive association between the size of migration flows between 172 countries and measures of overfishing, desertification, water scarcity, soil salinization, deforestation, air pollution, soil erosion, and soil pollution within nations. Thus, we can expect migration to be a common human response to environmental change, as it always has been.

Most studies of environmentally related migration rely on country-specific data rather than cross-national statistical analyses. In their study of migration in Guatemala and the Sudan, for example, Bilsborrow and DeLargy (1991) found that a decline in land productivity fostered rural out-migration, whereas Hitztaler (2004) found that resource-poor villages in Russia's Kamchatka region displayed greater rates of out-migration than those with stable resource bases. Massey, Axinn, and Ghimire (2010) similarly found that short-distance moves in Nepal were predicted by decreasing access to firewood, declines in agricultural productivity, and decreases in land cover. Bohra-Mishra and Massey (2011a) also found significant effects of population pressure, deforestation, and decreasing agricultural productivity on the likelihood of local mobility in Nepal, but found little evidence that environmental deterioration promoted long-distance migration.

In contrast, estimates derived by Feng, Krueger, and Oppenheimer (2010) suggested a strong relationship between declining crop yields and out-migration from Mexico to the United States; and Munshi (2003) documented a significant connection between the scarcity of rainfall and Mexico–U.S. migration, a connection also observed by Nawrotzki, Riosmena, and Hunter (2012). Donato and colleagues (2016) similarly found a strong association between lack of rainfall and internal migration in Bangladesh. In an era of global climate change, environmental disruptions carry significant potential to promote movement—clearly short distances but also likely over long distances and even internationally.

In addition to environmental change, another threat common to the contemporary world is civil violence, which emanates from diverse sources, including crime, political terrorism, narco-terrorism, guerilla insurgencies, revolutions, and state-sponsored repression. As with environmental change, aggregate-level studies generally uncover a strong connection between such violence and out-migration. Shellman and Stewart (2007) found that Haitian immigration to the United States was strongly correlated with surges in political violence in Haiti, holding economic conditions constant. Morrison (1993) found similar results in Guatemala, as did May and Morrison (1994) in Colombia. Jones (1989), however, found the effect of violence on migration was mainly indirect, with conflict producing local economic dislocations that, in turn, led to emigration. May and Morrison (1994) also found that conflict-related economic turmoil was more important than violence in predicting migration within Guatemala; but Schultz (1971) showed that the effect of violence on rural-urban migration in Guatemala was small compared to the effects of socioeconomic and demographic factors.

A growing number of investigators have examined the connection between violence and individual and household decisions to migrate. In Colombia, for example, both Engel and Ibáñez (2007) and Ibáñez and Vélez (2008) found that the threat of violence and the presence of paramilitary and guerilla groups were strongly associated with the likelihood of out-migration; and Silva and Massey (2014) have connected rising violence in Colombia to the growth of international migration. Both Lundquist and Massey (2005) and Massey, Durand, and Pren (2014) found that migration from Central America to the United States was strongly predicted by the intensity of the American Contra intervention. In their study of Nepal, Bohra-Mishra and Massey (2011b) found that civil violence had nonlinear effects on migration, such that low to moderate levels of violence reduced the likelihood of movement whereas high levels increased the probability of migration.

We have discussed climate change and violence as two independent threats, each of which potentially contributes to the flow of migrants around the world. Recent work suggests, however, that climate change and civil violence are, in fact, causally interrelated. Indeed, Hsiang, Meng, and Crane (2011) show that outbursts of civil violence are closely tied to variations in the El Niño Southern Oscillation (ENSO). Specifically, they found that the probability of a civil conflict erupting doubles during El Niño versus La Niña years and that the ENSO may have been behind 21 percent of all civil conflicts between 1950 and 2005. Given the potential of climate change to influence the frequency and severity of weather events such as El Niño, climate change not only has the potential to generate migration directly through displacement but also indirectly by triggering civil conflicts in affected areas throughout the world.

These findings contribute to a growing body of research that links international migration to environmental change and civil violence and, possibly, to a dynamic interplay between the two. In contrast to the recent past, therefore, threat evasion may soon come to dominate opportunity-seeking as the predominant motivation for immigration in the coming decades. Whereas opportunity seeking during the late twentieth and early twenty-first centuries produced a relatively small number of immigrants worldwide, threat evasion carries the potential for much larger outflows.

The decision to migrate under threat is more primal than rational. Harsher legal restrictions, enhanced border enforcement, and rising interdictions at sea may be sufficient to deter opportunity-seeking migrants, especially when the costs of movement are balanced against prospective gains that are only theoretical at the time of departure, cannot be foreseen with accuracy, and may or may not materialize in the wake of a move. It is doubtful, however, that the same policies will function as deterrents when the motivation is not a hypothetical gain but a very real, tangible, obvious, and quite immediate threat to the physical and emotional well-being of oneself and one's family. In this sense, the massive outflow of migrants from Syria, Iraq, and other chaotic zones in the Middle East during summer 2015 may simply be harbingers of greater movements to come as environmental change destabilizes governments and economies and creates immediate threats to well-being in poor nations throughout the world.

Research on Undocumented Migration

Thus, the potential for undocumented migration will, if anything, grow in the future. Understanding how irregular and undocumented migrants adapt and integrate into reluctant host societies while inhabiting tenuous legal statuses is thus a research question of the first order. In this volume, we bring together a series of studies that analyze how legal status affects labor market outcomes, a topic that has been extensively studied to date. It is, however, a question that raises formidable challenges with respect to data collection and analysis, for unauthorized migrants are rarely included in national statistical systems, whether based on censuses, surveys, or administrative databases.

The challenge became evident first in the United States, as undocumented migration from Mexico surged when opportunities for legal entry were curtailed after 1965. In 1978, Douglas Massey began to collaborate with an anthropologist, Joshua Reichert, who had just returned from a year of fieldwork in a rural Mexican village. In the course of his time there, Reichert compiled a notebook divided into sections; each section corresponded to a particular household and listed the basic demographic characteristics of each person living in each household as well as information on the first and last trips to the United States, including documentation. In addition, Reichert had compiled a detailed history of U.S. migration for each male household head and recorded basic information about the household itself, including landholdings, business ownership, home construction, and home amenities.

After seeing the richness of the data, Massey arranged for it to be entered into a computer. He and Reichert collaborated on several articles, using the data to study patterns and processes of migration to the United States. They found that three-quarters of all households contained migrants and 27 percent contained undocumented migrants (Reichert and Massey 1979, 1980). Impressed with the detail and quality of data on undocumented migration that could be compiled using ethnographic methods, Massey approached a group of Mexican anthropology students, and together they designed a project that combined ethnographic and survey methods to gather data from representative samples of strategically chosen Mexican communities—a methodological approach that came to be known as the ethnosurvey (Massey 1987).

The project was funded in late 1981 by the National Institute of Child Health and Human Development (NICHD), and in summer 1982 the team entered the field to carry out pilot surveys in four communities located in two of Mexico's top migrant-sending states: Jalisco and Michoacán. These studies ultimately produced a series of journal articles and the book *Return to Aztlán* (Massey et al. 1987). The success of the pilot effort was used as a springboard to submit a new proposed project to NICHD, to be directed jointly by Jorge Durand and Douglas Massey, that would use ethnosurvey methods to sample four to six Mexican communities each year, to compile over time a cumulative database on documented and undocumented migration to the United States.

That proposal was funded for a five-year period in 1987, launching what became known as the Mexican Migration Project (MMP). The MMP has been continuously funded by NICHD ever since (see Durand and Massey 2004) and was recently renewed to collect data through 2020. Over the years, the project has received supplemental funding from the Hewlett Foundation, the Mellon Foundation, the MacArthur Foundation, and the Russell Sage Foundation, but its principal source of support has always been NICHD. The MMP currently includes samples from 154 communities located in 23 Mexican states and data are made freely available to researchers via the project website,[1] which at last count had some 3,900 registered users. The database currently contains information on 25,658 households and 162,293 persons, including 25,918 migrants, 16,644 of whom were undocumented at the time of their last trip.

Given the success of the MMP and the rising migration from the Caribbean, Central America, and South America, in 1998 Durand and Massey submitted another proposal to NICHD to establish the Latin American Migration Project (LAMP), which sought to apply ethnosurvey methods developed by the MMP to communities in other countries throughout Latin America. The LAMP was funded for five years by NICHD and since 2003 has been funded by the MacArthur Foundation. To date, it has compiled survey data from eleven Latin American nations, including seven communities in Costa Rica, fourteen in Colombia, seven in the Dominican Republic, four in Ecuador, four in El Salvador, three in Guatemala, three in Haiti, nine in Nicaragua, two in Paraguay, and five each in Peru and Puerto Rico. Data are publicly available via the project website,[2] and at last count roughly 1,600 people had registered as data users.

Since 2000, the MMP investigators have collaborated with interested researchers at other universities throughout the world to launch comparable data collection efforts in other migrant-sending regions, leading to the creation of the China International Migration Project led by Zai Liang at SUNY, Albany; the Polish

Migration Project directed by Frank Kalter at Mannheim University; the Migration from Africa to Europe Project launched by Cris Beauchemin at France's Institut National d'Etudes Demographiques; the Bangladesh Environment and Migration Survey developed by Katharine Donato of Vanderbilt University; and the Gender, Migration, and Hispanic Health Project led by Emilio Parrado and Chenoa Flippen at the University of Pennsylvania.

Data collected by these projects form the basis for the studies reported in this volume. Together they address the challenge of studying undocumented migration and assess the effects of undocumented status, examining how illegality affects labor market outcomes among U.S. immigrants and the consequences of unauthorized migration for sending and receiving communities. Fernando Riosmena leads off by situating the MMP's ethnosurvey design in the broader context of studies on international migration, focusing in particular on the strengths and weaknesses of retrospective life history data and the importance of cross-case, comparative analysis.

Although prospective longitudinal surveys are often considered to be the gold standard for data collection, Riosmena points out that they are not necessarily the best approach when it comes to research on international migration because such surveys cannot readily assess the historical development and evolution of migration streams prior to the survey date. In reality, prospective and retrospective surveys have complementary advantages and disadvantages, a fact recognized by the Polish Migration Project, which combined retrospective data collection with prospective panel data that was gathered from the same people over time. In their analysis, Frank Kalter and Gisela Will cleverly exploit the two sources of data to study how social networks affect Polish labor migration to Germany, taking into account sources of unobserved heterogeneity that are typically left uncontrolled in retrospective event history analyses.

Consistent with their own previous findings and the work of many international migration scholars, Kalter and Will find that access to migration-specific social capital (through connections to people with migrant experience) is critical in predicting the likelihood of migrating from Poland to Germany. They expand knowledge about how social networks influence migration by demonstrating that the most important source of migration-specific capital initially is weak ties to prior German migrants within extended networks of friends and acquaintances. Such ties are instrumental in causing people to consider migration as a viable economic strategy in the first place. Once migration is within the calculus of conscious choice, potential Polish migrants draw on strong ties to facilitate a move to Germany for work.

Another feature of the ethnosurvey approach is parallel sampling—surveying respondents at places of both origin and destination. In his analysis, David Lindstrom refines the sampling procedure of the MMP by gathering information on the location of children of the household head, even those who have formed their own households. This enabled him to develop a new weighting scheme that makes an important distinction between temporary and settled migrants to correct for the underrepresentation of migrants who are more integrated in receiving communities. Pooling together binational data from western Guatemala and

Providence, Rhode Island, he estimates the relative size of the out-migrant set-tled population in the United States to create sample weights and pooled samples of nonmigrants, return migrants, and settled migrants across the two settings.

Although primarily a methodological analysis, like other articles in this volume, Lindstrom's data nonetheless reveal how a lack of legal status contributes to the social and economic marginalization of Guatemalan migrants, the vast majority of whom are undocumented. Even after reweighting to improve coverage of more integrated migrants, only 14 percent had a bank account, 19 percent had a credit card, and just half had taxes withheld from their pay. Only 17 percent said they spoke English a little or well, and just 5.5 percent reported having a white friend outside of work.

Following the foregoing methodological works, the remaining articles in the volume draw on various ethnosurvey-based studies to assess the economic situation of undocumented migrants from different countries in various destinations. The first set of studies focuses on Latino migrants in the United States, the largest recipient of immigrants throughout the twentieth century. Jorge Durand, Douglas Massey, and Karen Pren set the tone by documenting how the rise of illegal migration in the early 1970s, and a subsequent shift away from a predictable circular flow combined with continued strong undocumented in-migration, created a situation in which both the net volume of undocumented entries and the population of U.S. unauthorized immigrant residents grew, resulting in approximately 11 million persons now living in the United States without legal status. Their finding of a persistent deterioration in the wages of all Mexicans working in the United States is especially troubling given the failure of the U.S. Congress to reform immigration policy and offer a path for unauthorized migrants to regularize their status and become naturalized citizens.

In addition to the general decline in wages for Mexican immigrants, Durand and colleagues find that undocumented migrants are doubly disadvantaged. Because of their unauthorized status, they are channeled into the secondary labor market where wages are systematically lower than in the primary sector, and they earn lower wages than documented migrants regardless of sector of employment. Moreover, even migrants holding legal visas for temporary work in the United States are significantly disadvantaged in whatever sector they work. Although all Mexican immigrants are disadvantaged in the U.S. labor market, those without documents were more than twice as likely as legal immigrants to work in the secondary sector where wages were substantially lower. The authors estimate that this wage penalty yields an annual deficit of $2,655 for a full-time, year-round worker. Combined with unauthorized migrants' lower hourly wages and an additional annual deficit of $2,442, estimates suggest $5,097 in total annual income lost. Scaling this loss up across all unauthorized Mexican immigrants in the United States suggests that they bear an extremely high economic penalty, a burden likely to perpetuate poverty and disadvantage over time and into the next generation of American citizens.

In a separate article, Massey, Durand, and Pren build on these findings by combining data from the MMP and the LAMP to analyze how Mexican and non-Mexican Latino immigrants fare in the U.S. labor market. Because the large majority of Mexican and Central American immigrants today are in undocumented or marginal legal statuses, this analysis is especially important. Despite their higher levels of education and greater socioeconomic standing, non-Mexican Latino migrants—like their Mexican counterparts—have not fared very well in the U.S. labor market. Since the late 1980s, real wages have dropped for both groups. In addition to the wage penalty experienced by undocumented migrants, those who occupied liminal legal categories, such as Temporary Protected Status, also earned lower wages. Thus, the labor market positions of both Mexican and non-Mexican Latino immigrants are disadvantaged, uncertain, and insecure. Such precariousness is cause for great concern in the near future, as Latinos now represent 17 percent of the population and 25 percent of all births in the United States.

In her analysis of the employment and earnings of immigrant Hispanic women, Chenoa Flippen draws on ethnosurvey data collected in the new immigrant gateway of Durham, North Carolina. Although she finds that labor supply of Latina immigrants is driven mainly by family structure and to a lesser extent by human capital, their wages are determined more by legal status than anything else. She estimates that being without documents and concentrated in small firms reduces women's weekly wages by 25 percent. Furthermore, despite some variation in wages across jobs, approximately 40 percent of her sample reported earning less than the minimum wage. Hispanic immigrant women, therefore, experience multiple sources of disadvantage in the labor market and exist in the shadows in an especially precarious economic situation.

In a second article coauthored with Emilio Parrado, Flippen uses the same ethnosurvey dataset but focuses instead on how the recession and immigration enforcement influence the out-migration of Latino immigrants from Durham. Drawing on multiplicity sampling that relies on respondents' reports about the mobility of their siblings, they consider whether out-migration shifts over time, what precipitates the move (i.e., family considerations, accidents, economic conditions, or deportations), and whether individuals return to their country of origin or migrate internally to another U.S. destination. Their findings clearly demonstrate the power of the Great Recession: out-migration more than doubled after 2007 and migrants overwhelmingly returned home. Although noneconomic considerations related to families and accidents accounted for the majority of departures before the recession, economic considerations were dominant drivers of out-migration afterward. Migrants from Mexico and those with less human capital were more likely to leave, highlighting the selectivity of out-migration. Interestingly, despite stronger federal enforcement practices during this time, deportations accounted for a negligible share of all moves from Durham. Thus, Latin American migration, especially from Mexico, still involves some circularity, and the negligible effect of deportations as a reason for return suggests that deportations are less effective than voluntary return for regulating the size of immigrant populations.

The second set of articles considers whether and how legal status influences labor market outcomes for non-Hispanic immigrants and in destinations outside the United States. The study from Zai Liang and Bo Zhou considers the economic circumstances of Chinese immigrants in the New York metropolitan labor market, whereas the analysis from Erik Vickstrom focuses on African immigrants in Europe, and the study by Katharine Donato and colleagues examines whether and how legal status affects the international migration of Bangladeshis and their labor market experiences. These studies, like those in this volume that focus on U.S. immigrants, also reveal that legal status differentiates labor market outcomes, often by penalizing those without documents.

Using ethnosurvey data collected in New York City's Chinese community in 2004, Liang and Zhou examine the extent to which legal status affects Chinese immigrants' labor market performance and health status. They focus on five outcomes that are related to legal status of immigrants: wages, hours worked per week, location of employment, self-rated health, and health care utilization. They find that unauthorized immigrants were more likely than legal immigrants to work especially long hours and earn lower wages, and they were also more likely to work in U.S. communities far away from traditional immigrant enclaves in New York City. Undocumented migrants were also less likely than legal Chinese immigrants to use health care and see a doctor when sick.

Vickstrom draws on ethnosurvey data collected in Senegal and Europe to ask why immigrant women, many of whom have legal status, are initially less likely to work than men. He considers whether and how this difference reflects EU policies that create gendered channels of access to labor markets for Senegalese immigrants. He finds a strong association between legal status and employment for Senegalese women but not for men. Of the women who migrate from Senegal to Europe, most do so in a family reunification status that does not necessarily permit employment, and as a result, they are less likely than women in other legal statuses to be economically active upon arrival. Among Senegalese men, however, there is little association between legal status and their economic activity. However, Vickstrom observes that family reunification does not preclude women's labor market participation over the long term; most women with family-reunification profiles eventually transition into economic activity in their European destinations.

The final study in this volume, by Katharine Donato, Amanda Carrico, Blake Sisk, and Bhumika Piya, considers how legal status is associated with international migration from Bangladesh, a low-lying nation that has experienced dramatic environmental changes in recent decades and high rates of out-migration, which have led to contentious and deadly border conflicts with India. Using new ethnosurvey data collected in 2014 from approximately eighteen hundred households in nine villages, Donato and colleagues' findings reveal substantial variation by legal status and social capital in the chances of making a first international trip. For example, they report that men's chances of making an initial international trip by age 44 are highest if they are unauthorized and have a parent or sibling with prior international migrant experience. In addition, undocumented status is linked to fewer hours worked per week, a greater likelihood of using social contacts to find a job, and lower likelihoods of paying taxes or having a bank account in host nations. Thus, even among international migrants from Bangladesh, a nation with large-scale anthropogenic degradation, legal status operates in salient ways to stratify and differentiate the process of international migration.

Lessons Learned

The studies summarized above clearly illustrate that the laws, political narratives, and institutional social structures related to global migration in the early twenty-first century similarly affect the lives of international migrants, whether they originate in nations from which many immigrants seek economic opportunity; or in countries from which many leave to find refuge from conflict, environmental degradation, or other conditions. These studies also suggest that the paradox of twenty-first-century globalization, which created the new phenomenon of illegal migration, has also helped to create inequality among immigrants around the globe. Undocumented immigrants worldwide live and work at a considerable disadvantage, and when compounded by other characteristics, their disadvantage can only worsen the prospects for successful integration in new destinations. If the scale of future international migration grows as more find themselves in nations and communities that are untenable because of rising civil violence or environmental degradation, then the legal status disparities observed here are certain to widen. The mass exodus from the Middle East into Europe that made headlines in summer 2015 is likely a harbinger of things to come.

Notes

1. http://mmp.opr.princeton.edu/.
2. http://lamp.opr.princeton.edu/.

References

Afifi, Tamer, and Koko Warner. 2008. The impact of environmental degradation on migration flows across countries. Working Paper No. 5, United Nations University Institute for Environment and Human Security, Bonn, Germany.

Aysa-Lastra, María, and Lorenzo Cachón. 2015. *Immigrant vulnerability and resilience: Comparative perspectives on Latin American immigrants during the Great Recession.* New York, NY: Springer.

Berger, John, and Jean Mohr. 1975. *A seventh man.* New York, NY: Viking Press.

Bilsborrow, Richard E., and Pamela F. DeLargy. 1991. Population growth, natural resource use and migration in the third world: The cases of Guatemala and Sudan. *Population and Development Review* 16 (S): S125–S147.

Bohra-Mishra, Pratikshya, and Douglas S. Massey. 2011a. Environmental degradation and out-migration: New evidence from Nepal. In *Migration and climate change*, eds. Etienne Piguet, Antoine Pécoud, and Paul de Guchteneire, 74–101. Cambridge: Cambridge University Press.

Bohra-Mishra, Pratikshya, and Douglas S. Massey. 2011b. Individual decisions to migrate during civil conflict. *Demography* 48 (2): 401–24.

Castles, Stephen, and Godula Kosack. 1973. *Immigrant workers and class structure in Western Europe.* London: Oxford University Press.

Chavez, Leo R. 2001. *Covering immigration: Population images and the politics of the nation.* Berkeley, CA: University of California Press.

Chavez, Leo R. 2008. *The Latino threat: Constructing immigrants, citizens, and the nation.* Stanford, CA: Stanford University Press.

Clandestino Project. 2016. *Database on irregular migration [database online].* Vienna: International Centre for Migration Policy and Development. Available from http://irregular-migration.net/index.php?id=219 (accessed 14 January 2016).

Donato, Katharine M., Amanda R. Carrico, Blake Sisk, and Bhumika Piya. 2016. Migration, social capital and the environment in Bangladesh. Paper presented at the annual meeting of the Population Association of America, Washington, DC.

Donato, Katharine M., and Donna Gabaccia. 2015. *Gender and international migration: From the slavery era to the global age.* New York, NY: Russell Sage Foundation.

Durand, Jorge, and Douglas S. Massey. 2004. *Crossing the border: Research from the Mexican Migration Project.* New York, NY: Russell Sage Foundation.

Durand, Jorge, and Douglas S. Massey. 2010. New world orders: Continuities and changes in Latin American migration. *The ANNALS of the American Academy of Political and Social Science* 630 (1): 20–52.

El-Hinnawi, Essam. 1985. *Environmental refugees.* Nairobi: United Nations Environment Programme.

Engel, Stefanie, and Ana Maria Ibáñez. 2007. Displacement due to violence in Colombia: A household-level analysis. *Economic Development and Cultural Change* 55 (4): 335–65.

Feng, Shuaizhang, Alan B. Krueger, and Michael Oppenheimer. 2010. Linkages among climate change, crop yields and Mexico–U.S. cross-border migration. *Proceedings of the National Academy of Sciences* 107 (32): 14257–62.

Hatton, Timothy J., and Jeffrey G. Williamson. 1994. *Migration and the international labor market 1850–1939.* New York, NY: Routledge.

Hatton, Timothy J., and Jeffrey G. Williamson. 1998. *The age of mass migration: Causes and economic impact.* New York, NY: Oxford University Press.

Hitztaler, Stephanie. 2004. The relationship between resources and human migration patterns in central Kamchatka during the post-Soviet period. *Population and Environment* 25 (4): 355–75.

Hsiang, Solomon M., Kyle C. Meng, and Mark A. Crane. 2011. Civil conflicts are associated with the global climate. *Nature* 476:438–41.

Hugo, Graeme. 2008. *Migration, development and environment.* Geneva: International Organization for Migration.

Ibáñez, Ana Maria, and Carlos Eduardo Vélez. 2008. Civil conflict and forced migration: The micro determinants and welfare losses of displacement in Colombia. *World Development* 36 (4): 659–76.

Jones, Richard C. 1989. Causes of Salvadoran migration to the United States. *Geographical Review* 79 (2): 183–94.

Kershaw, Ian. 2015. *To hell and back: Europe 1914–1949.* New York, NY: Viking.

Klein, Herbert S. 1999. *The Atlantic slave trade.* Cambridge: Cambridge University Press.

Kunz, Egon F. 1973. The refugee in flight: kinetic models and forms of displacement. *International Migration Review* 7 (2): 125–46.

Lloyd, Martin. 2003. *The passport: The history of man's most traveled document.* Stroud, UK: The History Press.

Lundquist, Jennifer H., and Douglas S. Massey. 2005. Politics or economics? International migration during the Nicaraguan Contra War. *Journal of Latin American Studies* 37 (1): 29–53.

Martin, Philip L. 1980. *Guest-worker programs: Lessons from Europe.* Washington, DC: U.S. Department of Labor, Bureau of International Labor Affairs.

Martin, Philip L., and Zucher Gottfried. 2008. Managing migration: The global challenge. *Population Bulletin* 63 (1): 3–20.

Massey, Douglas S. 1987. Do undocumented migrants earn lower wages than legal immigrants? New evidence from Mexico. *International Migration Review* 21 (2): 236–74.

Massey, Douglas S. 1988. International migration and economic development in comparative perspective. *Population and Development Review* 14 (3): 383–414.

Massey, Douglas S. 2013. America's immigration policy fiasco: Learning from past mistakes. *Daedalus* 142 (3): 5–15.

Massey, Douglas S., Rafael Alarcon, Jorge Durand, and Humberto Gonzalez. 1987. *Return to Aztlan: The social process of international migration from Western Mexico.* Berkeley, CA: University of California Press.

Massey, Douglas S., Joaquín Arango, Graeme Hugo, Ali Kouaouci, Adela Pellegrino, and J. Edward Taylor. 1998 *Worlds in motion: International migration at the end of the millennium.* Oxford: Oxford University Press.

Massey, Douglas S., William G. Axinn, and Dirgha J. Ghimire. 2010. Environmental change and out-migration: Evidence from Nepal. *Population and Environment* 32 (2–3): 109–36.

Massey, Douglas S., Jorge Durand, and Nolan J. Malone. 2002. *Beyond smoke and mirrors: Mexican immigration in an age of economic integration*. New York, NY: Russell Sage Foundation.

Massey, Douglas S., Jorge Durand, and Karen A. Pren. 2014. Explaining undocumented migration. *International Migration Review* 48 (4): 1028–61.

Massey, Douglas S., Jorge Durand, and Karen A. Pren. 2015. Border enforcement and return migration by documented and undocumented Mexicans. *Journal of Ethnic and Migration Studies* 41 (7): 1015–40.

Massey, Douglas S., Jorge Durand, and Karen A. Pren. 2016. Why border enforcement backfired. *American Journal of Sociology* 121 (5): 1557–1600.

Massey, Douglas S. and Karen A. Pren. 2012. Unintended consequences of U.S. immigration policy: Explaining the post-1965 surge from Latin America. *Population and Development Review* 38 (1): 1–29.

May, Rachel A., and Andrew R. Morrison. 1994. Escape from terror: Violence and migration in post-revolutionary Guatemala. *Latin American Research Review* 29 (2): 111–32.

Menjívar, Cecilia. 2006. Liminal legality: Salvadoran and Guatemalan immigrants' lives in the United States. *American Journal of Sociology* 111 (4): 999–1037.

Morrison, Andrew R. 1993. Violence or economics: What drives internal migration in Guatemala? *Economic Development and Cultural Change* 41 (4): 817–31.

Munshi, Kaivan. 2003. Networks in the modern economy: Mexican migrants in the U.S. labor market. *Quarterly Journal of Economics* 118 (2): 549–97.

Nawrotzki, Raphael J., Fernando Riosmena, and Lori Hunter. 2012. Do rainfall deficits predict U.S.-bound migration from rural Mexico? Evidence from the Mexican Census. *Population Research and Policy Review* 32 (1): 129–58.

Oppenheimer, Stephen. 2003. *The real Eve: Modern man's journey out of Africa*. New York, NY: Carroll and Graf.

O'Rourke, Kevin, and Jeffrey G. Williamson. 1999. *Globalization and history: The evolution of a nineteenth-century Atlantic economy*. Cambridge, MA: MIT Press.

Reichert, Joshua S., and Douglas S. Massey. 1979. Patterns of migration from a central Mexican town to the United States: A comparison of legal and illegal migrants. *International Migration Review* 13 (4): 599–623.

Reichert, Joshua S., and Douglas S. Massey. 1980. History and trends in U.S.-bound migration from a Mexican town. *International Migration Review* 14 (4): 475–91.

Reichert, Joshua S., and Douglas S. Massey. 1982. Guestworker programs: Some evidence from Europe and the United States and some implications for U.S. policy. *Population Research and Policy Review* 1 (1): 1–17.

Sassen, Saskia. 1988. *The mobility of labor and capital: A study in international investment and labor flow*. New York, NY: Cambridge University Press.

Schultz, Paul T. 1971. Rural-urban migration in Colombia. *Review of Economics and Statistics* 53 (2): 157–63.

Shellman, Stephen M., and Brandon M. Stewart. 2007. Predicting risk factors associated with forced migration: An early warning model of Haitian flight. *Civil Wars* 9 (2): 174–99.

Silva, Adriana Carolina, and Douglas S. Massey. 2014. Violence, networks, and international migration from Colombia. *International Migration* 54 (5): 162–78.

Suhrke, Astri. 1994. Environmental degradation and population flows. *Journal of International Affairs* 47 (2): 473–96.

Stiglitz, Joseph E. 2002. *Globalization and its discontents*. New York, NY: W.W. Norton.

Thomas, Brinley. 1973. *Migration and economic growth: A study of Great Britain and the Atlantic economy*. Cambridge: Cambridge University Press.

United Nations. 2011. *International migration report 2009: A global assessment*. New York, NY: UN Department of Economic and Social Affairs, Population Division.

Williamson, Jeffrey G. 2004. *Migration and economic growth: A study of Great Britain and the Atlantic economy*. Washington, DC: AEI Press.

*The Challenge of Studying
Undocumented Migration*

The Potential and Limitations of Cross-Context Comparative Research on Migration

FERNANDO RIOSMENA

This article discusses major methodological challenges in the comparative study of the drivers of international mobility (between different times and places) when using household surveys. Noting the difference between the study of coterminous and stage-specific drivers of migration, I highlight the problems of obtaining data with adequate representation across periods and geographies, which are pressing for all social science research but especially for cross-local comparative endeavors. I discuss the advantages and drawbacks of a broad constellation of prospective and retrospective approaches, paying particular attention to the migration ethnosurvey. After briefly describing the general commonalities and differences of ethnosurvey approaches adopted around the world, I suggest how post hoc case selection and other adjustments can help to ameliorate retrospective biases and comparability problems. I conclude with ideas on a priori case selection that can help to bolster comparative migration studies.

Keywords: international migration; migration; ethnosurvey; survey research; survey methods

Theory validation and refinement as well as policy evaluation require systematic empirical work that encompasses a broad range of conditions in which migration is—and is not—produced. Because the circumstances in which international movement occurs seem to differ in some important ways across the globe (see Massey et al. 1998), contextual disparities may be fertile ground to test the range of migration theories and how they interact in different settings. This contextual dependence underscores the significance of empirical work across

Fernando Riosmena is an associate professor at the Population Program and the Geography Department at the University of Colorado at Boulder. His research looks at the role of U.S. immigration policy and social, economic, and environmental conditions in sending communities on the migration dynamics between Latin America and the United States.

Correspondence: Fernando.Riosmena@colorado.edu

DOI: 10.1177/0002716216650629

28
ANNALS, *AAPSS*, 666, July 2016

spatiotemporal scales that takes advantage of historical and cross-national variation in the drivers of mobility (see Clark, Hatton, and Williamson 2004, 2007; Donato and Gabaccia 2015; Fitzgerald and Cook-Martin 2014; Hatton and Williamson 1998; Fussell 2010; Fussell and Massey 2004; Garip 2012; Lindstrom and López Ramírez 2010; Massey and Sana 2003; Riosmena 2009).

Given the contemporary boom in individual/household survey data collection (despite ever-present challenges to migration measurement; see Beauchemin 2014; Raymer et al. 2008; Rogers, Little, and Raymer 2010), it is arguably more possible now than ever to perform cross-context comparative empirical research. Although data collection efforts have indeed fueled explicit cross-local and cross-national comparative studies, this research has mostly contrasted flows emanating from within the same world region, namely, Latin America and the Caribbean (e.g., Clark, Hatton, and Williamson 2004; Donato and León, forthcoming; Fussell 2010; Fussell and Massey 2004; Lindstrom and López-Ramírez 2010; Massey, Fischer, and Capoferro 2006; Massey and Sana 2003; Riosmena 2010), and in sub-Saharan Africa (e.g., Beauchemin et al. 2015; Castagnone et al. 2015; Toma and Vause 2014).

While a relatively small body of comparative studies have examined the causes of migration in different settings across world regions (Liu, Riosmena, and Creighton 2015; Massey, Kalter, and Pren 2008), more comparative research based on strategically chosen cases and strong research designs is necessary if we are to build a clear understanding of why the drivers of migration vary across places at a particular point in time, or why they diverge over time within particular places (for similar arguments on the understanding of the migration-development nexus, see Escobar et al. 2006; Iskander 2015). To build accurate theoretical models for evidence-based policy formulation, it is necessary not only to document differences in the drivers across periods and places, but more importantly to explain the reasons why the structural factors of migration are different across contexts and at different stages in the migration process.

As shown throughout this volume, over the last two decades relatively comparable household survey data have been collected using the "ethnosurvey" approach in particular communities located in China, Poland, Senegal, Ghana, the Congo, Bangladesh, Mexico, Guatemala, El Salvador, Nicaragua, Costa Rica, Puerto Rico, the Dominican Republic, Haiti, Paraguay, Peru, Ecuador, and Colombia. This approach blends survey methods with more in-depth qualitative interview styles to gather data in specific sending communities and foreign destinations, a centerpiece of its methodology being the compilation of retrospective life histories for both migrants and nonmigrants.

NOTE: The general ideas contained in this article were presented at the conference "The Ethnosurvey in Global Context" at Vanderbilt University in January 2015. I thank all conference participants for feedback and additional ideas provided during my presentation. Finally, I acknowledge partial support for this research from a Eunice Kennedy Shriver National Institute of Child Health and Human Development research infrastructure grant, 5R24 HD066613-03, to the University of Colorado Population Center in the Institute of Behavioral Science at the University of Colorado, Boulder.

Thanks to such data, scholars are increasingly able to advance systematic understandings of migration by directly contrasting and comparing how relevant individuals, families, households, and communities operate across carefully selected cases that generate different migratory outcomes. Although ethnosurvey methods hold much promise for migration research, comparative work using them highlights many methodological challenges, in some cases adding complications to those already prevalent in noncomparative research. Awareness of these problems and taking the appropriate countermeasures when designing research projects are necessary to avoid reaching incorrect conclusions, such as when cross-context differences in migration are taken to represent real differences in migrator dynamics.

Prior scholarship has discussed both the potential and limitations of applying survey and—to a lesser extent—other methods in comparative cross-national studies of migration, including issues of case selection (Fitzgerald 2012), data collection methods (Beauchemin and González-Ferrer 2011), and overall research design (Beauchemin 2014). This article contributes to this body of work by discussing the analytical challenges involved in comparing individual- and household-level survey data across settings. My aim is to provide a set of general guiding principles for a posteriori decisions about case selection, sample construction, and other adjustments that become necessary when datasets from different settings are combined. I also offer guidance for a priori case selection and data gathering choices that cross-context comparative researchers should bear in mind in future studies. These lessons do not apply solely to cross-national or interregional research but also to the study of migration to or from different sending or destination communities within the same country. As should be relatively clear, these reflections do not pertain exclusively to studies using ethnosurvey approaches but apply to any data collection effort aimed at describing and explaining the drivers of migration in different settings, and to retrospective data collection efforts in particular. I nonetheless pay specific attention to the ethnosurvey studies discussed throughout this volume, given that they represent perhaps the most promising avenue for direct cross-context comparative analysis.

The ethnosurvey is part of a long tradition of specialized migration surveys that seek to characterize and analyze drivers of migration at the individual, household, and community levels, all of which are important in understanding human mobility (Grasmuck and Pessar 1991; Massey and Espinosa 1997) and that together constitute the central units of analysis for migration theorists (see Massey et al. 1998, 17–59). Nonetheless, the ethnosurvey stands out from other migration surveys because its common principles have been applied more or less uniformly around the world. Within the universe of ethnosurveys, cross-context comparative work is particularly feasible because of common standards of sample design, questionnaire construction, variable definition, and data collection. However, the use of ethnosurvey data for comparative analysis is by no means unambiguously warranted. Before discussing its possibilities and limitations, I situate the migration ethnosurvey in a constellation of other large quantitative data collection techniques for the study of migration, summarizing the main advantages and limitations of each.

Capturing the Spatiotemporal Rhythms
with Migration Surveys

The rigor, scarcity, and inflexibility of prospective data
on international migration

Migration cannot be captured adequately by using cross-sectional survey or enumeration approaches that deal only with the here and now. To measure migration fully, data collection methods instead need to be able to capture the spatiotemporal rhythms of migration, which is achieved using true or quasi-longitudinal designs. True longitudinal approaches require the collection of data prospectively, prior to and after an event of interest, whereas quasi-longitudinal designs generally collect data at a single point by gathering retrospective histories.[1] Both rely on direct or proxy retrospective accounts of past events, though the short interwave recall window in most longitudinal surveys—particularly short-term panel studies—should yield less recall bias than purely retrospective approaches.

More important than better recall, however, is the fact that truly longitudinal approaches lessen interval censoring substantially in ways that retrospective approaches cannot, provided subjects are not lost to attrition between waves. Retrospective data collection is especially vulnerable to the loss of survey respondents from emigration, household dissolution, and family reconfiguration. Likewise, prospective longitudinal approaches allow for better and more direct measurement of premigration factors.[2] Finally, true longitudinal data increase the possibility of using a larger set of techniques to deal with unobserved heterogeneity, including the control of individual and household fixed effects. While other data collection techniques may allow for a modicum of these features, prospective approaches are likely to allow for a larger set of them and produce better quality information that is less affected by the aforementioned biases.

Nationally representative longitudinal surveys have become, in many ways, the gold standard of household data collection for a variety of topics. They are particularly powerful—and, indeed, most useful for migration studies—when they follow and collect information from individuals who move out of the original study area (for our purposes, to international locales; see Arenas et al. 2015; Goldman et al. 2014). At the very least, they need to offer the opportunity to identify the specific forms of movement that lead to a loss to follow-up to allow for the modeling of the drivers of migration, like some labor surveys do (Constant and Massey 2003; Villarreal 2014; Villarreal and Blanchard 2013).

Despite these clear potential advantages, longitudinal surveys around the world are oftentimes not designed to deal with many forms of spatial mobility, especially that spanning across national borders.[3] On a global or even regional basis, even in recent decades, short prospective panel data appropriate for migration studies are relatively scarce, while long-term panel surveys are virtually nonexistent. Even when existing, prospective data may have only been collected recently, and thus would be useful mainly for studying the drivers of coterminous contemporary migration flows, they leave important periods in the recent past unexplored. This further complicates the study drivers during specific stages of the migration "lifecycle" (see Jones 2013; Martin and Taylor 1996; Williamson 2015; Zelinsky 1971). Slight differences in the timing of the transition between these stages across settings are especially likely to be missed by prospective data collection methods.

Coterminous versus stage-specific drivers of migration

The examination of the drivers of migration from/to particular places (Massey and Espinosa 1997; Massey et al. 1998) and why these drivers differ over time (Garip 2012) and across places (Massey, Fischer, and Capoferro 2006) are arguably some of the most fundamental questions in migration studies. This assessment can be approached in at least two main ways, each yielding different substantive significance and policy relevance. Comparing the coterminous drivers of migration across places (i.e., during the same period) allows us to understand why migration rates may differ among sending nations and why immigration policies may be more effective on particular social groups (in terms of national origin or otherwise).[4]

The drivers of coterminous mobility could differ across sending areas because each is at a different "stage" of migration, so it seems logical to trace these histories and more precisely understand the differences in their evolution. Given these dynamics, a somewhat different question is how the causes of initiation, takeoff, maturation, or decline differ across places, each of which might have experienced these transitions during different times.[5] While the cross-context, comparative study of stage-specific drivers is scarcer than that of coterminous drivers (perhaps because of the difficulty of finding appropriate data to do so), I would argue such a design can further advance migration theory building and refinement in ways that the coterminous study of the drivers of mobility misses, or otherwise provides insufficient (e.g., counterfactual) proof.

The limitations and flexibility of retrospective measurement

Because the evolution of migration flows may differ considerably across communities, nations, and migratory systems, purely prospective data collection methods would need to rely on fortuitous timing to allow for the study of a particularly relevant period or stage in the migration process across settings. The comparative study of coterminous flows at similar stages but at different points in space and time requires even nimbler research designs to obtain a reasonable representation of the migration risk set prevailing in a specific spatiotemporal context. Flexibility is thus needed to allow for the comparison of migration dynamics at different places in the same period (Garip 2012) or at a particular stage in the migration process (Lindstrom and López-Ramírez 2010). Cross-sectional retrospective designs offer more flexibility to adjust sampling and instrumentation to cover significant differences in migration dynamics across time and places (as has occurred in Mexico-U.S. migration in recent years; see Massey, Durand, and Pren 2015; Villarreal 2014).[6]

Despite this potential flexibility, one cannot simply collect retrospective data using conventional sampling designs and expect them to fit any and all analytic needs, ipso facto, or to offer good representation of both current and past events. The main trade-off in prospective versus retrospective data collection methods lies in the information that is not collected by the latter,[7] from individuals and households not even sampled.[8] This is a problem that becomes more severe the further back in time the retrospective account aims to go. The left censoring of individuals who died or left the study area before the survey year—during periods that the analyst may be interested in studying—is thus the most pressing problem in retrospective data collection. While some experiences lost to left censoring might be recovered through de jure sampling or proxy interviews, these techniques are unlikely to overcome some of the attrition produced by the emigration, dissolution, or dramatic reconfiguration of complete households prior to the survey date (for the case of emigration, see Hamilton and Savinar 2015). The supplementary sampling of migrant households in destinations is probably the best way to overcome the problem (Beauchemin 2012; Liang et al. 2008; Parrado, McQuiston, and Flippen 2005); but destination sampling is less commonly used in migration surveys for many important practical reasons, such as a lack of a sampling frame and the cost and difficulty of reaching (e.g., undocumented) migrants.

Given these issues, representative surveys or even complete enumerations of a specific community will not necessarily yield a complete account of the population in times past, especially the distant past.[9] Quite surprisingly, statistical offices and researchers around the world still lack substantial knowledge about the past emigration of people and, especially, past reconfigurations of households and communities, rendering healthy skepticism about the usefulness of retrospective data. Although the potential biases might be relatively slight for some small number of years prior to the interview, we truly do not know the extent of the problem with much precision, or how biases might vary across communities, contexts, or countries. Depending on the net cumulative intensity of internal and international migration and return, and whose specific migration histories are in fact being collected, the problem likely varies in magnitude across places and, thus, hinders the study of particular communities in their own right, let alone in a comparative framework. These potential biases challenge cross-context comparative studies more than other forms of research. However, analyses that do not use communities or countries as units of analysis are hardly exempt from these problems.

At a national scale, statistical offices in a few countries (e.g., Burkina Faso, Senegal, and Mexico) have begun to use retrospective questions to capture the migration of members of sampled or enumerated households during some set period (usually one or five years) prior to the interview (e.g., Nawrotzki, Riosmena, and Hunter 2013). However, this approach is limited because censuses and related national surveys tend to collect a relatively limited amount of data, which, with few exceptions, are not retrospective. Thus, the wide coverage granted by census surveys comes at a nontrivial cost for those interested in household-level analysis, though they can be used to better understand the role of aggregate-level forces (e.g., at municipal or state scale-zonings; Barrios Puente, Perez, and Gitter

2015; Feng and Oppenheimer 2012). More importantly for cross-context comparative work, the typical question about migration in the past five years (or sometimes one year) is not always asked in censuses around the world; and even when it is asked, the resulting information suffers from several limitations, most notably the lack of comparable data on the experience of those who remained at points of destination.

Given the limitations of standard census and survey questions on migration, specialized retrospective surveys have been a recurrent methodological solution, offering quasi-longitudinal data to get at the reasons behind the international migration (e.g., Bohra and Massey 2009; Grasmuck and Pessar 1991; Gray and Bilsborrow 2013; Henry, Schoumaker, and Beauchemin 2004; Jones 1995, 2013; Lindstrom and Lauster 2001). In particular, the Mexican Migration Project's (MMP's) ethnosurvey approach has generated a continuous stream of community surveys over nearly three decades. Additional efforts using similar versions of the ethnosurvey conducted under the auspices of the Latin American Migration Project (LAMP) have allowed for a deeper understanding of flows to and from the Caribbean, Central America, and South America.

The resulting accumulation of data has allowed for a better understanding of the mobility of Mexican migrants to and from the United States (e.g., Massey et al. 1987; Massey, Durand, and Malone 2002; Massey, Durand, and Pren 2015; Massey and Espinosa 1997; Massey and Riosmena 2010), as well as migration between the island domains of Puerto Rico and the Dominican Republic and the U.S. mainland (and to a lesser extent Spain); migration from Nicaragua to Costa Rica and the United States; migration from Costa Rica, Haiti, Guatemala, and El Salvador to the United States (see Alvarado and Massey 2010; Donato 2010; Duany 2002; Lindstrom and López-Ramírez 2010; Lundquist and Massey 2005; Massey and Riosmena 2010; Massey and Sana 2003); and the international movement of Peruvians, Ecuadorans, and Colombians to the United States, Europe, and elsewhere in South America (e.g., Durand and Roa, forthcoming; Massey and Capoferro 2006; Takenaka and Pren 2010).

The general methodology of the ethnosurvey has also been the basis for collecting data on Paraguayan migration to Argentina (Parrado and Cerrutti 2003); Fujianese migration to the United States (Liang et al. 2008; Liang and Chunyu 2013); Polish-German migration (Kalter 2010; Massey, Kalter, and Pren 2008); and international migration from Senegal, the Congo, and Ghana to Europe, as well as to other African nations (Beauchemin et al. 2015; Castagnone et al. 2015; Liu 2013; Toma and Vause 2014; Vickstrom 2014). More recently, this approach has also been used to understand migration in Bangladesh (Donato et al., this volume). As such, the migration ethnosurvey stands out for cross-context comparative purposes because it has amassed data for a considerable number of communities in several countries across the world, which has opened up new possibilities for cross-local (Fussell and Massey 2004; Lindstrom and López-Ramírez 2010; Massey, Goldring, and Durand 1994; Riosmena 2009), cross-national (Donato and León, forthcoming; Massey, Fischer, and Capoferro 2006), and, increasingly, cross-regional comparative research (Liu, Riosmena, and Creighton 2015; Massey, Kalter, and Pren 2008).

Commonalities and Differences of Migration Ethnosurveys around the World

The migration ethnosurveys done to date share many items in common. With the general methodology discussed in more detail elsewhere (e.g., Massey 1987; Massey and Zenteno 2000; Massey and Capoferro 2004), here I consider several features common to nearly all ethnosurveys that are germane to comparative research on the drivers of migration. First, each survey aims to be representative at the local level, usually within specific sending communities that are selected to represent a range of migration and urbanization conditions (e.g., Massey, Kalter, and Pren 2008). This form of sampling—particularly if it draws less from communities with no prior history of migration whatsoever at a nonspecified sampling rate—makes it difficult to estimate national-level rates, for which a census (Giorguli and Gutiérrez 2012) or nationally representative survey (Hamilton and Savinar 2015; Villarreal 2014) are much better suited. Nevertheless, local representation and a mix of communities jointly allow for robust comparisons across contexts, helping to solve whether differences in the drivers of migration across nations are related to differences in drivers across particular settings in ways that are conducive to testing, and refining tenets in several migration theories (Fussell and Massey 2004; Riosmena 2009). This form of sampling also facilitates the selection of communities as case studies focused on a particular substantive interest, such as what explains the initiation of migration from particular places.

Second, all ethnosurveys include a basic sociodemographic profile and retrospective information on first and last internal and international moves for all people listed in the household roster. This may allow for more a complete representation of migratory behavior across different ages and cohorts because household rosters generally also include all children of the head regardless of their place of residence at the time of interview, which helps to reconstruct the prior history of migration in a community at a prior time point (e.g., Curran and Rivero-Fuentes 2003; Lindstrom 1996). The broad representation of age groups and cohorts and by gender also facilitates stage-specific or coterminous analyses in both present and past by covering individuals who migrate in different epochs (Donato, Durand, and Massey 1992; Donato 1993, 2010; Garip 2012; Kanaiaupuni 2000; Lindstrom 1996). The data also allow for analyses of the drivers of migration at both the household level (Hunter, Murray, and Riosmena 2013) and the family level (Liu, Riosmena, and Creighton 2015; Palloni et al. 2001). Rosters have permitted the construction of community-wide migration measures that have been instrumental in assessing the role of broader migrant networks in the migration process (Fussell 2010; Fussell and Massey 2004; Massey and Aysa-Lastra 2011; McKenzie and Rapoport 2007) and assess and model the takeoff point of migration (Lindstrom and López-Ramírez 2010; Massey, Goldring, and Durand 1994).

Finally, ethnosurveys also include more detailed retrospective migration and labor histories for at least one member of the household, which can be used to analyze the drivers of migration beyond first or last trips (e.g., Massey and

Espinosa 1997). More importantly, life histories allow for a deeper examination of the drivers of international mobility than is possible using household rosters alone. Histories of union formation and dissolution, fertility, property ownership, and migration by other family members generally collected in ethnosurveys can be usefully employed either as variables of interest or controls in event history analyses (e.g., Kalter 2010; Massey and Espinosa 1997; Massey and Riosmena 2010; Massey and Aysa-Lastra 2011; Riosmena 2009).

Despite these basic commonalities, cross-context comparative research is complicated by important differences in how some data are collected, perhaps reflecting differences in the spatiotemporal evolution of migration across settings. With respect to community sampling, for example, different ethnosurveys define local representation differently. In the Migration between Africa and Europe Project (MAFE),[10] the areas represented are the cities of Dakar, Senegal; Kinshasa, the Congo; and Accra and Kumasi, Ghana (Schoumaker and Mezger 2013). In contrast to the MAFE, the large city samples surveyed in the MMP and LAMP[11] are only representative of specific neighborhoods within these cities (see Fussell and Massey 2004). A final difference is that the MMP and LAMP, unlike the MAFE, also collected data in smaller cities, large towns, and smaller rural places, where samples are often representative of the whole community. These samples were selected via simple random sampling after own canvassing (Massey and Sana 2003). In slight contrast, the Fujianese ethnosurvey used stratified sampling in rural sending areas (Liang et al. 2008), while the Polish ethnosurvey used a multistage sampling procedure to oversample migrants in the sending communities selected (Kalter 2010).

Likewise, the size and, more importantly, structure of household rosters differ across projects because of the way each defines who is part of the household roster. For example, MMP and LAMP ethnosurveys perform a type of de jure enumeration in which the person who customarily serves as the head of household is generally counted in the roster as *head* even if he or she is outside the sending community at the time of the interview.[12] In contrast, the enumeration and structure in the MAFE project follows more of a de facto approach as headship is assigned to an individual residing in the household at time of the survey.[13] This difference is particularly important to bear in mind when making cross-context comparisons, as it may define who the children of the head listed in the household roster are, thereby yielding differences in who is counted in the household roster in different settings. While these differences might be surmountable technically (see Liu, Riosmena, and Creighton 2015; Massey, Kalter, and Pren 2008), they should not be glossed over or assumed away.

Finally, ethnosurveys differ in terms of which individuals' detailed retrospective histories are collected. For instance, in Senegal, Ghana, and the Congo (Beauchemin and González-Ferrer 2011), as well as in Poland (Kalter 2010), they were gathered from a randomly chosen individual; whereas in Latin American and Fujianese ethonsurveys, they were compiled for household heads and their spouses (e.g., Donato 2010; Liang et al. 2008; Massey, Fischer, and Capoferro 2006). A random selection of individuals ensures a clearer representation of people across age groups and stages of the life course as of the survey date, not to mention across gender and other large social groups. In contrast, given that heads are usually older, on average, than the general adult population, the selection of household heads provides a better representation of migration-age individuals in years prior to the interview (at least in settings with nontrivial return migration, or when destination samples are systematically collected), making it more likely to capture early stages of the migration process. Depending on the timing of transitions to adulthood (union formation in particular) and on the social rules governing family headship in different settings, sampling individuals who have become household heads by the time of the interview may actually not yield a representative cross-section of people exposed to the risk of migration in the few years preceding the survey year. Also, depending on the prevalence of marital dissolution, the life histories of spouses will be more or less representative of any particular social group, for example, women in patriarchal systems where males are generally assigned the role of, or assumed to be, the household heads (as in the Mexican case).

A litany of checks and adjustments

Analysts should be aware of these nontrivial differences in research designs across ethnosurveys (and other surveys) and how prior histories of both internal and international migration may amplify or reduce the relevance of these differences. Indeed, any study—but cross-context comparative studies in particular—should strive for accurate representation of each community and time period of interest, which may need to be achieved with different instruments or by focusing attention on specific cohorts or social groups across communities.

The differences featured here require careful case and subsample selection based both on the substantive goals of the project (Fitzgerald 2012) and an understanding of the methodological limitations inherent in retrospective data collection (see also Beauchemin 2014). Once cases and subsamples are selected, checks and adjustments for retrospective biases are needed. As Curran and Rivero-Fuentes (2003, 294–95) pointed out, logistic regression in particular may allow for the estimation of robust coefficients (but not of the true migration rate) when using the ethnosurvey design, though this likely assumes a well-specified model with trivial unobserved heterogeneity, something that is impossible to guarantee in any study. Whenever possible, checks for the robustness of findings should be implemented, for instance, by varying the retrospective window of analysis and examining effects across different communities and social groups to assess if patterns go in the expected direction. Alternatively, post hoc adjustments such as case-control/matching, or propensity score–based methods, such as matching, stratification, or inverse proportional treatment weighting (e.g., Lanza, Moore, and Butera 2013), should be implemented to assess whether the drivers of migration differ when assuming a different representation of cohorts or social groups presumed to be more likely to be underrepresented in the data due to left censoring. This allows for testing the robustness of regression-based approaches that assume representation of these groups is adequate.

Conclusion: An Agenda for Comparative
Data Collection and Analysis

This article has provided a broad overview of the strengths and weaknesses of prospective and retrospective approaches to the measurement and understanding of migration. I placed particular emphasis on the comparative study of the drivers of international mobility, as the proper measurement and understanding of these drivers through comparative research of carefully selected cases are necessary for effective theory building and policy-making and are essential to the analysis of related phenomena such as economic development (see De Haas [2010] on the migration-development nexus). I also considered several important weaknesses of retrospective as opposed to prospective data collection methods, especially with respect to the added complications of left censoring produced by the emigration of individuals (either internationally or internally) and the dissolution and reconfiguration of households prior to the time of the survey.

Despite these weaknesses and their potential biases—the true extent of which are surprisingly unknown—retrospectively collected data from ethnosurveys have been and will continue to be quite valuable in advancing knowledge on the drivers of past migration that have not been effectively captured by prospective approaches. Retrospective data collection is particularly valuable for comparative research given the relative lack of comparable prospective data on migrants around the world, which hinders, in particular, the study of specific stages of migration in different periods and nations. Thus, I argue for the need and usefulness of retrospectively collected data for the comparative study of migration.

Although transitions between specific stages in the migration process and what drives them are a matter of some debate (cf. Jones 2013; Martin and Taylor 1996; Williamson 2015; Zelinsky 1971), most models include an initiation or takeoff stage (which Lindstrom and López-Ramírez 2010 see as different from one another); a stage of maturity, with some ebb-and-flow; and, given sufficient time, a declining or winding down stage (Massey 1995). The most influential review and synthesis of migration theories (Massey et al. 1998) clearly identified the theoretical mechanisms in sending and receiving societies posited to account for the initiation versus the continuation of migratory flows. Because these mechanisms are probabilistic rather than deterministic, they should also inform when flows fail to take off and when they are likely to decline, thus arguably accounting for what has come to be known as the migration "hump." Stage-specific analyses of the drivers of migration in different contexts would further advance theoretical understanding and place the more commonly studied differences in coterminous migration into better perspective.

Among the many retrospective data collection efforts, those using the migration ethnosurvey stand out for gathering and continuing to collect data in hundreds of communities in several countries across the globe. Because of their extensive application, the ethnosurveys covered in this volume will remain a key data source for the study of migration in the future, especially for cross-regional studies and other cross-context comparative work. Despite their large recent and past contributions and further promise, the potential biases of retrospective data are accentuated in comparative studies because of their clear need to have adequate representation across the different settings under study: differences in sampling and retrospective life history collection between ethnosurveys may limit the extent or hinder the quality of comparative work. To deal with these challenges, sensible strategies should generally undertake community selection based on the substantive motivation behind the analysis while remaining aware of extant differences between cases. They should also identify the cohorts and social groups that best represent the period or migration stage of interest, and construct survey modules that best serve this representation. Finally, robustness checks and post hoc adjustments, including reweighting and matching, can further bolster these examinations.

Looking forward, the challenge will be to keep migration data collection evolving to keep pace with the increasing elusiveness of human mobility and the changing nature of migration flows, while ideally keeping the current impetus toward comparative research. Retrospective data collection as part of cross-sectional or longitudinal surveys offers advantages relative to prospective approaches because of its flexibility. This plasticity is evinced in instruments such as the ethnosurvey, where the experience of many migration cohorts is captured through basic migration histories compiled for all individuals included in the household roster, in no small part because the rosters often include information for all children of the head regardless of their current location. Representation is also aided because ethnosurveys either provide proxy reporting on absent migrant members or secure émigré representation using destination-based sampling (Beauchemin 2012; Parrado, McQuiston, and Flippen 2005).

Additional flexibility can be provided by stratified sampling approaches that overrepresent individuals most likely to be part of the risk set of core immigrant generations (e.g., Guveli et al. 2015) or during migration stages of particular interest. Such designs would allow a more accurate portrayal of generations, periods, or stages while also reflecting contemporary flows by drawing oversamples of older groups (including proxy reports on the deceased) and providing weights for the representation of both population and oversampled groups, greatly facilitating cross-context and historical research and enabling theory testing and development. In addition, reconstructing the household structure during years before the survey might also provide invaluable data to evaluate the extent of left censoring biases, something that would be useful not only to migration studies but to any social science–based retrospective survey or census data. Although the challenges for comparative research are many, its contributions to the understanding of migration flows and theory refinement have been and will continue to be of very high value. Thus, we must continue to develop data and methods that facilitate comparative work.

Notes

1. As such, panel surveys may include both truly longitudinal as well as quasi-longitudinal information, with cross-sectional surveys comprising only the latter.

2. In addition to these, some projects deal with internal migration across the world in similar fashion, most notably including Demographic Surveillance Systems in several developing countries. However, none of these to date follow international migrants (but indeed gather data on internal moves, e.g., Collinson et al. 2006; Kuhn 2003; VanWey 2005), though some may be able to identify them within the reasons of loss to follow-up.

3. With few exceptions, movement out of the study area is treated as attrition rather than outcome, meaning that registration of a move, when it happens, may not lead to very detailed measurement (of, e.g., specific migrant destinations). Even sophisticated long panel studies designed for (Telles and Ortiz 2008) or with clear applications (and invaluable contributions) to migration studies (Angel et al. 2010) do not quite study the causes of mobility in itself but rather its consequences. Limitations on definitions of what is a migration trip/move, and on the windows covered in the data might also limit cross-context analysis.

4. For instance, comparative research of contemporary undocumented flows to the United States under a coterminous, contemporary lens would look at why irregular Mexican migration slowed down during the last eight years, while that from El Salvador, Honduras, and Guatemala did not (Passel, Cohn, and Gonzalez-Barrera 2013). This examination would provide nuance for several migration theories, by testing the limits or nonlinearities in cost-benefit calculations characteristic of neoclassical economics (Massey et al. 1998) or by providing empirical guidance to build a more robust institutional theory that takes into account the capacity and effectiveness of states in influencing migration flows and their selectivity (Fitzgerald and Cook-Martin 2014; Orrenius and Zavodny 2005).

5. Using the prior example of unauthorized migration from Mexico and Central America, the research question under this approach would be to understand the differences in the takeoff of flows from Honduras in the 1990s; from those from El Salvador and Guatemala in the 1980s; from those of Mexico in the 1940s, when they were "reactivated" by the Bracero Program, or even from the early 1900s, when they first took off during the "Enganche" Era (Massey, Durand, and Malone 2002).

6. In addition, cross-sectional retrospective collection is much cheaper than longitudinal approaches. While this may appear to be an important advantage in high-uncertainty funding environments where seeking to renew a project and thus fund more than two to three waves of collection (in, say, a 10-year span, a reasonable one) may be a bit risky, finding funding to collect additional cross-sections of retrospective data over a longer span is perhaps just as difficult.

7. Recalling the timing and sequencing of events long before interview is challenging and can be influenced by how interviewers probe on the issues (see Belli et al. 1994). People's memories tend to fail when they have made several short moves (Auriat 1991; Redstone and Massey 2004). Yet overall, individuals do tend to remember the timing and sequencing of (arguably, most) migrations, especially in relation to other important life transitions (Smith and Thomas 2003).

8. Although nonresponse (i.e., noncontact + refusal) rates are a growing concern in large-scale social science surveys (see De Heer 1999), this is not overall a major problem in most census enumerations and surveys that gather migration data, including the migration ethnosurvey (e.g., Kalter 2010, 560; Massey and Capoferro 2004, Table 1).

9. Just as cross-sectional data may not provide a representative snapshot of the population of a given area in the past when used retrospectively, longitudinal data may not provide a representative snapshot of this population at future waves. However, the difference between these two types of data collection lies in that prospective approaches do allow for the possibility of adding individuals to the original sample to reach this representation (e.g., Wong et al. 2015).

10. See http://mafeproject.site.ined.fr/en/.

11. See MMP (2012), http://mmp.opr.princeton.ede and http://lamp.opr.princeton.edu.

12. This individual, who is absent due to being in the "middle" of a migration trip, is presumed to be temporarily away or, at least, still fully connected to the household and engaged with its economic survival and power structure (which may be true in settings where core family members do remain behind; Sana and Massey 2005; and other times may not be; e.g., Nobles 2013).

13. MAFE surveys also differ from most other ethnosurveys (particularly those collected over the last 15–20 years) in that they include supplementary destination-based samples collected with the goal of directly capturing the experience of individuals not interviewed in the sending country precisely because of their migration (Beauchemin 2012). In contrast the MMP and LAMP samples rely more on proxy reporting and on the notion that individuals are linked to sending areas in some fashion.

References

Alvarado, Steven Elías, and Douglas S. Massey. 2010. Search of peace: Structural adjustment, violence, and international migration. *The ANNALS of the American Academy of Political and Social Science* 630 (1): 137–61.

Angel, Ronald J., Jacqueline L. Angel, Carlos D. Venegas, and Claude Bonazzo. 2010. Shorter stay, longer life: Age at migration and mortality among the older Mexican-origin population. *Journal of Aging and Health* 22 (7): 914–31.

Arenas, Erika, Noreen Goldman, Anne R. Pebley, and Graciela Teruel. 2015. Return migration to Mexico: Does health matter? *Demography* 52 (6): 1853–68.

Auriat, Nadia. 1991. Who forgets? An analysis of memory effects in a retrospective survey on migration history. *European Journal of Population* 7 (4): 311–42.

Barrios Puente, Gerónimo, Francisco Perez, and Robert J. Gitter. 2015. The effect of rainfall on migration from Mexico to the U.S. *International Migration Review*. doi:10.1111/imre.12116.

Beauchemin, Cris. 2012. Migrations between Africa and Europe: Rationale for a survey design. MAFE Methodological Note No. 5. Available from http://www.ined.fr/fichier/s_rubrique/21396/note.5_mafe_rationale_for_a_survey_design.fr.pdf.

Beauchemin, Cris. 2014. A manifesto for quantitative multi-sited approaches to international migration. *International Migration Review* 48 (4): 921–38.

Beauchemin, Cris, and Amparo González-Ferrer. 2011. Sampling international migrants with origin-based snowballing method. *Demographic Research* 25 (3): 103–34.

Beauchemin, Cris, Jocelyn Nappa, Bruno Schoumaker, Pau Baizan, Amparo González-Ferrer, Kim Caarls, and Valentina Mazzucato. 2015. Reunifying versus living apart together across borders: A comparative analysis of sub-Saharan migration to Europe. *International Migration Review* 49 (1): 173–99.

Belli, Robert F., D. Stephen Lindsay, Maria S. Gales, and Thomas T. McCarthy. 1994. Memory impairment and source misattribution in postevent misinformation experiments with short retention intervals. *Memory & Cognition* 22 (1): 40–54.

Bohra, Pratikshya, and Douglas S. Massey. 2009. Processes of internal and international migration from Chitwan, Nepal. *International Migration Review* 43 (3): 621–51.

Castagnone, Eleanora, Tiziana Nazio, Laura Bartolini, and Bruno Schoumaker. 2015. Understanding transnational labour market trajectories of African-European Migrants: Evidence from the MAFE survey. *International Migration Review* 49 (1): 200–231.

Clark, Ximena, Timothy J. Hatton, and Jeffrey G. Williamson. 2004. What explains emigration out of Latin America? *World Development* 32 (11): 1871–90.

Clark, Ximena, Timothy J. Hatton, and Geffrey G. Williamson. 2007. Explaining U.S. immigration, 1971–1998. *Review of Economics and Statistics* 89 (2): 359–73.

Collinson, Mark, Stephen M. Tollman, Kathleen Kahn, Samuel J. Clark, and Michel Garenne. 2006. Highly prevalent circular migration: Households, mobility and economic status in rural South Africa. In *Africa on the move: African migration and urbanisation in comparative perspective*, eds. Marta Tienda, Sally E. Findley, Stephen Tollman, and Eleanor Preston-Whyte, 194–216. Witwatersrand, South Africa: Wits University Press.

Constant, Amelie, and Douglas S. Massey. 2003. Self-selection, earnings, and out-migration: A longitudinal study of immigrants to Germany. *Journal of Population Economics* 16 (4): 631–53.

Curran, Sara R., and Estela Rivero-Fuentes. 2003. Engendering migrant networks: The case of Mexican migration. *Demography* 40 (2): 289–307.

De Haas, Hein. 2010. Migration and development: A theoretical perspective. *International Migration Review* 44 (1): 227–64.

De Heer, Wim. 1999. International response trends: results of an international survey. *Journal of Official Statistics-Stockholm* 15 (2): 129–42.

Donato, Katharine M. 1993. Current trends and patterns in female migration: Evidence from México. *International Migration Review* 27 (4): 748–71.

Donato, Katharine M. 2010. U.S. migration from Latin America: Gendered patterns and shifts. *The ANNALS of the American Academy of Social and Political Science* 630 (1): 78–92.

Donato, Katharine M., Amanda R. Carrico, Blake Sisk, and Bhumika Piya. 2016. Different but the same: How legal status affects international migration from Bangladesh. *The ANNALS of the American Academy of Political and Social Science* (this volume).

Donato, Katharine M., Jorge Durand, and Douglas S. Massey. 1992. Stemming the tide? Assessing the deterrent effects of the Immigration Reform and Control Act. *Demography* 29 (2): 139–57.

Donato, Katharine M., and Donna Gabaccia. 2015. *Gender and international migration*. New York, NY: Russell Sage Foundation.

Donato, Katharine M., and Gabriela León. Forthcoming. Educación, Género, y Migración de Colombia y México a Estados Unidos. In *Colombia en la Encrucijada: El Proyecto LAMP-Colombia sobre Migración*, eds. Jorge Durand and María Gertrudis Roa. Cali: Universidad del Valle.

Duany, Jorge. 2002. *The Puerto Rican nation on the move: Identities on the island & in the United States*. Chapel Hill, NC: University of North Carolina Press.

Durand, Jorge, and María Gertrudis Roa, eds. Forthcoming. *Colombia en la Encrucijada: El Proyecto LAMP-Colombia sobre Migración*. Cali: Universidad del Valle.

Escobar, Agustín, Kay Hailbronner, Philip Martin, and Liliana Meza. 2006. Migration and development: Mexico and Turkey. *International Migration Review* 40 (3): 707–18.

Feng, Shuaizhang, and Michael Oppenheimer. 2012. Applying statistical models to the climate–migration relationship. *Proceedings of the National Academy of Sciences* 109 (43): E2915.

Fitzgerald, David S. 2012. A comparativist manifesto for international migration studies. *Ethnic and Racial Studies* 35 (10): 1725–40.

Fitzgerald, David S., and David Cook-Martin. 2014. *Culling the masses: The democratic origins of racist immigration policy in the Americas*. Cambridge, MA: Harvard University Press.

Fussell, Elizabeth. 2010. The cumulative causation of international migration in Latin America. *The ANNALS of the American Academy of Political and Social Science* 630:162–77.

Fussell, Elizabeth, and Douglas S. Massey. 2004. The limits to cumulative causation: International migration from Mexican urban areas. *Demography* 41 (1): 151–71.

Garip, Filiz. 2012. Discovering diverse mechanisms of migration: The Mexico-U.S. stream 1970–2000. *Population and Development Review* 38 (3): 393–433.

Giorguli, Silvia E., and Edith Y. Gutiérrez. 2012. Migration et développement. De l'ambivalence à la désillusion? *Hommes et migrations* 1296:22–33.

Grasmuck, Sherri, and Patricia R. Pessar. 1991. *Between two islands: Dominican international migration*. Berkeley, CA: University of California Press.

Gray, Clark, and Richard Bilsborrow. 2013. Environmental influences on human migration in rural Ecuador. *Demography* 50 (4): 1217–41.

Goldman, Noreen, Anne R. Pebley, Matthew J. Creighton, Graciela Teruel, Luis N. Rubalcava, and Chang Chung. 2014. The consequences of migration to the United States for short-term changes in the health of Mexican immigrants. *Demography* 51 (4): 1159–73.

Guveli, Ayse, Harry Ganzeboom, Lucinda Platt, Bernhard Nauck, Helen Baykara-Krumme, Şebnem Eroğlu, Sait Bayrakdar, Efe K. Sözeri, and Niels Spierings. 2015. *Intergenerational consequences of migration: Socio-economic, family and cultural patterns of stability and change in Turkey and Europe*. Basingstoke, UK: Palgrave Macmillan.

Hamilton, Erin R., and Robin Savinar. 2015. Two sources of error in data on migration from Mexico to the United States in Mexican household-based surveys. *Demography* 52 (4): 1345–55.

Hatton, Timothy J., and Jeffrey G. Williamson. 1998. *The age of mass migration: Causes and economic impact*. New York, NY: Oxford University Press.

Henry, Sabine, Bruno Schoumaker, and Cris Beauchemin. 2004. The impact of rainfall on the first out-migration: A multi-level event-history analysis in Burkina Faso. *Population and Environment* 25 (5): 423–60.

Hunter, Lori M., Sheena Murray, and Fernando Riosmena. 2013. Rainfall patterns and U.S. migration from rural Mexico. *International Migration Review* 47 (4): 874–909.

Iskander, Natasha. 2015. *Creative state: Forty years of migration and development policy in Morocco and Mexico*. Ithaca, NY: Cornell University Press.

Jones, Richard C. 1995. *Ambivalent journey: U.S. migration and economic mobility in North-Central Mexico*. Tucson, AZ: University of Arizona Press.

Jones, Richard C. 2013. Migration stage and household income inequality: Evidence from the Valle Alto of Bolivia. *Social Science Journal* 50 (1): 66–78.

Kalter, Frank. 2010. Social capital and the dynamics of temporary labour migration from Poland to Germany. *European Sociological Review* 27 (5): 555–69.

Kanaiaupuni, Shawn M. 2000. Reframing the migration question: An analysis of men, women, and gender in Mexico. *Social Forces* 78 (4): 1311–47.

Kuhn, Randall. 2003. Identities in motion: Social exchange networks and rural-urban migration in Bangladesh. *Contributions to Indian Sociology* 37 (1–2): 311–37.

Lanza, Stephanie T., Julia E. Moore, and Nicole M. Butera. 2013. Drawing causal inferences using propensity scores: A practical guide for community psychologists. *American Journal of Community Psychology* 52 (3–4): 380–92.

Liang, Zai, and Miao David Chunyu. 2013. Migration within China and from China to the USA: The effects of migration networks, selectivity, and the rural political economy in Fujian Province. *Population Studies* 67 (2): 209–23.

Liang, Zai, Miao David Chunyu, Guotu Zhuang, and Wenzhen Ye. 2008. Cumulative causation, market transition, and emigration from China. *American Journal of Sociology* 114 (3): 706–37.

Lindstrom, David P. 1996. Economic opportunity in Mexico and return migration from the United States. *Demography* 33 (3): 357–74.

Lindstrom, David P., and Nathanael Lauster. 2001. Local economic opportunity and the competing risks of internal and U.S. migration in Zacatecas, Mexico. *International Migration Review* 35 (4): 1232–56.

Lindstrom, David P., and Adriana López Ramírez. 2010. Pioneers and followers: Migrant selectivity and the development of U.S. migration streams in Latin America. *The ANNALS of the American Academy of Political and Social Science* 630 (1): 53–77.

Liu, Mao-Mei. 2013. Migrant networks and international migration: Testing weak ties. *Demography* 50 (4): 1243–77.

Liu, Mao-Mei, Fernando Riosmena, and Matthew Creighton. 2015. Family position and family networks in Mexican and Senegalese migration. Paper presented at the annual meetings of the Population Association of America, San Diego, CA.

Lundquist, Jennifer H., and Douglas S. Massey. 2005. Politics or economics? International migration during the Nicaraguan Contra War. *Journal of Latin American Studies* 37 (1): 29–53.

Martin, Philip L., and J. Edward Taylor. 1996. The anatomy of a migration hump. In *Development strategy, employment, and migration: Insights from models*, ed. J. Edward Taylor, 43–62. Paris: OECD Development Centre.

Massey, Douglas S. 1987. The ethnosurvey in theory and practice. *International Migration Review* 21 (4): 1498–1522.

Massey, Douglas S. 1995. The new immigration and ethnicity in the United States. *Population and Development Review* 21 (3): 631–52.

Massey, Douglas S., Rafael Alarcón, Jorge Durand, and Humberto González. 1987. *Return to Aztlan: The social process of international migration from Western Mexico.* Berkeley, CA: University of California Press.

Massey, Douglas S., Joaquín Arango, Graeme Hugo, Ali Kouaouci, and Adela Pellegrino. 1998. *Worlds in motion: Understanding international migration at the end of the millennium.* Oxford: Oxford University Press.

Massey, Douglas S., and Maria Aysa-Lastra. 2011. Social capital and international migration from Latin America. *International Journal of Population Research* 2011:1–18. doi:10.1155/2011/834145.

Massey, Douglas S., and Chiara Capoferro. 2004. Measuring undocumented migration. *International Migration Review* 38 (3): 1075–1102.

Massey, Douglas S., and Chiara Capoferro. 2006. Sálvese quien pueda: Structural adjustment and emigration from Lima. *The ANNALS of the American Academy of Political and Social Science* 606:116–27.

Massey, Douglas S., Jorge Durand, and Nolan J. Malone. 2002. *Beyond smoke and mirrors: Mexican immigration in an era of economic integration.* New York, NY: Russell Sage Foundation.

Massey, Douglas S., Jorge Durand, and Karen A. Pren. 2015. Border enforcement and return migration by documented and undocumented Mexicans. *Journal of Ethnic and Migration Studies* 41 (7): 1015–40.

Massey, Douglas S., and Kristen E. Espinosa. 1997. What's driving Mexico-U.S. migration? A theoretical, empirical, and policy analysis. *American Journal of Sociology* 102 (4): 939–99.

Massey, Douglas S., Mary J. Fischer, and Chiara Capoferro. 2006. International migration and gender in Latin America: A comparative analysis. *International Migration* 44 (5): 63–91.

Massey, Douglas S., Luin Goldring, and Jorge Durand. 1994. Continuities in transnational migration: An analysis of nineteen Mexican communities. *American Journal of Sociology* 99 (6): 1492–1533.

Massey, Douglas S., Frank Kalter, and Karen A. Pren. 2008. Structural economic change and international migration from Mexico and Poland. *Kölner Zeitschrift fur Soziologie und Sozialpsychologie* 60 (48): 134–61.

Massey, Douglas S., and Fernando Riosmena. 2010. Undocumented migration from Latin America in an era of rising U.S. enforcement. *The ANNALS of the American Academy of Political and Social Science* 630:294–321.

Massey, Douglas S., and Mariana Sana. 2003. Patterns of U.S. migration from Mexico, the Caribbean, and Central America. *Migraciones Internacionale* 2 (2): 5–39.

Massey, Douglas S., and René Zenteno. 2000. A validation of the ethnosurvey: The case of Mexico-U.S. migration. *International Migration Review* 34 (3): 765–92.

McKenzie, David, and Hillel Rapoport. 2007. Network effects and the dynamics of migration and inequality: Theory and evidence from Mexico. *Journal of Development Economics* 84 (1): 1–24.

Mexican Migration Project. 2012. The Mexican Migration Project weights. Available from http://mmp.opr .princeton.edu/databases/pdf/MMP%20and%20LAMP%20Weights%202012.pdf.

Nawrotzki, Raphael J., Fernando Riosmena, and Lori Hunter. 2013. Do rainfall deficits predict U.S.-bound migration from rural Mexico? Evidence from the Mexican census. *Population Research and Policy Review* 32 (1): 129–58.

Nobles, Jenna. 2013. Migration and father absence: Shifting family structure in Mexico. *Demography* 50 (4): 1303–14.

Orrenius, Pia M., and Madeline Zavodny. 2005. Self-selection among undocumented immigrants from Mexico. *Journal of Development Economics* 78 (1): 215–40.

Palloni, Alberto, Douglas S. Massey, Miguel Ceballos, Kristin Espinosa, and Michael Spittel. 2001. Social capital and international migration: A test using information on family networks. *American Journal of Sociology* 106 (5): 1262–98.

Parrado, Emilio A., and Marcela Cerrutti. 2003. Labor migration between developing countries: The case of Paraguay and Argentina. *International Migration Review* 37 (1): 101–32.

Parrado, Emilio A., Chris McQuiston, and Chenoa A. Flippen. 2005. Participatory survey research integrating community collaboration and quantitative methods for the study of gender and HIV risks among Hispanic migrants. *Sociological Methods & Research* 34 (2): 204–39.

Passel, Jeffrey S., D'Vera Cohn, and Ana Gonzalez-Barrera. 2013. *Population decline of unauthorized immigrants stalls, may have reversed*. Washington, DC: Pew Hispanic Center.

Raymer, James, Frans Willekens, Dorota Kupiszewska, and Beata Nowok. 2008. Comparability of statistics on international migration flows in the European Union. In *International migration in Europe: Data, models and estimates*, eds. Dorota Kupiszewska and Beata Nowok, 41–71. New York, NY: Wiley.

Redstone, Ilana, and Douglas S. Massey. 2004. Coming to stay: An analysis of the U.S. Census question on immigrants' year of arrival. *Demography* 41 (4): 721–38.

Riosmena, Fernando. 2009. Socioeconomic context and the association between marriage and Mexico-U.S. migration. *Social Science Research* 38 (2): 324–37.

Riosmena, Fernando. 2010. Policy shocks: On the legal auspices of Latin American migration to the United States. *The ANNALS of the American Academy of Political and Social Science* 630:270–93.

Rogers, Andre, Jani Little, and James Raymer. 2010. *The indirect estimation of migration: Methods for dealing with irregular, inadequate, and missing data*. New York, NY: Springer.

Sana, Mariano, and Douglas S. Massey. 2005. Household composition, family migration, and community context: Migrant remittances in four countries. *Social Science Quarterly* 86 (2): 509–28.

Schoumaker, Bruno, and C. Mezger. 2013. Sampling and computation weights in the MAFE surveys. MAFE Methodological Note No. 6. Available from http://www.ined.fr/fichier/s_rubrique/21396/ note_6_mafe_nale_for_samplingandcomputationweights.fr.pdf.

Smith, James P., and Duncan Thomas. 2003. Remembrances of things past: Test-retest reliability of retrospective migration histories. *Journal of the Royal Statistical Society: Series A (Statistics in Society)* 166 (1): 23–49.

Takenaka, Ayumi, and Karen A. Pren. 2010. Determinants of emigration: Comparing migrants' selectivity from Peru and Mexico. *The ANNALS of the American Academy of Political and Social Science* 630:178–93.

Telles, Edward E., and Vilma Ortiz. 2008. *Generations of exclusion: Mexican-Americans, assimilation, and race*. New York, NY: Russell Sage Foundation.

Toma, Sorana, and Sophie Vause. 2014. Gender differences in the role of migrant networks: Comparing Congolese and Senegalese migration flows. *International Migration Review* 48 (4): 972–97.

VanWey, Leah K. 2005. Land ownership as a determinant of international and internal migration in Mexico and internal migration in Thailand. *International Migration Review* 39 (1): 141–72.

Vickstrom, Erik. 2014. Pathways into irregular status among Senegalese migrants in Europe. *International Migration Review* 48 (4): 1062–99.

Villarreal, Andrés. 2014. Explaining the decline in Mexico-U.S. migration: The effect of the Great Recession. *Demography* 51 (6): 2203–28.

Villarreal, Andrés, and Sarah Blanchard. 2013. How job characteristics affect international migration: The role of informality in Mexico. *Demography* 50 (2): 751–75.

Williamson, Jeffrey G. 2015. World migration in historical perspective: Four big issues. In *Handbook of the economics of international migration, 1A: The immigrants*, eds. Barry A. Chiswick and Paul W. Miller, 89–101. Amsterdam: North Holland-Elsevier.

Wong, Rebeca, Alejandra Michaels-Obregón, Alberto Palloni, Luis M. Gutiérrez-Robledo, César González-González, Mariana López-Ortega, Marta M. Téllez-Rojo, and Laura R. Mendoza-Alvarado. 2015. Progression of aging in Mexico: The Mexican Health and Aging Study (MHAS) 2012. *Salud Pública de México* 57 (S1): s79–s89.

Zelinsky, Wilbur. 1971. The hypothesis of the mobility transition. *Geographical Review* 61 (2): 219–49.

Social Capital in Polish-German Migration Decision-Making: Complementing the Ethnosurvey with a Prospective View

By
FRANK KALTER
and
GISELA WILL

In this article we use a combination of retrospective and prospective data from the Polish Migration Project to examine the effect of social capital on the likelihood of migrating to Germany. We derive hypotheses from social capital theory about how personal connections to people with migratory experience affect the probability of migration, and we specify models to be estimated using both the retrospective and prospective data. Estimates of retrospective event history models confirm prior findings about social capital's influence on migration decisions, and these findings are also generally confirmed using prospective data, even when potentially confounding variables are controlled. The prospective data also enable estimation of a two-stage decision model in which people first come to consider migration as an option and then rationally consider whether to depart. The estimates suggest that weak social ties are especially influential in predicting whether migration is considered, while strong ties are important in the decision to move.

Keywords: social capital; migration; prospective panel design; two-stage decision model

The role that social networks play in migration processes has received much attention in research in recent decades and has been one of the most important contributions to migration theory. The basic idea about the role of social networks could be sharpened by combining it with the general framework of

Frank Kalter is a professor of sociology at the School of Social Sciences at the University of Mannheim, Germany. Currently, he also serves as the director of the Mannheim Centre for European Social Research (MZES). His major research interests include migration, the integration of immigrants and their children, and the formal modelling of social processes.

Gisela Will is a senior research fellow at the Leibniz Institute for Educational Trajectories (LIfBi) at the University of Bamberg, which carries out the National Educational Panel Study (NEPS). Within NEPS, she contributes to the area "Education Acquisition of Persons with Migration Background Across the Life Span."

Correspondence: kalter@uni-mannheim.de

DOI: 10.1177/0002716216643506

social capital theory (Massey and Espinosa 1997) to address the underlying mechanisms and permit the derivation of content-rich hypotheses that allow for stricter empirical testing.

From its beginning, the Mexican Migration Project (MMP) (Massey 1987; Durand and Massey 2004) has informed this line of research. The project's unique data provide retrospective longitudinal information on the lives and migration histories of respondents and related others and have enabled significant methodological progress. On one hand, the project has clearly demonstrated that social processes are a crucial element of many facets of past and contemporary Mexican-U.S. migration. On the other hand, the MMP data have accounted for many of the strictest empirical confirmations of causal social capital effects that are available in migration research (Palloni et al. 2001). Moreover, the MMP has, as witnessed by this special issue of *The ANNALS*, inspired a series of sister studies, conducted in other migration contexts all over the world, which have underpinned the potential generality of many social capital assumptions (Fussell 2010; Massey and Aysa-Lastra 2011; Massey and Riosmena 2010).

Among these studies is our own Polish Migration Project (PMP), which confirms the importance of social capital processes for temporary labor migration from Poland to Germany (Kalter 2011; Will 2016). Our study closely followed the general ideas of the MMP, modifying them only slightly to satisfy the specific needs of the context conditions and data collection restrictions. We also added a major new component: in addition to the traditional retrospective design, we implemented a prospective element by reinterviewing the respondents about one year after the first interview. Because the retrospective and prospective perspectives have some different advantages and disadvantages, the prospective element can further improve the empirical evidence for and our theoretical understanding of social capital effects.

In this article, we use the panel portion of our PMP survey to augment research on social capital in three ways. First, we use the prospective longitudinal information to cross-validate typical findings from the standard retrospective approach. Our study is, to the best of our knowledge, the first one to allow for similar models from both perspectives to be run. Second, building upon this cross-validation, we consider important independent variables that are necessary to control for but that are hard, or impossible, to measure retrospectively. Third, and most important, we try to make progress in understanding the deeper mechanisms underlying social capital effects in migration. Thus we use the panel design to gain further insights into the decision-making process of nonmigrants and migrants and try to identify where, exactly, in this process different kinds of social capital might be crucial, and why. We begin with a brief sketch of the theoretical background of and the empirical challenges to our approach. We continue by describing the background and the major methodological features of our PMP. We then present and discuss our analyses, which are structured according to the three aims described above, and conclude by summarizing the major insights and conclusions.

Theoretical Background and Empirical Challenges

Emphasizing that migration is very much a "social process" and that networks play an important role in explaining its dynamics has been important to migration research over the last decades. The two overarching and interwoven tasks of migration research have been to detect the deeper theoretical mechanisms underlying the social processes of migration and to provide the strictest empirical evidence for it. There is no doubt that there has been great and impressive progress on both counts, and there is likewise little doubt that the data and thoughts developed within the MMP have played a major part in achieving this progress.

Progress has been made on the theoretical side by treating migration as having a social contagion effect, using the more general framework of social capital theory. In their seminal paper, Massey and Espinosa (1997, 952) formulated what can be regarded as the basic social capital hypothesis of migration: "Nonmigrants are hypothesized to draw on the social capital embedded in ties to migrants to lower their costs and risks of movement. ... As a result of these raised benefits and lowered costs and risks, some people decide to migrate. ..." It is this reference to micro-theory, in this case the general cost-benefit framework, that gives the hypothesis its analytical power. It allows the idea to be wedded to other important tools in migration theory, most notably the human capital model, and helps researchers to understand and specify more precisely the mechanisms behind the influence of social networks. The well-known hypotheses of "affinity," "information," and "facilitating" as formulated by Ritchey (1976), for example, can easily be reconstructed as auxiliary hypotheses, or "bridge" assumptions, about how social ties affect basic parameters of a subjective utility model, including value-expectations, probabilities, and costs (Kalter 2011).

The explicit reference to general social capital theory allows integration of some of its important insights, thereby enabling further specifications of the mechanisms by which networks operate and yielding more fine-grained, testable hypotheses. For example, the well-known differentiation between strong ties, which may provide resources more reliably (Coleman 1990; Lin 2001), and weak ties, which are more far-reaching (Granovetter 1973; Burt 1992), suggests that with respect to migration the former might have more to do with Ritchey's (1976) facilitating mechanisms, whereas the latter might relate especially to information mechanisms (Will 2016).

While the merits of social capital theory in migration seem closely intertwined with a basic cost-benefit or rational-choice framework, the rational-choice framework has nonetheless fallen into some disrepute in recent years. Empirical research has increasingly revealed that the basic assumptions of rational choice do not always represent a realistic model of actual behavior (Kroneberg and Kalter 2012). This caveat holds for many different fields of application, and migration seems to be no exception. In fact, it has already been stated in classic migration theories, such as those posited by Fairchild (1925) or Lee (1966), both of which observe that migration behavior often involves a puzzling "inertia" that seems to contradict the notion of rational action.

Speare (1971, 130) has explicitly critiqued the rational choice (RC) model, noting that "the biggest problem with the application of a cost-benefit model to human migration may not be the crudeness of the actual calculation, but the fact that many people never make any calculation at all." Moreover "a large proportion of the non-migrants had never considered moving, and many of these … would have gained by moving" (Speare 1974, 174). To consider the consequences drawn from these observations, Speare (1971, 130) models migration decision-making as a multistep process in which the first crucial step is whether actors consider migration at all (see Brown and Moore [1970], Rossi [1980], and Sell and DeJong [1983] for similar proceedings). Only if this first step is taken does the rational choice portion of the process start and potentially lead to a decision to move after careful cost-benefit calculations (Speare 1974; Speare, Goldstein, and Frey 1975).

Speare's formulation suggests that social mechanisms, such as the three distinguished by Ritchey (1976) mentioned above, might be expected to be relevant especially in the latter step, when actors have already overcome their inertia and begun to weigh the pros and cons of migration in more detail. Social capital mechanisms cannot be assumed to be absent during the first step, however, when actors consider whether migration is an option at all. Although Speare (1974) relied on a rather vague satisfaction concept to capture this step, Kalter (1997) has suggested that it can also be modeled using rational choice theory. He assumes that the first step in the decision-making process should be understood as a kind of meta-decision as to whether to engage in a more detailed decision process at all. Accordingly, people consider migration if they expect the utility of migration (at this point rather un-reflected-upon and weighted by the subjective probability that consideration will eventually lead to an actual decision to migrate) to outweigh the costs of consideration. The model has been successfully applied empirically to internal migration within Germany in two independent larger studies (Kalter 1997; Kley 2009; Kley and Mulder 2010).

Modeling the first step as an RC model is not just a scholastic exercise; it also preserves the basic merits of RC theory, namely, its precision and analytical power (Kroneberg and Kalter 2012). With respect to hypotheses derived from social capital theory, it immediately leads to a more fine-grained specification of potential mechanisms. Most importantly, the bridge assumptions that social capital affects value expectations, probabilities, and costs (as implicit in the hypotheses of Ritchey [1976]) can be transferred to the respective parameters of the consideration model. That is, the migration experiences of others might signal the high potential gains of migration, so that it becomes worth considering. In other words, earlier decisions by the former migrants offer proof that migration might, in fact, turn out to be the preferred option (Neff and Constantine 1979; McHugh 1984).

In addition, the presence of migrants in one's personal network means that the costs of gathering information on migration are highly reduced (Goodman 1981). Accordingly research has shown that migrant social capital might be behind non-migrants' consideration to migrate at all, that they include migration in the set of alternatives, and thus overcome their basic inertia. Following the arguments above, one could expect that this might be a mechanism that is particularly related to the impact of weak ties (Will 2016).

On the empirical side, the unique data structure of the MMP has overcome many common limitations of other empirical approaches (Massey et al. 1998), such as small sample sizes, nonrandom sampling, and inadequate reference groups. The MMP's large-scale comprehensive quantitative information on migration and life histories of respondents, together with those of their relevant social ties, allows for sophisticated longitudinal methods to be employed, which provide comparably strict evidence for the causal impact of social networks (Palloni et al. 2001). The information was collected with a retrospective approach, and the combination of standardization and ethnographic methods in the interviews—the trademark of an ethnosurvey—has been the key to ensuring data quality.

While the retrospective approach in general offers many advantages (Featherman 1979), such as covering relatively long periods of time and being cost-efficient, it also comes with some disadvantages. One of the common issues is how much the sample at the time of the survey and its past behavior are truly representative of the behavior of the population at large in the past (Goldstein and Goldstein 1983). This is especially a problem when studying migration (Massey, Goldring, and Durand 1994). A second larger concern pertains to the limits of the respondent's memory and the validity of the retrospective information. Migration behavior itself, being an especially "hard" fact, is usually remembered comparably well (Donato, Durand, and Massey 1992; Smith and Thomas 2003; McKenzie and Rapoport 2007). There are also indications that information on important events in the life of persons in their close network is relatively reliable (Anderson and Silver 1986), though, to the best of our knowledge, there are no specific studies that have tested the reliability of migration information given by others.

The problem can be more severe, however, with respect to other independent variables that one would like to include in the analyses, either to control for unobserved heterogeneity or to assess mediating mechanisms. In the first case, when testing whether the migration experience of others has a causal effect on decisions to migrate, it might be wise to control for other destination-specific capital, such as destination-country language skills. Such a control would help to exclude the alternative explanation that the correlation between one's own migration behavior and that of others is spurious because language skills are decisive and shared. Language skills, however, can hardly be measured in a retrospective design. Second, reliable measurement of whether migration was merely considered in the past, maybe years ago, seems almost impossible.

These limitations call to mind a principal alternative to retrospective data collection: a prospective panel design. In fact, the prospective view has been the design of choice in most classical and in more recent studies that focus on the deeper mechanisms of the decision-making process (Bach and Smith 1977; Coulter, van Ham, and Feijten 2011; De Jong 2000; Landale and Guest 1985; Kalter 1997; Kley and Mulder 2010; Sell and De Jong 1983; Speare 1974; Speare, Goldstein, and Frey 1975; Speare, Kobrin, and Kingkade 1982). Most of these studies have been conducted within the context of internal migration processes, however, as implementing panel studies for international migration processes is, as a rule, prohibitively expensive. Moreover, as opposed to the retrospective design, the prospective design for studying migration bears further relative disadvantages, such as covering much shorter periods of time, right-censoring, and panel mortality (Buck 2000;

Featherman 1979; Smith and Thomas 2003). Therefore we sought to combine both perspectives and thus complement the traditional design of the ethnosurvey with a prospective element. The specific context and the major details of our study are briefly described in the next section.

The Polish Migration Project

Migration between Poland and Germany has a long history that can be traced back to the nineteenth century. In the postwar period, the fall of the Iron Curtain marked a turning point in the dominant pattern of migration. Prior to 1990, migration from Poland to Germany was predominantly permanent, with so-called Aussiedler (ethnic Germans) accounting for a large part of this migration. Temporary forms of migration existed, of course, but occurred to a lesser extent and mainly between Poland and the former German Democratic Republic (GDR). Since 1990, however, permanent migration has declined sharply and temporary labor migration has become the predominant form of migration between Poland and the Federal Republic of Germany. In 2004 the number of officially registered temporary stays of Polish workers in Germany exceeded three hundred thousand for the first time, and even after Poland's admission to the European Union temporary migration has remained at a high level (Bundesministerium des Innern 2007).

A great deal of research has been conducted on the substantive importance of Polish-German migration (see Iglicka 2000; Okólski 2001, 2004; Pallaske 2002). Although the impact of social networks has also been addressed in several ways (Elrick and Lewandowska 2008; Grzymała-Kazłowska 2001; Kaczmarczyk 2001; Korczyńska 2001; Münst 2008; Osipowicz 2002), few studies have been able to test potential social capital effects on migration in a rigorous way (Kalter 2011). To overcome these shortcomings, we initiated the PMP in 2004, transferring the ideas and basic design features of the MMP to the Polish-German context.

In line with the tradition of the MMP, we first drew a deliberate sample of communities. We wanted to include both rural and urban contexts, as well as regions near to and far away from the Polish-German border. Thus, we selected the following four communities: the city of Poznań in western Poland, and the nearby rural municipality of Jaraczewo; and the city of Kielce in southeastern Poland, and the nearby community of Pawłów. In each of these four communities about one hundred migrants and one hundred nonmigrants were interviewed. The target population consisted of residents aged 18 to 65.

To draw random samples, in selected households in Jaraczewo, the target person was singled out via the last-birthday method. In the other three communities, we drew a random sample from the electronic population register system, PESEL. Since migrants are a relatively rare group in the population, a stratified sample was constructed. In the first phase, all selected persons were interviewed. In the second phase, as soon as one hundred nonmigrants had been interviewed, a short screening interview was implemented, and full interviews were conducted with migrants only. A person was defined as being a migrant if she or he

TABLE 1
Sampling Information for Surveys of Four Polish Communities

	All Interviews	Full Interviews			Response Rate	Follow-Up Interview	
		Nonmigrants	Migrants	Total		N	Percentage
Jaraczewo	495	101	59	**160**	88.4%	140	87.5%
Poznań	603	105	54	**159**	67.8%	109	68.6%
Pawłów	320	101	104	**205**	89.1%	176	85.9%
Kielce	596	102	101	**203**	85.9%	149	73.4%
Total	**2,014**	**409**	**318**	**727**	**80.5%**	**574**	**79.0%**

had ever traveled to Germany for work between 1980 and 2004. Table 1 shows the realized interviews and the response rates in the four communities.

As in the MMP, the full interviews gathered extensive information on biographies of the respondents. These biographical data include information on the family situation, periods of employment and unemployment, and the acquisition of property. For the aims of this article, two sets of information are particularly important. The first is the migration history of the respondent. Here, more detailed information on the timing was gathered for up to seven working trips to Germany between 1980 and 2003. Working stays in 2004 were gathered on a daily basis. The second important set of information is the migration experience of the respondents' social ties or, more precisely, whether, and if so, when, for the first time a working trip or even a permanent move to Germany was ever made by significant others. These "others" include all household members, all children of the head living outside the household, as well as other members of the immediate family (brothers, sisters, parents) or extended family (e.g., aunts, uncles, cousins, grandparents, and partner's family).

In contrast to the MMP, these data were collected using an almost completely standardized questionnaire, as previous studies in Poland have shown the feasibility of this approach (Frejka, Okólski, and Sword 1998; Jaźwińska and Okólski 1996). However, this standardized procedure had a limitation in that detailed information on the migration trips could be gathered for only five people per group (household members, children, and other family). Analysis of the data has determined, however, that in only a very few cases did more than five relatives ever work in Germany.

As mentioned above, not all variables can be measured reliably in a retrospective way, and this is the case for "softer" variables such as subjective language skills. It is especially true for attitudes such as intentions to migrate. Migration experiences of nonfamily are also considered not very well remembered facts over the life course. These kinds of information were therefore gathered at the time of the first interview only. To test whether these factors determine migration within the year after the initial interview, a follow-up survey was conducted. Table 1 shows the number of successful follow-up interviews. Whereas the probability of reaching migrants and nonmigrants again was nearly the same (results not shown), the response rate for respondents who lived in urban communities was lower in the second panel wave. All in all, 574 people could be interviewed a second time, and 570 of these cases are used for the prospective analyses.

Retrospective Analyses

As outlined above, retrospective longitudinal analyses have been the most common approach for testing social capital effects with ethnosurvey data. More precisely, discrete-time event history models (Allison 1984) have become the major workhorse and have proven to be particularly helpful. We start by using this principal tool for a first test of whether network effects are an important element of the forces behind recent migration patterns from Poland to Germany.

To do so, the comprehensive longitudinal information of the respondents was transformed into a data file that included all person-years from 1990 to 2004.[1] People were followed starting at age 18, resulting in a dataset with 7,829 person-years to provide the cases for retrospective analysis. The dependent variable is whether the respondent went to Germany for work-related reasons during the person-year in question. Migration was coded as 1 if such a trip was made in a given year t and 0 otherwise. We ran discrete-time event history analyses, controlling for a rich set of independent variables on the macro and micro levels.[2]

The explanatory variable of specific interest is migration-specific social capital, and in the first model depicted in Table 2, this concept is operationalized as simply as possible, using only a dummy variable to indicate whether anyone in the respondent's family (household members, immediate family, and extended family) had ever migrated by year $t - 1$. We found that migration experience in the family significantly increased the likelihood of making a working trip to Germany, as measured by average marginal effect (see model 1). Thus, our analysis shows the general relevance of migrant-specific social capital in the Polish-German migration context. This confirms earlier findings (Kalter 2011) that used somewhat different model specifications.

To further check the robustness of this finding and to get some indication of the potential mechanisms behind it, we ran the same analysis with other measures of the migration-specific social capital. Model 2 shows that the significance of the impact was somewhat increased when social capital was measured by the number of prior family-member migrants to Germany. The overall model fit is also better in model 2, but only slightly. Including the number in nonlinear ways (not shown here) did not significantly improve the fit. Model 3 distinguishes between several kinds of family members: the partner, immediate family members, and other relatives within the extended family. While the partner's prior migration experience hardly had any effect, we found that migration-specific capital in both the immediate and extended family led to an increase in the likelihood that the respondent would make a trip, with almost equal strength.

To make the analyses comparable to later analyses discussed below, model 4 combines the partner and the immediate family members into one category, now labeled "strong ties." The effect of this dummy is significant at the 10 percent

TABLE 2

Discrete-Time Event History Analysis: Risk of Making a Working Trip to Germany—
Influence of Migration-Specific Social Capital (Average Marginal Effects) Using
Different Operationalizations

	Model 1	Model 2	Model 3	Model 4	Model 5
Measure of migration-specific social capital					
Any migrant in family (dummy)	.0155°°				
	(.0064)				
Number of migrants in family		.0105°°°°			
		(.0021)			
Partner a migrant			.0085		
			(.0105)		
Migrant in immediate family			.0223°°°		
			(.0080)		
Migrant in extended family			.0239°°°		
			(.0073)		
Migrant among strong ties				.0134°	
				(.0073)	
Migrant among weak ties				.0261°°°°	
				(.0073)	
Index of permanent migration experience in family					.0146
					(.0093)
Index of temporary migration experience in family					.0149°°°°
					(.0038)
N person-years	7,829	7,829	7,829	7,829	7,829
N persons	677	677	677	677	677
Wald χ^2	546.49	562.07	555.35	553.57	560.14
Pseudo r^2	.1555	.1592	.1596	.1584	.1588

NOTE: Average marginal effects controlling for community, year (dummies), age, age squared, sex, human capital, migration-specific human capital, and location-specific capital. Standard errors in parentheses.
°$p < .10$. °°$p < .05$. °°°$p < .01$. °°°°$p < .001$.

level. The second dummy for "weak ties" captures the extended family members as in model 3, but is relabeled. In the last variant (model 5), we apply two indices, which were introduced by Espinosa and Massey (1997). These indices consider not only the degree of relationship (the closeness of ties as measured by steps between interviewed person and the particular relative) but also whether the relevant person lives in the country of destination permanently or whether she or he is just a temporary migrant laborer. We found that the effect strength of permanent and nonpermanent migration-specific social capital was almost the same, though only the latter turned out to be significantly different from zero given the underlying variances.

Prospective Analyses

As mentioned earlier, the retrospective approach has many advantages, but it also comes with some built-in disadvantages. Therefore, in the second step of our analyses, we used the prospective longitudinal information to cross-validate our findings from the standard retrospective approach above. Specifically, we ran logistic regression models for all respondents who were reinterviewed in the second wave of our survey (n = 570). The dependent variable here is whether migration occurred between the first and the second interview, that is, between 2005 and 2006. The variable was defined as 1 if a person had migrated to Germany and 0 otherwise. A total of fifty-nine respondents did migrate to Germany between the first and the second wave. The analyses controlled for the same set of independent variables as the retrospective analyses above, apart from the year of course, and the variables are constructed in exactly the same way.

Table 3 shows clearly that in the prospective analysis as well there was a strong and robust positive effect of migrant-specific social capital on the respondent's likelihood of migrating in the following years. As in the retrospective model, both the dummy variable and the number of prior migrants in the family had a significant positive effect on the likelihood of taking a working trip to Germany within one year of the first interview. In the third model, however, we observe some differences between the two approaches. Contrary to the retrospective analysis in the prospective model, prior migration experience of the partner had a significant positive effect on one's own likelihood to migrate.

In addition, whereas social capital provided by close family members played a significant role in both approaches, more distant relatives influenced the likelihood of migrating in the retrospective model only, as reflected in the results of model 4. Whereas in the retrospective analysis weak ties had a more significant effect, in the prospective model only strong ties seemed to provide migration-specific social capital. Results once again differ with regard to measures of permanent versus nonpermanent migration-specific social capital. As in the retrospective design, only the effect of social capital provided by temporary migrants turns out to be significant.

Building upon this cross-validation, we can consider other important independent variables, which are crucial, but hard or impossible to measure in retrospect. The most important aspect in this context is surely German-language skills. In the first interview the respondents were asked to estimate their German skills (understanding, speaking, reading, and writing) on a scale from 1 (*not at all*) to 4 (*very good*). One index of these four dimensions was constructed and included in the analysis. In the prospective approach it is also possible to construct several independent variables in a more sophisticated way. For example, homeownership can be measured more exactly, because people who live in their parents' or grandparents' house can be identified. We can also differentiate between children over 18 who have already moved out and those who still live in the parental home. In addition, other adults living in the respondent's household as well as unmarried partners can be considered in the analyses.

TABLE 3
Logistic Regression: Risk of Making a Working Trip to Germany—Influence
of Migration-Specific Social Capital (Average Marginal Effects),
Using Different Operationalizations

	Model 1	Model 2	Model 3	Model 4	Model 5
Measure of migration-specific social capital					
Any migrant in family (dummy)	.0770***				
	(.0239)				
Number of migrants in family		.0178***			
		(.0056)			
Partner a migrant			.0873**		
			(.0350)		
Migrant in immediate family			.1188****		
			(.0245)		
Migrant in extended family			.0054		
			(.0267)		
Migrant among strong ties				.1115****	
				(.0242)	
Migrant among weak ties				.0118	
				(.0261)	
Index of permanent migration experience in family					.0199
					(.0414)
Index of temporary migration experience in family					.0358****
					·(.0103)
N	570	570	570	570	570
Wald χ²	82.82	92.13	80.00	77.23	90.56
Pseudo r²	.2862	.2786	.3230	.3110	.2902

NOTE: Average marginal effects controlling for community, age, age squared, sex, human capital, migration-specific human capital, and location-specific capital. Standard errors in parentheses.
*p < .10. **p < .05. ***p < .01. ****p < .001.

Model 2 in Table 4 adds these new and reconstructed variables to the analysis. As expected, German-language skills had a strong and significant positive effect on the likelihood of migrating. Moreover, the reconstructed variable of home-ownership had a significant inhibitory effect. But what is more important, we now see that the relevance of migration-specific social capital (included as a simple dummy variable) remains even upon inclusion of these additional variables. This result is robust to the particular operationalization of migration-specific social capital (results not shown). Thus, the prospective approach confirmed even more the impact of social capital because we were able to control for unobserved heterogeneity, which cannot be controlled for in the traditional retrospective design.

So far we have concentrated on migration-specific social capital within the family. From a theoretical point of view, social capital that is provided by friends or acquaintances can be valuable as well (Bagchi 2001; Giulietti, Wahba, and Zenou 2014; Will 2016; Wong and Salaff 1998). Since the migration behavior of weak ties is not retrospectively measurable, the social capital of weak ties can be considered only when using a prospective approach. Model 3 in Table 4 adds two variables that measure nonfamilial social capital. The first variable indicates the number of people in one's circle of acquaintances who went to Germany to work but were now living in Poland. The second variable counts all known people outside the family living in Germany permanently.

This analysis reveals that only the number of temporary migrant laborers had a significant effect on the probability of migration. The effect of the migrant-specific social capital provided by relatives again remained unchanged. The resources that social capital from strong and weak ties provides are different. Variables to discriminate between these kinds of social capital were already introduced (see model 4 in Tables 2 and 3); but by considering nonfamilial ties, the variable measuring social capital from weak ties can be defined more exactly. Model 4 includes the original indicator, whereas model 5 employs the new variable. In both analyses, only social capital that is provided by strong ties significantly raised the respondent's chances of migrating.

Social Capital in Migrant Decision-Making

As the final step in our analyses, we sought to add a deeper understanding of the mechanisms underlying social capital effects by taking further advantage of the panel. Specifically, we sought to identify more exactly where in the decision-making process are different types of social capital most crucial. Following the earlier theoretical discussion, we divide the process of migration into two basic steps. The first step is whether the respondent considers migration as an option at all. We measured this in the first interview in 2005 by asking: "Have you, recently, seriously thought about working abroad or living there for a longer period of time?" The respondent could answer with "yes" or "no," coded as 1 or 0, respectively.

Based on this dummy variable, which we labeled "considerations," we ran a number of logistic regressions to disentangle the effects of migration-specific social capital at different points in the decision process, controlling for migration-specific human capital in addition to other independent variables, as shown in Table 5. The first column shows the effects of migration-specific (social) capital variables when looking at actual migration (between the first and the second interview). Basically, this is the same as model 5 in Table 4, though the coefficients marginally differ owing to slightly different sets of control variables. As we have already seen and discussed, migration experience among strong family ties had a clear impact on one's likelihood of making a trip to Germany to work.

Looking at the likelihood of considering migration in column 2, we found here that migration experience among weak ties seemed especially important. This is

TABLE 4
Logistic Regression: Risk of Making a Working Trip to Germany—Control of Additional
Variables (Average Marginal Effects) in the Prospective Approach

	Model 1	Model 2	Model 3	Model 4	Model 5
Human capital					
German-language skills		.0613****	.0602****	.0586****	.0586****
		(.0177)	(.0178)	(.0174)	(.0174)
Location-specific capital					
Homeownership	−.0092				
	(.0278)				
Homeownership (new)		−.0931****	−.0924****	−.0914****	−.0892***
		(.0275)	(.0270)	(.0270)	(.0273)
Internal migration	−.0584	−.0481	−.0485	−.0543	−.0564
	(.0399)	(.0402)	(.0386)	(.0391)	(.0389)
Married	−.0783*				
	(.0434)				
Partner		−0.0680*	−0.0715*	−0.0840**	−0.0850**
		0.0381	0.0387	0.0361	0.0364
Child < 6 years	−.0074	−.0041	−.0090	.0061	.0062
	(.0397)	(.0375)	(.0378)	(.0348)	(.0354)
Child 6–17 years	.0591*	.0485	.0506*	.0470	.0473
	(.0330)	(.0300)	(.0301)	(.0288)	(.0289)
Child >17 years	.0972**				
	(.0411)				
Child in household >17 years		.1006***	.0919**	.1050***	.1060***
		(.0381)	(.0373)	(.0371)	(.0373)
Adults in household		.0012	.0017	.0008	.0010
		(.0103)	(.0105)	(.0103)	(.0104)
Migration-specific social capital					
Any migrant in family (dummy)	.0770***	.0812****	.0766***		
	(.0239)	(.0234)	(.0240)		
Number of temporary migrants outside the family			.0028**		
			(.0014)		
Number of permanent migrants outside the family			−.0026		
			(.0044)		
Migrant among strong ties				.1086****	.1104****
				(.0224)	(.0226)
Migrant among weak ties				.0179	
				(.0264)	
Migrant among weak ties (new)					.0050
					(.0227)
N	570	570	570	570	570
Wald χ^2	82.82	89.72	90.99	95.96	96.01
Pseudo r^2	.2862	.3419	.3537	.3655	.3644

NOTE: Average marginal effects controlling for community, age, age squared, sex, human capital, migration-specific human capital, and location-specific capital. Standard errors in parentheses.
*$p < .10$. **$p < .05$. ***$p < .01$. ****$p < .001$.

TABLE 5

Logistic Regressions: Influence of Migration-Specific Social Capital (Average Marginal Effects) in Different Steps of the Decision-Making Process

	Migration (All Respondents)	Considerations (All Respondents)	Considerations (Nonmigrants)	Considerations (Migrants)	Migration if Considerations
Migration-specific human capital					
German-language skills	.0570***	.0438**	.0747***	−.0196	.1087***
	(.0188)	(.0223)	(.0272)	(.0368)	(.0401)
(Prior) Migrant	.1194****	.1111***			.2268****
	(.0259)	(.0340)			(.0671)
Number of prior trips				.0414***	
				(.0140)	
Migration-specific social capital					
Migrant among strong ties	.1058****	.0032	.0142	−.0114	.3486****
	(.0230)	(.0391)	(.0505)	(.0632)	(.0488)
Migrant among weak ties	.0114	.1149****	.1013***	.0902*	−.1070*
	(.0239)	(.0312)	(.0375)	(.0511)	(.0553)
N	570	708	400	308	160
Wald χ^2	97.20	102.49	62.90	47.33	43.12
Pseudo r^2	.3136	.1758	.2306	.1641	.3938

NOTE: Average marginal effects controlling for city, age, age squared, sex, human capital, migration-specific human capital, and location-specific capital. Standard errors in parentheses.

*$p < .10$. **$p < .05$. ***$p < .01$. ****$p < .001$.

exactly what we anticipated given the basic arguments in the social capital litera-ture. Next to migration-specific social capital, migration-specific human capital is also important at this step in the decision-making process. German-language skills and one's own prior migration experience both significantly increased the likelihood of considering migration. The latter seemed especially obvious, as migration had proven to be in the respondents' set of alternatives before. One could thus expect the impact of weak ties to be especially strong for nonmigrants who lack migration experience of their own. But comparing the models for non-migrants (third column) and former migrants (fourth columns) showed that the effect strength was almost the same; it was just that the effect for migrants did not reach the same significance level. There was, however, a clear interaction with respect to German-language skills, which were an important determinant of whether one considered migration, but only for nonmigrants.

The last column in Table 5 shows the effects of a model for the likelihood of migration only for those who considered migration the year before. We look at the determinants that lead from considerations to actual moves. We found that the effects of German-language skills and former migration experience were especially strong. Migration-specific human capital is thus particularly relevant when weighing the pros and cons of migration in the second step of the decision-making process. Even more important, we found a strong effect of migration experience among strong ties, indicating that strong ties are important when it comes to realizing migration possibilities already under consideration. This find-ing supports the assumption that strong ties are closely related to the facilitating mechanism. Interestingly, the effect of weak ties was slightly negative in this model. So, it seems that while weak ties are influential in overcoming inertia, supporting their relevance in the information mechanisms, they are not sufficient to actually lead to migration. On the contrary, the slightly negative effect suggests that they are prone to lead to considerations, which turn out to be unrealistic options in the end.

Summary and Conclusion

The analyses in this article have shown that complementing the traditional retro-spective design of an ethnosurvey with a prospective panel component can increase the evidence for and the understanding of social network effects on migration. Implementing a follow-up interview with the respondents to the PMP, we were able to show that prospective analyses confirm, and thus cross-validate, the basic finding that migration-specific social capital has been an important fac-tor in generating temporary migration from Poland to Germany. While replicat-ing findings with different approaches and methods is valuable in its own right, the prospective approach also allowed us to include important variables that are hard to measure in retrospect. Thus one can better account for some sources of unobserved heterogeneity, making the findings even more reliable.

Most importantly, the prospective approach allowed for analysis of the role that migration-specific capital plays in the decision process of potential migrants.

We find that weak ties are especially relevant in the first step—considering migration at all—while strong ties are more important in the second step—transforming such considerations into actual migration. This finding is in line with basic expectations deriving from social capital theory and supports the fruitfulness of this general framework.

Notes

1. Although the data of the PMP cover both time periods, before and after 1990, in this article we focus on temporary labor migration after 1990. The main reason for this is that some crucial independent variables are available only for the later years.

2. The included variables are community, year (dummies), age, age squared, sex, level of education (according to CASMIN), employment status (according to ISCO main groups), unemployment, migration-specific human capital (number of prior migration trips, number of prior migration trips squared), and location-specific capital: homeownership (dummy), prior internal migration (dummy), married, children under 6 (dummy), children between 6 and 17 (dummy), or children aged 18 and older (dummy).

References

Allison, Paul D. 1984. *Event history analysis: Regression for longitudinal event data*. Newbury Park, CA: Sage Publications.

Anderson, Barbara, and Brian Silver. 1986. The validity of survey responses: Interviews of multiple respondents in a household from a survey of Soviet emigrants. Research Report No. 86-89, University of Michigan, Population Studies Center, Ann Arbor, MI.

Bach, Robert L., and Joel Smith. 1977. Community satisfaction, expectations of moving, and migration. *Demography* 14 (2): 147–67.

Bagchi, Ann D. 2001. Migrant networks and the immigrant professional: An analysis of the role of weak ties. *Population Research and Policy Review* 20 (1–2): 9–31.

Brown, Lawrence A., and Eric G. Moore. 1970. The intra-urban migration process: A perspective. *Geografiska Annaler, Series B, Human Geography* 52 (1): 1–13.

Buck, Nicholas. 2000. Using panel surveys to study migration and residential mobility. In *Researching social and economic change: The uses of household panel studies*, ed. David Rose, 250–72. London: Routledge.

Bundesministerium des Innern. 2007. *Migrationsbericht des Bundesamtes für Migration und Flüchtlinge im Auftrag der Bundesregierung. Migrationsbericht 2006*. Berlin: Bundesministerium des Innern.

Burt, Ronald S. 1992. *Structural holes: The social structure of competition*. Cambridge, MA: Harvard University Press.

Coleman, James S. 1990. *Foundations of social theory*. Cambridge, MA: Belknap Press.

Coulter, Rory, Maarten van Ham, and Peteke Feijten. 2011. Partner (dis)agreement on moving desires and the subsequent moving behavior of couples. IZA Discussion Paper, No. 5277, Bonn, Germany.

De Jong, Gordon F. 2000. Expectations, gender, and norms in migration decision-making. *Population Studies* 54 (3): 307–19.

Donato, Katharine M., Jorge Durand, and Douglas S. Massey. 1992. Stemming the tide? Assessing the deterrent effects of the Immigration Reform and Control Act. *Demography* 29 (2): 139–57.

Durand, Jorge, and Douglas S. Massey, eds. 2004. *Crossing the border: Research from the Mexican Migration Project*. New York, NY: Russell Sage Foundation.

Elrick, Tim, and Emilia Lewandowska. 2008. Matching and making labour demand and supply: Agents in Polish migrant networks of domestic elderly care in Germany and Italy. *Journal of Ethnic and Migration Studies* 34 (5): 717–34.

Espinosa, Kristen, and Douglas S. Massey. 1997. Undocumented migration and the quantity and quality of social capital. In *Transnationale Migration. Soziale Welt, Sonderband 12*, ed. Ludger Pries, 141–62. Baden-Baden: Nomos Verlagsgesellschaft.

Fairchild, Henry P. 1925. *Immigration: A world movement and its American significance*. New York, NY: MacMillan.

Featherman, David. 1979. Retrospective longitudinal research: Methodological considerations. CDE Working Paper, 79-19, University of Wisconsin at Madison.

Frejka, Tomas, Marek Okólski, and Keith Sword, eds. 1998. *In-depth studies on migration in Central and Eastern Europe: The case of Poland*. New York, NY: United Nations.

Fussell, Elizabeth. 2010. The cumulative causation of international migration in Latin America. *The ANNALS of the American Academy of Political and Social Science* 630:162–77.

Giulietti, Corrado, Jackline Wahba, and Yves Zenou. 2014. Strong versus weak ties in migration. IZA Discussion Paper, No. 8089, Bonn, Germany.

Goldstein, Sidney, and Alice Goldstein. 1983. *Migration and fertility in peninsular Malaysia: An analysis using life history data*. Santa Monica, CA: Rand Corporation.

Goodman, John L. 1981. Information, uncertainty, and the microeconomic model of migration decision making. In *Migration decision making*, eds. Gordon F. De Jong and Robert W. Gardner, 130–48. New York, NY: Pergamon Press.

Granovetter, Mark S. 1973. The strength of weak ties. *American Journal of Sociology* 78 (6): 1360–80.

Grzymała-Kazłowska, Aleksandra. 2001. Dynamika sieci migranckich: Polacy w Brukseli. In *Ludzie na huśtawce. Migracje między peryferiami Polski i Zachodu*, eds. Ewa Jaźwińska and Marek Okólski, 272–302. Warszawa: Scholar.

Iglicka, Krystyna. 2000. Mechanisms of migration from Poland before and during the transition period. *Journal of Ethnic and Migration Studies* 26 (1): 61–73.

Jaźwińska, Ewa, and Marek Okólski, eds. 1996. *Causes and consequences of migration in Central and Eastern Europe*. Warsaw: ISS/Friedrich-Ebert-Stiftung.

Kaczmarczyk, Paweł. 2001. Uwarunkowania procesów migracyjnych z perspektywy społeczności wysyłającej. In *Ludzie na huśtawce: Migracje miedzy peryferiami Polski i Zachodu*, eds. Ewa Jaźwińska, and Marek Okólski, 303–30. Warszawa: Wydawnictwo Naukowe Scholar.

Kalter, Frank. 1997. *Wohnortwechsel in Deutschland*. Opladen: Leske und Budrich.

Kalter, Frank. 2011. Social capital and the dynamics of temporary labour migration from Poland to Germany. *European Sociological Review* 27 (5): 555–69.

Kley, Stefanie A. 2009. *Migration im Lebensverlauf. Der Einfluss von Lebensbedingungen und Lebenslaufereignissen auf den Wohnortwechsel*. Wiesbaden: VS Verlag für Sozialwissenschaften.

Kley, Stefanie A., and Clara H. Mulder. 2010. Considering, planning, and realizing migration in early adulthood. The influence of life-course events and perceived opportunities on leaving the city in Germany. *Journal of Housing and the Built Environment* 25 (1): 73–94.

Korczyńska, Joanna. 2001. Individuelle Kosten und Nutzen der Saisonarbeit der Polen in Deutschland: Analyse und Ergebnisse einer empirischen Untersuchung 1999/2000 In *Die migration von Polen nach Deutschland: Zu Geschichte und Gegenwart eines Europäischen migrationssystems*, ed. Christoph Pallaske, 205–25. Baden-Baden: Nomos Verlagsgesellschaft.

Kroneberg, Clemens, and Frank Kalter. 2012. Rational choice theory and empirical research: Methodological and theoretical contributions in Europe. *Annual Review of Sociology* 38:73–92.

Landale, Nancy S., and Avert M. Guest. 1985. Constraints, satisfaction and residential mobility: Speare's model reconsidered. *Demography* 22 (2): 199–222.

Lee, Everett S. 1966. A theory of migration. *Demography* 3 (1): 47–57.

Lin, Nan. 2001. *Social capital: A theory of social structure und action*. Cambridge: Cambridge University Press.

Massey, Douglas S. 1987. Understanding Mexican migration to the United States. *American Journal of Sociology* 92 (6): 1372–1403.

Massey, Douglas S., Joaquín Arango, Graeme Hugo, Ali Kouaouci, Adela Pellegrino, and J. Edward Taylor. 1998. *Worlds in motion. Understanding international migration at the end of the millennium*. Oxford: Clarendon Press.

Massey, Douglas S., and María Aysa-Lastra. 2011. Social capital and international migration from Latin America. *International Journal of Population Research*. doi:10.1155/2011/834145.

Massey, Douglas S., and Kristen E. Espinosa. 1997. What's driving Mexico-U.S. migration? A theoretical, empirical, and policy analysis. *American Journal of Sociology* 102 (4): 939–99.

Massey, Douglas S., Luin Goldring, and Jorge Durand. 1994. Continuities in transnational migration: An analysis of nineteen Mexican communities. *American Journal of Sociology* 99 (6): 1492–1533.

Massey, Douglas S., and Fernando Riosmena. 2010. Undocumented migration from Latin America in an era of rising U.S. enforcement. *The ANNALS of the American Academy of Political and Social Science* 630:294–321.

McHugh, Kevin E. 1984. Explaining migration intentions and destination selection. *The Professional Geographer* 36 (3): 315–25.

McKenzie, David, and Hillel Rapoport. 2007. Network effects and the dynamics of migration and inequality: Theory and evidence from Mexico. *Journal of Development Economics* 84 (1): 1–24.

Münst, Agnes S. 2008. Social capital in migration processes of Polish undocumented care- and household workers. In *Migration and mobility in an enlarged Europe. A gender perspective*, eds. Sigrid Metz-Göckel, Mirjana Morokvasić, and Agnes Senganata Münst, 203–24. Farmington Hills, MI: Barbara Budrich Publishers.

Neff, James Alan, and Robert J. Constantine. 1979. Community dissatisfaction and perceived residential alternatives: An interactive model of the formulation of migration plans. *Journal of Population* 2 (1): 18–32.

Okólski, Marek. 2001. Incomplete migration: A new form of mobility in Central and Eastern Europe. The case of Polish and Ukrainian migrants. In *Patterns of migration in Central Europe*, eds. Claire Wallace and Dariusz Stola, 105–28. New York, NY: Palgrave.

Okólski, Marek. 2004. Przepływ siły roboczej w świetle niemiecko-polskiej umowy dwustonnej o pracownikach sezonowych. In *Polscy pracownicy na rynku Unii Europejskiej*, eds. Kaczmarczyk Paweł and Wojciech Łukowski, 23–37. Warszawa: Wydawnictwo Naukowe Scholar.

Osipowicz, Dorota. 2002. *Rola sieci i kapitału społecznego w migracjach Międzynarodowyc: Przykład Moniek*. Seria Prace Migracyjne No. 46. Warszawa: Instytut Studiów Społecznych.

Pallaske, Cristoph. 2002. *Migrationen aus Polen in die Bundesrepublik Deutschland in den 1980er und 1990er Jahren*. Münster: Waxmann.

Palloni, Alberto, Douglas S. Massey, Miguel Ceballos, Kristen Espinosa, and Michael Spittel. 2001. Social capital and international migration: A test using information on family networks. *American Journal of Sociology* 106 (5): 1262–98.

Ritchey, P. Neal. 1976. Explanations of migration. *Annual Review of Sociology* 2:363–404.

Rossi, Peter H. 1980. *Why families move*. Beverly Hills, CA: Sage Publications.

Sell, Ralph R., and Gordon De Jong. 1983. Deciding whether to move: Mobility, wishful thinking and adjustment. *Sociology and Social Research* 67 (2): 146–65.

Smith, James P., and Duncan Thomas. 2003. Remembrances of things past: Test-retest reliability of retrospective migration histories. *Journal of the Royal Statistical Society Series A* 166 (1): 23–49.

Speare, Alden, Jr. 1971. A cost-benefit model of rural to urban migration in Taiwan. *Population Studies* 25 (1): 117–30.

Speare, Alden, Jr. 1974. Residential satisfaction as an intervening variable in residential mobility. *Demography* 11 (2): 173–88.

Speare, Alden, Jr., Sidney Goldstein, and William H. Frey. 1975. *Residential mobility, migration, and metropolitan change*. Cambridge, MA: Ballinger Publishing Company.

Speare, Alden, Jr., Frances Kobrin, and Ward Kingkade. 1982. The influence of socioeconomic bonds and satisfaction on interstate migration. *Social Forces* 61 (2): 551–74.

Will, Gisela. 2016. *Die Bedeutung sozialen Kapitals für Migrationsprozesse: Darstellung am Beispiel des polnisch-deutschen Migrationsgeschehens*. Wiesbaden: Springer VS.

Wong, Siu-Lun, and Janet W. Salaff. 1998. Network capital: emigration from Hong Kong. *British Journal of Sociology* 49 (3): 358–74.

This analysis draws on binational data from an ethno-survey conducted in Guatemala and in the United States in Providence, Rhode Island, to develop a refinement of the weighting scheme that the Mexican Migration Project (MMP) uses. The alternative weighting procedure distinguishes between temporary and settled migrants by using a question on household location in the Guatemala questionnaire that is not used in the MMP. Demographic characteristics and integration experiences of the most recent U.S. trip are used to assess the composition and representativeness of the U.S. sample. Using a composite index of migrant integration to compare the impact of alternative U.S. sample weights on point estimates, I find that although the U.S. sample is broadly representative across a range of background characteristics, the MMP sample weighting procedure biases estimates of migrant integration downward.

Keywords: migration; Mexico; snowball samples; immigrant integration

How Representative Are Snowball Samples? Using the Ethnosurvey to Study Guatemala-U.S. Migration

By
DAVID P. LINDSTROM

M easuring the social and economic processes of migration has always been a challenge, particularly when migrants are dispersed across international borders. The challenges are even greater in the case of undocumented migrants who have a powerful incentive to avoid detection and conceal their status in places of destination (Hill 1985). Recent efforts to measure the stock and flow of Mexico-U.S. migrants have relied on combinations of census data and nationally representative surveys from both countries (Hill and Wong 2005; Rendall, Brownell, and Kups

David P. Lindstrom is a professor in and the chair of the Department of Sociology and a faculty associate of the Population Studies and Training Center at Brown University. His research examines the determinants and consequences of migration in economically developing societies, the transition into adulthood, and the changing dynamics of reproductive health and behavior.

Correspondence: David_Lindstrom@Brown.edu

DOI: 10.1177/0002716216646568

2011). Studying the social and economic dynamics of migration, however, requires specialized migration surveys that collect a greater breadth of data at the individual and household level than do censuses and national surveys (Escobar and Roberts 1998).

To study the full range of mobility patterns and appropriately estimate migration probabilities, migration surveys need to include households in the place of origin that have no migrants, households in the place of origin that have active or return migrants, individual migrants in the place of destination, and migrant households in the place of destination (Groenewold and Bilsborrow 2008, 295). Sample surveys conducted in places of origin miss out-migrant households, and sample surveys conducted in places of destination miss migrants and migrant households that return back to their place of origin. Binational surveys conducted in migrant places of origin and destination, what Rallu (2008) calls "both-ways migration surveys," reduce the bias found in origin or destination surveys caused by the omission of settled or return migrants.

A major challenge to surveying migrants in places of destination is finding them, especially if they are a small minority of the destination population. In the case of undocumented migration, the problem is compounded by the fact that the migrants may not want to be found. The Mexican Migration Project (MMP) ethnosurvey overcomes many of the problems of migrant underenumeration through the use of simple random sampling in Mexican origin communities and snowball sampling in U.S. places of destination to construct a binational sample (Durand, Massey, and Zenteno 2001; Massey 1985; Massey and Capoferro 2004; Massey and Zenteno 1999). Snowball or other referral sampling methods have been proven to be effective for recruiting hidden or hard-to-find populations such as undocumented migrants (Sudman and Kalton 1986). However, because they are nonprobabilistic samples, snowball samples suffer from potential problems of sample bias due to the undernumeration or overenumeration of particular segments of the target population (McKenzie and Mistiaen 2009). A closely related problem is determining the size of the out-migrant community in the destination country to appropriately weight the destination sample for pooled analysis with the origin sample. The MMP has developed a method for calculating U.S. sample weights that uses information on the prevalence of U.S. migration among the independent adult children of household heads interviewed in the origin community to estimate the size of the out-migrant community.

In this article, we use binational data from an MMP-style ethnosurvey conducted in Guatemala and in the United States in Providence, Rhode Island, to develop a refinement of the MMP sample weights. Our proposed weighting procedure makes an important distinction between temporary and settled migration status by using a question on household location in the Guatemala questionnaire that is not used in the MMP. We use selected demographic characteristics and experiences of economic and social integration on the most recent U.S. trip to assess the composition and representativeness of the U.S. sample. We also develop a composite index of migrant integration to compare the impact of alternative U.S. sample weights on point estimates. We find that although the U.S. sample is broadly representative of adult U.S. migrant children of household heads on a range of background characteristics, the MMP sample weights bias downward estimates of migrant integration in the United States.

Guatemala Study Design

The Guatemala Survey of Population Dynamics collected data from 552 randomly sampled households in two adjacent municipalities in the department of Quiche, western Guatemala, between 2000 and 2002. The sample included the two municipal town centers and five rural communities. An additional twenty surveys were completed in 2002 in the primary U.S. destination area, Providence, Rhode Island, using snowball sampling. The Guatemala interviews were completed by a team of male and female bilingual interviewers (Spanish-Quiche) who were enrolled in a regional satellite degree program of the University of San Carlos. The interviewers were not members of the study communities but were familiar with the indigenous Mayan dialects spoken in the communities. The interviews in the United States were completed by one of the survey field supervisors. The Guatemala sample interviews were conducted in Quiche or Spanish depending upon the preference of the respondent. The questionnaires were printed in Spanish, and simultaneous translation from Spanish into Quiche was conducted with Quiche-speaking respondents. Intensive interviewer training before the start of interviewing and daily supervision and team meetings in the field ensured consistency in translations and the application of the questionnaire.

At the outset of fieldwork in each community, permission was secured to conduct the interviews from the town mayors and the village authorities. In the rural communities the research team donated school supplies to the local primary school prior to the start of interviewing. No compensation was provided to survey respondents. Following the standard practice of the MMP, sampling frames for the communities were constructed by conducting a street-by-street enumeration of dwellings, and then using a random number generator to randomly select households for interviews. In four of the five rural communities, attempts were made to interview all households. The response rates were generally high and ranged from 85 to 95 percent in six of the seven communities, with corresponding low refusal rates ranging from 2 to 10 percent. In one rural community, the refusal rate was 27 percent. At the time of the survey, this small indigenous community had recently been defrauded of funds that had been raised to finance the electrification of the community. As a consequence, the interviewers encountered considerable suspicion and resistance to being interviewed.

Interviewing for the U.S. sample was conducted over a four-week period during the months of October and November using snowball sampling. Initial telephone contact was made with several migrants using phone numbers provided by family members resident in the origin municipality. These initial interviews led to referrals to other migrants from the study area. Migrants from the study area were concentrated in one neighborhood of Providence, and in several instances migrants occupied multiple apartments in the same building. This spatial concentration of migrants also made it possible to recruit respondents from the study area through direct contact in apartment buildings and in public places in the neighborhood.

The survey questionnaire followed the standard format of the MMP ethnosurvey and used a household registry to collect basic demographic characteristics and information about first and last U.S. trips for all household members and independent adult children of the household head who were members of other households. The questionnaire also collected detailed information about the most recent U.S. trip for migrant household heads. In contrast to the standard ethnosurvey questionnaire, the Guatemala Survey of Population Dynamics recorded the primary place of residence of the households of independent adult children with the question: "Where does [NAME] normally live, that is where is his/her home and family located?" This question on usual place of residence in combination with the standard MMP questions on household membership and current migration status allows us to distinguish between independent adult children who are in the United States and have families resident in Guatemala and independent adult children who are settled with their families in the United States. This distinction is important for identifying settled migrants in the United States among all migrants in the United States at the time of the survey.

Sample Characteristics

All of the migrants interviewed in the U.S. sample came from one of the two surveyed municipalities. In this article, we restrict our analysis to the 302 households in the town and two rural communities from this municipality, in addition to the 20 households in the U.S. sample. We begin our analysis by using data on adult children of the household head age 16 and older recorded in the household registries of the Guatemala sample. Table 1 presents the distribution of these 662 adult children by U.S. migration status, current household membership status, and usual place of residence. We define three migration statuses: nonmigrants who have never been to the United States, return migrants who have been to the United States and are back in Guatemala at the time of the survey, and migrants who are in the United States at the time of the survey. These three migration statuses are cross-tabulated by four household membership and residency statuses: adult children who are nonhead members of households in the origin municipality, adult children who are members of other households in the origin municipality, adult children who are members of households resident in other places in Guatemala, and adult children who are members of households resident in the United States. Four adult children in the sample were resident in countries other than Guatemala and the United States and are included in the other places in the Guatemala category. If we assume that all adult children who are members of independent households are either the heads of those households or the spouse of the head, then the bottom three rows of the table constitute a parallel sample of household heads and spouses to the Guatemala sample of household

TABLE 1
U.S. Migration Experience of Adult Children Age 16 and Older of Household Heads by
Household Membership Status and Current Place of Residence, Guatemala Sample,
Guatemala Population Dynamics Survey, 2000–2002

	(1) Nonmigrants	(2) Return Migrants	(3) In the United States
Nonhead members of sample households in origin municipality	38.4%	2.1%	5.6%
Members of independent households in origin municipality	30.2%	1.4%	0.5%
Members of independent households in other places in Guatemala	12.8%	1.2%	
Members of independent households in the U.S.			7.9%
Total	81.4%	4.7%	13.9%
Number of observations	539	31	92

heads and spouses. However, in contrast to the survey sample of household heads and spouses, the independent adult children sample contains household heads and spouses who have moved away from the community to other locations in Guatemala and the United States.

Approximately 14 percent of adult children of household heads were in the United States at the time of the survey, with slightly more than one-half of these children reported as members of independent households resident in the United States. These independent adult children in U.S. households correspond to the household heads and spouses who are missed by surveys conducted in origin communities and who are the primary target of the MMP U.S. sample. The smallest group of adult migrant children (0.5 percent) was made up of members of households resident in the origin municipality. This group of migrants corresponds to migrant heads of households in the origin community for whom the spouse is a proxy respondent. In terms of migration categories, these two groups roughly correspond to settled and temporary migrants. This distinction is made possible by the inclusion in the Guatemala survey of the question on household place of residence for independent (nonmember) adult children. The distinction is relevant for estimating the size of the out-migrant settled community in the United States and can be consequential for calculating sample weights.

The sample of all adult children in the United States at the time of the survey shown in the third column of Table 1 is approximately the population of migrants from the origin municipality who are at risk of inclusion in the U.S. sample. We use these migrants as a reference group for making comparisons with the adult migrants captured in the U.S. sample. Table 2 compares the sample of adult migrant children reported in the Guatemala sample (column 3 of Table 1), to the sample of adults age 16 and older from the origin municipality who were reported in the household registry of the U.S. sample as resident in the United States. This

TABLE 2

Adult U.S. Migrant Children Age 16 and Older Reported in the Guatemala Sample
and Adults from the Origin Municipality Captured in the U.S. Sample,
Guatemala Population Dynamics Survey, 2000–2002

	(1) Adult Children of Household Heads: Guatemala Sample	(2) Adults from Guatemala: U.S. Sample
Nonhead members of sample households in origin municipality	40.2%	25.0%
Members of independent households in origin municipality	3.3%	21.9%
Members of independent households in the U.S.	56.5%	53.1%
Number of observations	92	32

comparison is informative of the relative inclusion of different types of migrants
in the U.S. sample. For example, roughly one-half of each of the respective samples of migrants comprises settled migrants, that is, migrants living in the United
States with their households. However, the U.S. sample contains a much higher
percentage of household heads separated from their spouse and children in
Guatemala (21.9 percent) compared to the Guatemala sample of adult children
(3.3 percent), and it contains a smaller percentage of nonhead adult children
separated from their parents (25.0 percent compared to 40.2 percent).

The differences in the two samples in the relative percentages of household
heads and nonheads who are members of households resident in Guatemala are
due to differences in sampling error, selection probabilities, and how respondents in Guatemala and in the United States identify household membership status and usual place of residence. It is notable that the U.S. sample includes a
broad cross-section of migrants of different household membership and residency statuses. At a minimum, 53.1 percent of the U.S. sample are settled
migrants, and some portion of the 25.0 percent of adult children who identify
themselves as nonhead members of households in Guatemala appear to be settled migrants in the sense that they will not return to Guatemala. Although a
portion of the 21.9 percent of migrant heads of households resident in Guatemala
may eventually be joined in the United States by other household members, none
could be considered settled migrants at the time of the survey based on the location of their spouse and children.

Household membership status and place of primary residency are dynamic
and to a degree ambiguous statuses that are open to different definitions and
understandings, especially when comparing self-reports and proxy respondent
reports. In many cases, there is no clear moment in time that marks the transition
from temporary to settled status or, in the case of unmarried adult migrant children, that marks the transition into independence. As alternative points for comparison, we use the background and migration experiences of the Guatemala

TABLE 3
Selected Sample Characteristics of Adult U.S. Migrant Children Age 16 and Older
Reported in the Guatemala Sample and Adults from the Origin Municipality Captured in
the U.S. Sample, Guatemala Population Dynamics Survey, 2000–2002

	(1) Adult Children of Household Heads: Guatemala Sample	(2) Adults from Guatemala: U.S. Sample	(3) Adult Children of Household Heads and Member of Independent Household in U.S.: Guatemala Sample	(4) Adults from Guatemala and Member of Independent Household in U.S.: U.S. Sample
Male	79.3%	68.8%	75.0%	47.1%
Mean age	27.5 (8.8)	30.8 (10.5)	31.1 (9.5)	32.8 (7.6)
Mean years of education	6.6 (4.3)	4.2 (4.1)	7.0 (4.8)	6.0 (4.6)
Mayan	37.0%	50.0%	26.9%	35.3%
Currently married/ consensual union	51.1%	71.9%	71.2%	94.1%
Mean number of U.S. trips	1.0 (0.3)	1.2 (0.5)	1.0 (0.2)	1.4 (0.7)
Undocumented in U.S.	85.4%	75.0%	78.0%	58.8%
Number of observations	92	32	52	17

NOTE: Standard deviations in parentheses.

adult migrant children sample and the U.S. sample. Table 3 presents means and percentages for selected sociodemographic characteristics and U.S. migration experience reported in the household registry. Column 1 contains the Guatemala sample that was presented in column 1 of Table 2, and column 2 contains the U.S. sample that was presented in column 2 of Table 2.

The Guatemala sample of adult migrant children has a slightly higher percentage of males (79.3 percent) than the U.S. sample (68.8 percent), and it has a lower percentage of currently married (51.1 percent compared to 71.9 percent). Adult migrant children in the Guatemala sample also tend to be slightly younger and more educated on average than migrants in the U.S. sample. The two samples also differ with respect to ethnic composition, with the U.S. sample containing a higher percentage of Mayans than the Guatemala sample. With respect to U.S. migration experience, the mean number of trips in both samples is similar, with the large majority of migrants making only one trip. The vast majority of migrants in both samples are also in the United States without legal documentation, although the prevalence of U.S. documents is higher among migrants in the U.S. sample. Overall, the U.S. sample is more heavily weighted than the Guatemala sample of migrant children toward characteristics that are typically associated with settlement in the United States, such as a higher prevalence of women, older ages, more currently married, and a greater prevalence of documentation. The greater prevalence of Mayans in the U.S. sample may stem from the ethnic composition of the initial seeds in the U.S. snowball sample. Social relations in Guatemala are highly ethnically stratified. Because snowball sampling relies on social networks to recruit respondents, ethnic divisions present in the origin community are likely to lead to ethnically differentiated social networks in the destination, making it difficult to survey both ethnic groups in the United States in proportions that are similar to their respective proportions in the origin community.

In the MMP study design, the destination snowball sample is intended to capture settled migrants rather than a cross-section of all active migrants. Columns 3 and 4 of Table 3 present only members of U.S. resident households among independent adult children in the Guatemala sample and adults in the U.S. sample, respectively. These two groups are the same groups shown in the bottom row of Table 2 and are subsets of columns 1 and 2 in Table 3. Based on household place of residence, they are considered settled migrants and are missed by household surveys conducted in the origin community. Similar to what we found in the comparisons of all migrants, settled migrants in the U.S. sample compared to the Guatemala sample have a higher prevalence of characteristics typically associated with settlement, and even more so than was the case with the entire U.S. sample. In particular, 41 percent of the adult settled migrants in the U.S. sample have legal documents, and approximately one-half are women.

If we treat the independent adult children of household heads in the Guatemala sample who are resident in the United States (column 3) as the group the U.S. sample is designed to capture, then it is the U.S. sample of all adults, irrespective of household membership or residency status (column 2), that comes closest to matching this group on most sample characteristics. On five of the seven characteristics listed in Table 3, the full U.S. sample is closer to the sample of adult out-migrant children in the Guatemala sample than the restricted U.S. sample of settled migrants. Even though the full U.S. sample captures a broad cross-section of temporary and settled migrants, at least on the background and migration characteristics reviewed in Table 3, the sample matches relatively well out-migrant adult children reported in the Guatemala survey. In part, this result may reflect the fact that the distinction between temporary and permanent migration is not hard and fast. Not all the migrants in the U.S. sample who identify themselves as members of households resident in Guatemala will return to Guatemala, and some of the migrant households that are defined as settled in the United States will return to Guatemala. Temporary and settled migrants may also not be differentially selected on these observed characteristics.

Calculating Sample Weights

The MMP uses the relative prevalence of U.S. migration among independent adult children of household heads in the origin community to calculate sample weights for households in the U.S. sample. The relative prevalence of out-migration, defined as households that leave the home community for the United States, is estimated by forming the ratio of the number of independent adult children of household heads who are in the United States at the time of the survey to the number of independent adult children who are in the origin community. We have shown that the sample of independent adult migrant children in the Guatemala sample contains temporary and settled migrants in proportions that are different from the U.S. sample, and that the U.S. sample also contains migrants who still consider themselves as members of their parent's household in Guatemala. Nevertheless, we also show that for the purpose of representing the settled out-migrant community in the United States, this mismatch may not be very consequential. In our final exercise we present selected characteristics of the last U.S. trip for household heads and compare the pooled Guatemala and U.S. samples using alternative sample weights. This exercise is designed to assess the sensitivity of survey results to sample weights based on alternative ways of treating the different categories of migrants in the two samples.

Table 4 presents fourteen selected characteristics of last U.S. trip for household heads. Many of these characteristics have been used in other studies to measure immigrant integration and can be divided into four domains of integration: financial, employment, social, and linguistic (Barry 2001, 2005; Bijl et al. 2008; Entzinger and Biezeveld 2003; Kurthen and Heisler 2009; Rhine and Greene 2006). Financial integration is measured by whether the migrant had a bank account and a credit card in the United States. Employment integration is measured by whether the migrant was paid with a check, had social security taxes withheld, had federal taxes withheld, and submitted a tax return. Social integration is measured by whether the migrant was friends outside of work with African Americans, Asians, and whites. Linguistic integration is measured by whether the migrant used some or a lot of English at home, at work, with friends, and in the neighborhood. The percentages shown in Table 4 are based on binary versions of the friendship and English usage variables, which in their original form are ordinal variables. We also used principal components analysis to construct a composite index of integration from the fourteen characteristics using the ordinal versions of the nonbinary variables.

Column 1 presents results for the unweighted pooled Guatemala and U.S. sample of migrant household heads. In general, the results reveal relatively low levels of integration and are indicative of the undocumented status of most of the migrants. Approximately one in ten migrants had a credit card, and even fewer had a bank account in the United States. Although two-thirds of the migrants reported being paid with a check, a minority thought that social security and federal taxes were withheld from their pay, and only 10 percent submitted tax returns. Virtually none of the migrants reported friendships with African Americans, Asians, or whites outside of work; and while most migrants reported using some or a lot of English at work, only 8 percent reported speaking and understanding English a little or well. Cronbach's alpha, which provides a measure of the intercorrelations of the fourteen items, is relatively high at .836. With a range of 0 to 1, values of Cronbach's alpha between .8 and .9 indicate a good level of internal consistency among the items and are good candidates for a composite index (Jackman 2008, 124–25). We used principal components analysis to

TABLE 4
Experiences on Last U.S. Trip, Household Heads/Respondents Pooled
Guatemala and U.S. Sample with Alternative Weights, Guatemala
Population Dynamics Survey, 2000–2002

On last U.S. trip:	(1) Pooled Guatemala and U.S. Sample: Unweighted (%)	(2) Pooled Guatemala and U.S. Sample: MMP Weights (%)	(3) Pooled Guatemala and U.S. Sample: Mixed Weights (%)
Had bank account	8.3	8.7	13.9
Had credit card	10.4	11.6	19.4
Was paid with check	66.7	66.3	76.2
Social security taxes withheld	43.8	40.3	50.4
Federal taxes withheld	39.6	34.7	44.1
Submitted tax return	10.4	14.1	22.8
Friends with African Americans outside of work	4.2	5.6	11.0
Friends with Asians outside of work	2.1	2.8	5.5
Friends with whites outside of work	2.1	2.8	5.5
Speaks and understands English a little or well	8.3	11.2	17.3
Used some or a lot of English at home	12.5	16.9	28.3
Used some or a lot of English at work	64.6	62.2	66.7
Used some or a lot of English with friends	29.2	29.4	35.5
Used some or a lot of English in the neighborhood	45.8	39.4	43.9
Cronbach's alpha for 14 items	.836	.853	.867
Mean integration index: Guatemala sample	−.059	−.084	−.378
Mean integration index: U.S. sample	.082	.065	.265
Observations	48	48	48

construct a standard normal integration index. The mean values of the composite index for the Guatemala and U.S. samples, calculated from the unweighted pooled sample, are very close to one another (−.059 and .082, respectively), indicating that the two samples are also close to one another on the fourteen measures of integration.

Column 2 of Table 4 presents the results for the pooled Guatemala and U.S. sample using sample weights based on the MMP procedure. Using MMP sample weights has a relatively small impact on the pooled sample point estimates, with many of the estimates remaining virtually the same as in the unweighted pooled sample. The difference in the mean values of the integration index for the Guatemala and U.S. samples is also small. The closeness of the composite index for the two samples and the relative absence of any impact of the MMP weights suggest that the experience of Guatemala migrants in the study area who returned to Guatemala and those who were in the United States at the time of the survey are on the whole very similar. This result is also consistent with the fact that the U.S. sample, as already noted, contains a cross-section of migrants and not only settled migrants.

The MMP procedure for calculating the U.S. sample weights assumes that the independent adult migrant children reported in the Guatemala survey and the adult migrants captured in the U.S. survey are members of U.S.-based households. We have seen that for both samples this assumption is not true. We next derive alternative U.S. sample weights that treat migrants in the United States who are members of households in Guatemala differently from migrants who are members of U.S.-based households. Our distinction between Guatemala and U.S.-based migrants enters into the calculation of sample weights at two points. First, in the estimation of the prevalence of U.S. migration among independent adult children reported in the Guatemala sample, we include in the numerator only independent adult children who are members of U.S.-based households, rather than all independent adult children in the United States. Second, in the calculation and assignment of weights for the U.S. sample, we base the calculation only on the number of U.S.-based households in the U.S. sample and not all respondents in the U.S. sample. We also apply the U.S. sample weights only to the nine U.S.-based households in the U.S. sample, and we apply the weights from the Guatemala sample to the remaining eleven households in the U.S. sample for whom the respondents report being either members of their parents' household or heads of households in the origin municipality. These eleven Guatemala-based U.S. migrant households are represented by the Guatemala sample, and by assigning the Guatemala sample weights to them; we are in effect treating the respondents as substitutes for household heads who were away in the United States at the time of the Guatemala survey and reported on by their spouse.

Column 3 of Table 4 presents point estimates from the pooled sample using these alternative, mixed sample weights. This alternative sample weight design places more relative weight on settled migrants in the U.S. sample compared to the MMP weights, and therefore will generate point estimates different from the MMP weights only to the extent that settled migrants have different integration experiences than temporary migrants. The estimates presented in column 3 do indeed suggest higher degrees of integration among settled U.S. migrants than temporary migrants. On all fourteen items, the percentages in column 3 are larger than the percentages in column 2 that are based on the MMP weights; and on half the items, the percentages are 50 to 100 percent larger. The difference in the integration index between the Guatemala and U.S. samples also increases from .149 to .643.

Discussion

The independent adult migrant children reported in the household registries of the origin community survey include temporary migrants who are members of households in the origin community and settled migrants who are in the United States with their own household. The failure to differentiate between these two groups will generate overestimates of the size of the U.S. out-migrant community. Snowball samples of migrants in the United States will potentially include three groups of migrants: temporary migrants who are members of their parent's household in the origin community, temporary migrants who are heads of households still resident in the origin community, and settled migrants who are members of households in the United States. Weighting all respondents in the U.S. sample as if they were settled migrants will generate point estimates that are biased toward temporary migrants since the experiences of temporary migrants are represented in both the origin community sample through the use of proxy respondents, and in the U.S. sample, where they are also overweighted. The distinction between temporary and settled migrants among the independent adult children of household heads cannot be made with the current MMP data because no information is collected on the households of these children.

Restricting interviewing in the U.S. snowball sample to settled migrant households, the intended target of the sample, is too costly given the difficulty and already high cost of securing interviews with migrants, many of whom are undocumented. The very nature of snowball sampling is likely to yield a cross-section of different types of migrants. Removing temporary migrants from the U.S. sample at the analysis stage throws away valuable and difficult-to-secure information. An alternative solution that we present here involves the differential weighting of temporary and settled migrants in the U.S. sample. The distinction between temporary and settled migrants can be made in the U.S. sample with the current MMP data using information on the migration experience of all household members recorded in the household registry.

In our analysis of the binational Guatemala Survey of Population Dynamics, we found that on a range of sociodemographic characteristics the U.S. sample was very close in composition to the independent adult migrant children reported in the Guatemala sample. This finding suggests that temporary and settled migrants are not differentially selected on these variables. We also suggested that the cross-section of migrants represented in the U.S. sample represents migrants at different stages in the settlement process, with at least some of the temporary migrants eventually transitioning into settled status. However, temporary and settled migrants differ with respect to their degree of financial, economic, social, and linguistic integration in the United States. Our comparison of point estimates of integration using the MMP weights and our proposed weights indicated that the MMP weights bias downward estimates of migrant integration in a pooled sample. An alternative solution to the use of weights when assessing migrant integration and experiences in the United States is to stratify the analysis by temporary-settled migration status when the number of observations permits. The results that we present here are for just one community. The sensitivity of point estimates of a broad range of background characteristics and measures of migration experience will vary by the relative proportions of temporary and settled migrants in the origin community sample and in the U.S. sample.

References

Barry, Declan T. 2001. Development of a new scale for measuring acculturation: The East Asian accul-turation measure (EAAM). *Journal of Immigrant Health* 3 (4): 193–97.

Barry, Declan T. 2005. Measuring acculturation among male Arab immigrants in the United States: An exploratory study. *Journal of Immigrant Health* 7 (3): 179–84.

Bijl, Rob V., Aslan Zorlu, Roel P. W. Jennissen, and Martine Blom. 2008. The integration of migrants in the Netherlands monitored over time: Trend and cohort analyses. In *International migration in Europe: New trends and new methods of analysis*, eds. Corrado Bonifazi, Marek Okolski, Jeannette Schrool, and Patrick Simon, 199–223. Amsterdam: Amsterdam University Press.

Durand, Jorge, Douglas S. Massey, and René Zenteno. 2001. Mexican immigration to the United States: Continuities and changes. *Latin American Research Review* 36 (1): 107–27.

Entzinger, Han, and Renske Biezeveld. 2003. *Benchmarking in immigrant integration*. Report for the European Commission. Rotterdam: European Research Centre on Migration and Ethnic Relations, Erasmus University Rotterdam.

Escobar, Agustín, and Bryan Roberts. 1998. Surveys as instruments of modernization. *American Behavioral Scientist* 42 (2): 237–51.

Groenewold, George, and Richard Bilsborrow. 2008. Design of samples for international migration sur-veys: Methodological considerations and lessons learned from a multi-country study in Africa and Europe. In *International migration in Europe: New trends and new methods of analysis*, eds. Corrado Bonifazi, Marek Okolski, Jeannette Schrool, and Patrick Simon, 293–312. Amsterdam: Amsterdam University Press.

Hill, Kenneth. 1985. Some methodological issues in analyzing data on immigration. In *Immigration statis-tics: A story of neglect*, eds. Donald B. Levine, Kenneth Hill, and Robert Warren, 203–54. Washington, DC: National Academies Press.

Hill, Kenneth, and Rebeca Wong. 2005. Mexico-U.S. migration: Views from both sides of the border. *Population and Development Review* 31 (1): 1–18.

Jackman, Simon. 2008. Measurement. In *The Oxford handbook of political methodology*, eds. Janet M. Box-Steffensmeier, Henry E. Brady, and David Collier, 119–51. Oxford: Oxford University Press.

Kurthen, Hermann, and Barbara S. Heisler. 2009. Immigrant integration: Comparative evidence from the United States and Germany. *Ethnic and Racial Studies* 32 (1): 139–70.

Massey, Douglas S. 1985. The settlement process among Mexican migrants to the United States: New methods and findings. In *Immigration statistics: A story of neglect*, eds. Donald B. Levine, Kenneth Hill, and Robert Warren, 255–92. Washington, DC: National Academies Press.

Massey, Douglas S., and Chiara Capoferro. 2004. Measuring undocumented migration. *International Migration Review* 38 (3): 1075–1102.

Massey, Douglas S., and René Zenteno. 1999. A validation of the ethnosurvey: The case of Mexico-U.S. migration. *International Migration Review* 34 (3): 766–93.

McKenzie, David J., and Johan Mistiaen. 2009. Surveying migrant households: A comparison of census-based, snowball and intercept point surveys. *Journal of the Royal Statistical Society A* 172 (Part 2): 339–60.

Rallu, Jean Louis. 2008. One-way or both-ways migration surveys. In *International migration in Europe: New trends and new methods of analysis*, eds. Corrado Bonifazi, Marek Okolski, Jeannette Schrool, and Patrick Simon, 273–92. Amsterdam: Amsterdam University Press.

Rendall, Michael S., Peter Brownell, and Sarah Kups. 2011. Declining return migration from the United States to Mexico in the late-2000s recession: A research note. *Demography* 48 (3): 1049–58.

Rhine, Sherrie L. W., and William H. Greene. 2006. The determinants of being unbanked for U.S. immi-grants. *Journal of Consumer Affairs* 40 (1): 21–40.

Sudman, Seymour, and Graham Kalton. 1986. New developments in the sampling of special populations. *Annual Review of Sociology* 12:401–29.

Undocumented Latinos in the United States

Double Disadvantage: Unauthorized Mexicans in the U.S. Labor Market

JORGE DURAND,
DOUGLAS S. MASSEY,
and
KAREN A. PREN

From 1988 to 2008, the United States' undocumented population grew from 2 million to 12 million persons. It has since stabilized at around 11 million, a majority of whom are Mexican. As of this writing, some 60 percent of all Mexican immigrants in the United States are in the country illegally. This article analyzes the effect of being undocumented on sector of employment and wages earned in the United States. We show that illegal migrants are disproportionately channeled into the secondary labor market, where they experience a double disadvantage, earning systematically lower wages by virtue of working in the secondary sector and receiving an additional economic penalty because they are undocumented. Mexican immigrants, in particular, experienced a substantial decline in real wages between 1970 and 2010 attributable to their rising share of undocumented migrants in U.S. labor markets during a time when undocumented hiring was criminalized.

Keywords: undocumented migrants; illegal migration; Mexican immigrants; wages; labor markets

The current era of Mexican migration to the United States began in 1942 when the U.S. government approached authorities in Mexico to propose a binational agreement known as the Bracero Accord. Faced with labor shortages because of war mobilization and the initiation of a military draft, U.S. officials sought to arrange for the yearly importation of Mexican laborers on temporary visas for seasonal work

Jorge Durand is a senior research professor in the Department for the Study of Social Movements at the University of Guadalajara and codirector of the Mexican Migration Project. He is a member of the Mexican Academy of Sciences and a foreign associate of the U.S. National Academy of Sciences.

Douglas S. Massey is the Henry G. Bryant Professor of Sociology and Public Affairs at Princeton University, where he directs the Office of Population Research in addition to serving as codirector of the Mexican Migration Project.

Correspondence: j.durand.mmp@gmail.com

DOI: 10.1177/0002716216643507

ANNALS, *AAPSS*, 666, July 2016

north of the border. Although originally envisioned as a temporary wartime measure, tight labor markets persisted in the postwar years and prompted the U.S. Congress to extend and expand the program. During the late 1950s, some 450,000 Bracero migrants were entering the United States each year, along with about 50,000 legal permanent residents who were not, at that point, subject to numerical limitation (Massey, Durand, and Malone 2002).

During the 1960s, however, Congress began to scale back the Bracero program, and at the end of 1964 Congress let it expire despite Mexican government protests. In the following year, Congress amended U.S. immigration law to apply numerical limits on permanent immigration from the Western Hemisphere for the first time. Legislation steadily tightened these restrictions until 1976, when immigration from the Americas was capped at twenty thousand persons per country per year. The cancellation of the Bracero Accord and these restrictive changes to U.S. immigration law were enacted as civil rights reforms—abandoning discriminatory quotas enacted in the 1920s against Southern and Eastern Europeans while ending prohibitions on immigration from Asia and Africa and eliminating what had come to be seen as an exploitive labor program. Little thought was given to what would happen to the annual inflow of half a million Mexicans when access to legal visas was suddenly curtailed (Massey and Pren 2012b).

What happened, of course, was the continuation of migration, but it was largely undocumented. By the late 1970s, the annual migratory flows of the late 1950s had essentially been reestablished, only this time the migrants were "illegal aliens" rather than legally authorized workers. Since the migrants were "illegal," they were by definition "criminals" and "lawbreakers" and, thus, could be readily portrayed as a grave threat to the nation by immigration bureaucrats eager to increase agency budgets and cynical politicians seeking to mobilize voters for political purposes (Massey and Pren 2012a). The resulting "Latino Threat Narrative" framed Mexican immigration either as a "rising tide" that threatened to "flood" the United States and "drown its culture," or as an "alien invasion" in which "outgunned" border patrol officers valiantly sought to "hold the line" against "banzai charges" of Mexicans seeking to "reconquer" the United States (Chavez 2001, 2008; Santa Ana 2002).

Over time, this narrative gave rise to a new politics of immigration restriction and border enforcement that brought about the progressive militarization of the Mexico-U.S. border (Dunn 1996; Nevins 2001). Between 1986 and 2010, the budget of the U.S. Border Patrol increased by a factor of twelve in real terms and the number of officers increased by a factor of almost six, even though the volume of inflow had stabilized by around 1979 (Massey, Durand, and Pren 2016). Prior to 1986, undocumented Mexican migration to the United States was overwhelmingly circular, with 85 percent of entries between 1965 and 1985 being offset by departures (Massey and Singer 1995). The militarization of the border,

Karen A. Pren is the manager of the Mexican Migration Project and the Latin American Migration Project at Princeton University and the University of Guadalajara.

NOTE: The authors thank the MacArthur Foundation (grant 12-102305-000-CFP) and the National Institute of Child Health and Human Development (grants R01 HD035643 and P2C HD047879-11) for their support of this research.

however, sharply increased the costs and risks of unauthorized border crossing, and in response, migrants minimized border crossing, not by remaining in Mexico in the first place, but by staying in the United States once they had achieved entry (Massey, Durand, and Pren 2015).

In the end, the strategy of border enforcement backfired by reducing the volume of undocumented out-migration while having no effect at all on the volume of unauthorized in-migration (Massey, Durand, and Pren 2016). From 1988 to 2008, the size of the undocumented population rose from 2 million to 12 million. Although the undocumented population fell by around a million persons between 2008 and 2009 in the wake of the Great Recession, since then it has stabilized at around 11 million (Passel, Lopez, and Cohn 2014). Not since the days of slavery have so many residents of the United States lacked any social, economic, or political rights and enjoyed so few legal protections (Massey 2013).

Prior to 1986, undocumented status had no significant effect on the wages earned by Mexican migrants in the U.S. labor market (Massey 1987). In that year, however, the Immigration Reform and Control Act criminalized the hiring of undocumented workers, and in this context the growing population of unauthorized migrants created a pool of exploitable workers that put downward pressure on the wages of all immigrants, but especially those without documents (Donato and Massey 1993; Phillips and Massey 1999; Donato and Sisk 2013; Massey and Gentsch 2014). Here we demonstrate how undocumented workers continue to be doubly disadvantaged in the United States. Not only are they selected into the most disadvantaged sector of the labor market but, whatever sector they work in, they earn lower wages than other migrants.

Modeling Undocumented Employment and Earnings

Following Massey et al. (1998), we combine the theoretical perspectives of Piore (1979) and Portes (1987) to define a labor market structure of three sectors: a primary sector characterized by formal employment in "good" jobs, a secondary sector defined by informal employment in "bad" jobs, and an enclave sector of people employed by immigrant entrepreneurs. According to Piore, capital is a fixed factor of production that can be idled by lower demand but not laid off, meaning that business owners bear the costs of its unemployment. In contrast, labor is a variable factor of production that can be released when demand falls, forcing workers to bear the cost of their unemployment. For this reason, whenever possible owners employ capital-intensive methods to meet the stable, reliable portion of demand and labor-intensive methods to accommodate the seasonal, fluctuating component of demand, thereby creating two classes of jobs: one characterized by regular employment at high wages and another characterized by unstable employment and low wages. Here we operationally define *secondary sector employment* as working for a non-Mexican employer and being paid cash with no taxes withheld.

Portes (1987) expanded segmented labor market theory by hypothesizing a third sector of employment consisting of immigrant-owned or managed businesses that are interconnected with one another and rely mainly on other immigrants as workers. Within the enclave, common social origins and cultural values create solidarity and trust that rewards migrant workers for their efforts and loyalty, over time yielding opportunities for economic mobility and earnings (Portes and Bach 1987). We operationally define *enclave employment* as working in a business owned or managed by a Mexican, whatever the terms of employment. These definitions of the secondary and enclave sectors leave *primary sector employment* as the reference category, implicitly defining it as working for a non-Mexican employer in a job paid by check and subject to tax withholdings.

Our leading hypothesis is that migrants without legal status will be disproportionately channeled away from primary sector employment into secondary sector jobs and that in whatever jobs they hold, undocumented migrants will earn less money. We define legal status in terms of three categories. *Legal immigrants* serve as the reference category and include naturalized U.S. citizens and persons holding legal permanent residence in the United States. *Undocumented migrants* include persons who entered the country without authorization or who entered on a tourist visa and subsequently violated its terms by taking paid employment. *Temporary migrants* are those who entered with a temporary work visa that authorized work for a specific employer while in the United States for a set period of time. We argue that temporary legal workers will be channeled away from the enclave sector because of the restrictive terms of their temporary work visas. We expect to observe lower earnings in secondary sector jobs compared with primary sector jobs, but we predict that earnings in the enclave sector will approximate those in the primary sector. As already noted, whatever their sector of employment, we expect undocumented migrants to experience lower earnings because of their vulnerable status and poor bargaining position.

We measure earnings in terms of real hourly wages defined in 2010 inflation-adjusted dollars. While examining the effect of legal status on sector of employment and wages, we control for a variety of independent variables, including indicators of demographic background (gender, age, marital status), human capital (education, occupational skill, U.S. experience, and English language ability), social capital (connection to a migrant parent or sibling and the prevalence of U.S. migration in the origin community), how the job was obtained (by oneself or through a relative, acquaintance, or contractor), and degree of integration within U.S. society (whether the migrant reported having social relations with Anglo-Americans or holding a formal bank account).

Data and Methods

Our data come from the Mexican Migration Project (MMP [MMP154 database]) compiled from random surveys conducted between 1982 and 2015 in 154 communities located in twenty-three states throughout Mexico. Each year, four to six communities were purposively selected to increase the geographic coverage, socioeconomic diversity, and demographic range of the dataset. Dwellings within the selected communities were then enumerated to create a sampling frame from which households were randomly selected for a personal interview using a semistructured questionnaire. In the course of an ethnographically informed conversation, interviewers gathered basic information about the household head, spouse, all children of the head, and any other household residents to compile basic demographic, social, and economic information about each person along with information about that person's first and most recent trip to the United States. Household heads and spouses additionally provided life histories that included a complete history of migration and border crossing; household heads also answered a series of detailed questions about their most recent U.S. trip. The accuracy, reliability, and validity of the MMP data have been validated by direct comparisons with data from nationally representative samples (Massey and Zenteno 2000; Massey and Capoferro 2004).

Our working dataset includes 5,564 household heads, each of whom provided information on jobs held in the United States from 1970 through 2010. Table 1 presents means and standard deviations for independent and dependent variables included in the analysis. As can be seen, the average migrant earned $10.21 per hour in constant 2010 dollars, and in rough terms around 60 percent held jobs in the primary sector and 20 percent each held jobs in the enclave and secondary sectors. Nearly three-quarter of the migrants were undocumented; whereas 21 percent were U.S. citizens or legal permanent residents; and just 3 percent held temporary work visas, though the relative frequency of legal temporary visas has risen dramatically in recent years (Massey, Durand, and Pren 2015). Males composed 95 percent of all respondents with an average age of about 33 years, though only 36 percent were married or in a union at the time of the last trip.

As one might expect, the migrants generally came from modest socioeconomic backgrounds, with average schooling of just 6.2 years, a quarter working in agriculture, and nearly two-thirds being unskilled manual laborers. The average migrant had made some 2.5 prior trips to the United States and at the time of the most recent visit had accumulated an average of 77 months of U.S. experience. Only 27 percent said they spoke and understood English well, though 37 percent said they did speak and understand some English; about a third reported no English ability at all. Some 19 percent of respondents reported having a parent with U.S. experience, and 39 percent said they had a sibling who had been to the United States. In the typical community, around 22 percent of all persons aged 15 and older had been to the United States at the time of the most recent U.S. trip. Most respondents obtained their job either through a relative (31 percent) or an acquaintance (28 percent), but relatively few obtained work through a labor contractor (just 0.9 percent). The typical migrant was not very well integrated into the United States, with only 35 percent reporting a social relationship with an Anglo-American and just 16 percent holding a bank account. Most of the U.S. trips took place between 1980 and 2004, with the greatest concentration (22 percent) occurring between 1990 and 1994.

Legal Status, Employment, and Wages

Table 2 presents a multinomial logit model estimated to predict sector of employment for migrants in the MMP154 dataset. As shown in the top panel of the table, holding a temporary work visa has a strong negative effect on the likelihood

TABLE 1
Means and Standard Deviations of Variables Used in the Analysis
of Unauthorized Mexicans in the U.S. Labor Force

Variable	Mean	Standard Deviation
Earnings		
Hourly wage (2010 dollars)	10.21	5.62
Sector of employment		
Primary	0.599	0.599
Secondary	0.199	0.399
Enclave	0.202	0.401
Documentation		
Legal resident or citizen	0.207	0.405
Temporary work visa	0.034	0.181
Undocumented	0.740	0.439
Demographic background		
Female	0.052	0.223
Age at last trip	33.17	11.95
Married or union	0.362	0.481
Education		
School years completed	6.175	3.958
Occupation		
Agriculture	0.248	0.432
Unskilled	0.653	0.476
Skilled	0.041	0.198
U.S. experience		
Number of prior U.S. trips	2.491	4.902
Months of U.S. experience	77.05	86.73
English ability		
Does not speak or understand English	0.335	0.472
Speaks and understands some English	0.368	0.482
Speaks and understands much English	0.271	0.445
Social capital		
Parent a migrant	0.192	0.394
Sibling a migrant	0.386	0.487
Community migration prevalence	22.45	14.54
How job obtained		
By oneself	0.260	0.439
Relative	0.311	0.463
Acquaintance	0.284	0.451
Contractor	0.009	0.092
Integration		
Has relations with Anglos	0.349	0.477
Has bank account	0.159	0.366

(continued)

TABLE 1 (CONTINUED)

Variable	Mean	Standard Deviation
Period		
1970–1974	0.061	0.240
1975–1979	0.094	0.292
1980–1984	0.106	0.308
1985–1989	0.175	0.380
990–1994	0.222	0.416
1995–1999	0.177	0.382
2000–2004	0.114	0.317
2005–2010	0.051	0.219

of enclave employment, an effect that occurs because temporary visas are tied to specific employers. People holding such a visa are only around 60 percent as likely to work in the enclave sector compared with legal immigrants (determined by computing $\exp[-0.506] = 0.603$). Consistent with our leading hypothesis, being undocumented strongly predicts the likelihood of working in the secondary sector. Indeed, lacking legal papers increases the odds of secondary sector employment by a factor of 2.3 (determined by computing $\exp[0.817] = 2.264$). Thus, legal status plays a key role in channeling migrants into distinct sectors of the labor market.

Turning to other variables in the model, we see that sector of employment is not affected by a migrant's demographic characteristics, education, or period of migration, though there is some indication of a decline in the likelihood of secondary sector employment after the year 2000. With respect to occupation status, unskilled manual workers are only 78 percent as likely to work in the enclave sector but are 95 percent more likely to work in the secondary sector compared to agricultural workers. Being a skilled worker likewise increases the odds of working in the secondary sector by 90 percent. With each prior trip to the United States, the likelihood of employment in the enclave sector rises by around 3.6 percent. In contrast, each additional month of prior U.S. experience lowers the likelihood of enclave employment by around 0.2 percent and reduces the odds of working in the secondary sector by 0.5 percent. In general, English language ability lowers the likelihood of enclave employment and increases the probability of employment in the secondary sector. Thus, speaking and understanding much English reduces the odds of enclave employment by 29 percent and increases the odds of secondary sector employment by 20 percent.

In terms of social capital, as the prevalence of migration in the origin community rises, the odds of enclave employment increase by around 1.2 percent, while the odds of secondary sector employment decrease by 1.4 percent. In contrast, having a migrant sibling decreases the odds of enclave employment by 99 percent but increases the odds of secondary sector employment by a factor of 2.2. In addition, obtaining a job through a relative increases the odds of enclave

TABLE 2
Multinomial Logit Model Predicting Sector of Employment
for Mexican Migrants to the United States

Variable	Sector=Enclave		Sector=Secondary	
	B	SE	B	SE
Documentation				
Legal	—	—	—	—
Temporary	−0.506°°°	0.214	0.228	0.277
Undocumented	−0.143	0.129	0.817°°°°	0.127
Demographic Background				
Female	−0.093	0.237	0.351	0.223
Age	0.011	0.018	−0.001	0.016
Age squared	0.000	0.001	0.000	0.000
Married or in union	0.105	0.188	0.069	0.185
Education				
School years completed	−0.014	0.012	−0.017	0.011
Occupation				
Agriculture	—	—	—	—
Unskilled	−0.244°°°	0.093	0.667°°°°	0.090
Skilled	−0.351	0.219	0.641°°°	0.208
U.S. experience				
Number of prior U.S. trips	0.035°°°	0.015	0.010	0.012
Total months of U.S. experience	−0.002°°°	0.001	−0.005°°°°	0.001
English ability				
Does not speak or understand English	—	—	—	—
Speaks and understands some English	−0.099	0.095	0.331°°°°	0.092
Speaks and understands much English	−0.346°°°	0.122	0.185°	0.113
Social capital				
Parent a migrant	0.057	0.136	−0.125	0.100
Sibling a migrant	−7.152°°°°	1.005	0.768°°°°	0.103
Community migration prevalence	0.012°°°°	0.003	−0.014°°°°	0.003
How job obtained				
By oneself	—	—	—	—
Relative	0.478°°°°	0.096	0.046	0.089
Acquaintance	0.200°°°	0.100	0.000	0.089
Contractor	0.301	0.402	0.550	0.352
Integration				
Relations with Anglos	−0.162°	0.099	−0.092	0.081
Bank account	−0.224°°	0.129	−1.102°°°°	0.157
Period				
1970–1974	—	—	—	—
1975–1979	−0.015	0.233	−0.163	0.179
1980–1984	0.291	0.225	−0.266	0.179

(continued)

TABLE 2 (CONTINUED)

Variable	Sector=Enclave		Sector=Secondary	
	B	SE	B	SE
1985–1989	0.240	0.214	0.065	0.166
1990–1994	0.122	0.213	0.028	0.163
1995–1999	0.184	0.206	–0.167	0.177
2000–2004	0.288	0.212	–0.424°°°	0.201
2005–2010	0.386	0.241	–0.392	0.259
Intercept	–0.661	0.435	–1.766°°°°	0.403
Likelihood ratio	1,921.68°°°°			
Wald score	588.021°°°°			
Observations	5,564			

°p = .10. °°p < .10. °°°p < .05. °°°°p < .001.

employment by 61 percent, whereas becoming employed through an acquaintance increases the odds of working in the enclave sector by 22 percent. Finally, greater integration within U.S. society generally reduces the likelihood of employment in both the enclave and the secondary sectors. Having a bank account reduces the odds of enclave employment by around 20 percent and lowers the odds of secondary sector employment by 67 percent.

Table 3 presents an ordinary least squares regression of the natural log of the real hourly wage on sector of employment, legal status, and other independent variables. In a logged wage regression, coefficients indicate the percentage increase or decrease in wages associated with a unit change in the variable in question. As shown in the top panel, working in the secondary sector is associated with a 12.5 percent reduction in real wages while being undocumented reduces them by another 11.5 percent. Thus undocumented migrants are doubly disadvantaged, first because their lack of legal papers raises the odds of secondary sector employment, which itself carries a 12.5 percent wage penalty; and second by lowering wages directly by another 11.5 percent whatever sector they work in. Within the secondary sector, respondents to the MMP report stiff competition from undocumented Central Americans, who continue to arrive in significant numbers; and a relative saturation of local labor markets, which drives down wages and undermines working conditions.

As is typical in earnings regressions, wages vary in curvilinear fashion with respect to age (rising up to age 29 and declining thereafter) and are 18 percent lower for women. Each year of education increases real wages by 1.1 percent, and holding an unskilled manual job carries an 11.5 percent wage premium compared to an agricultural occupation, whereas holding a skilled job boosts wages by 23.1 percent. Wages rise by 0.6 percent with each additional prior trip and are 4.8 percent greater for those who speak and understand some English and 8.8 percent greater for those who speak and understand a lot of English. Each

TABLE 3
OLS Regression of Logged Wages on Selected Independent Variables

Variable	B	SE
Sector of employment		
Enclave	−0.022	0.020
Secondary	−0.125°°°°	0.018
Documentation		
Legal	—	—
Temporary	−0.114°°°	0.045
Undocumented	−0.115°°°°	0.021
Demographic background		
Female	−0.180°°°°	0.044
Age	0.011°°°	0.003
Age squared	−0.0002°°°°	0.000
Married or in union	0.033	0.032
Education		
School years completed	0.011°°°°	0.002
Occupation		
Agriculture	—	—
Unskilled	0.115°°°°	0.017
Skilled	0.231°°°°	0.037
U.S. Experience		
Number of prior U.S. trips	0.006°°°	0.002
Total months of U.S. experience	0.000	0.000
English ability		
Does not speak or understand English	—	—
Speaks and understands some English	0.048°°°	0.018
Speaks and understands much English	0.088°°°°	0.021
Social capital		
Parent a migrant	0.019	0.018
Sibling migrated	−0.107°°°°	0.020
Community migration prevalence	0.002°°°	0.001
How job obtained		
By oneself	—	—
Relative	−0.013	0.017
Acquaintance	−0.013	0.017
Contractor	0.045	0.073
Integration		
Relations with Anglos	0.005	0.015
Bank account	0.180°°°°	0.022
Period		
1970–1974	—	—
1975–1979	−0.127°°°°	0.036

(continued)

TABLE 3 (CONTINUED)

Variable	B	SE
1980–1984	−0.219°°°°	0.035
1985–1989	−0.295°°°°	0.033
1990–1994	−0.348°°°°	0.033
1995–1999	−0.375°°°°	0.035
2000–2004	−0.300°°°°	0.039
2005–2010	−0.400°°°°	0.048
Intercept	2.221°°°°	0.079
Adjusted R-squared	0.184	
Number of observations	4,146	

°$p = .10$. °°$p < .10$. °°°$p < .05$. °°°°$p < .001$.

point increase in the prevalence of migration in the origin community raises wages by 0.2 percent, whereas having a migrant sibling is associated with a 10.7 percent wage reduction. In contrast, having a U.S. bank account is associated with an 18 percent wage premium. A particularly noteworthy result is the progressive decline in the real value of wages over time for all immigrants, which according to Massey and Gentsch (2014) reflects the downward pressure on wages that stems from a rising share of undocumented workers in labor markets where undocumented hiring is criminalized.

Summary and Conclusion

During the Second World War the United States negotiated a binational treaty known as the Bracero Accord to bring Mexican workers into the United States on temporary visas for short-term work. The program grew to sustain around 450,000 annual entries by the late 1950s. At this time legal permanent immigration was not restricted numerically, and around 50,000 additional permanent immigrants entered each year. In 1965, however, the U.S. Congress chose not to renew the Bracero Accord and imposed the first-ever numerical limits on immigration from the Americas. The drastic reduction of opportunities for legal entry did not end large-scale migration from Mexico to the United States, however. Instead, the flows continued and reestablished themselves under undocumented auspices.

The rise of "illegal" migration, in turn, created a new "Latino Threat Narrative" in public discourse that after 1986 led to an unprecedented militarization of the Mexico-U.S. border. Prior to this time, undocumented migration had been overwhelmingly circular; but the rising costs and risks of undocumented border crossing increasingly induced migrants to cease moving back and forth, and rates of return migration to Mexico fell sharply. However, because rates of undocumented in-migration were unaffected by the militarization of the border, the net volume of undocumented entries increased and the unauthorized population grew rapidly. Since 2008, the number of undocumented residents has stabilized at around 11 million persons. Here we documented the labor market consequences of persistent undocumented status for this large, disenfranchised population.

Our results confirm earlier studies, documenting a steady decline in the wages of all Mexicans working in the United States over time, as well as the significant penalty paid by migrant workers who lack full legal status. In addition to the general decline in wages for Mexican immigrants, we found undocumented migrants to be doubly disadvantaged, being channeled into the secondary labor market where wages are systematically lower than in the primary sector, and then earning lower wages than documented migrants regardless of sector of employment. In addition, we found migrants holding temporary work visas were also significantly disadvantaged. Rather than being channeled away into the secondary sector, however, they were channeled away from employment in immigrant enclaves, a sector of the labor market in which greater opportunities prevailed and wages roughly equaled those in the primary sector; but like undocumented migrants, they earned lower wages in whatever sector they worked.

In sum, this empirical analysis clearly demonstrates the disadvantaged position of Mexican immigrants, in general, and undocumented Mexicans, in particular, within the U.S. labor market and highlights the importance of legal status in determining economic welfare in the United States. Undocumented migrants were more than twice as likely as legal immigrants to work in the secondary sector, where wages were 12.5 percent lower than in the primary or enclave sector. Evaluated at the mean wage of $10.21 per hour, this wage penalty yields an annual deficit of $2,655 for a full-time, year-round worker (i.e., 40 hours per week, 52 weeks a year). Holding sector of employment constant, moreover, undocumented migrants earn 11.5 percent less per hour than legal immigrants, resulting in an annual deficit of $2,442. For those migrants who were unfortunate enough to be channeled into the secondary sector (49 percent of those without documents, on average, according to model predictions), the total loss of annual income would be $5,097, out of a base income of $21,237 working at the mean wage.

Millions of undocumented Mexicans currently working in the U.S. labor force therefore earn systematically less than they otherwise would if they were fully documented, inevitably depressing the earnings of households to which they belong, which increasingly contain U.S.-born (citizen) children. According to Passel and Taylor (2010), in 2009, the children of undocumented migrants living in the United States included 4 million U.S. citizens who, because of the undocumented wage penalty, could not have received the same level of parental investment as their counterparts with documented parents. If each of these children had an undocumented parent working full time at the average wage, the total disinvestment would equal $9.8 billion. Very clearly, then, the economic penalty associated with a lack of legal status not only constitutes a burden for currently undocumented adults but carries the very real risk of perpetuating poverty and disadvantage over time and into the next generation of American citizens.

References

Chavez, Leo R. 2001. *Covering immigration: Population images and the politics of the nation*. Berkeley, CA: University of California Press.

Chavez, Leo R. 2008. *The Latino threat: Constructing immigrants, citizens, and the nation*. Stanford, CA: Stanford University Press.

Donato, Katharine M., and Douglas S. Massey. 1993. Effects of the immigration reform act on the wages of Mexican migrants. *Social Science Quarterly* 74 (3): 523–41.

Donato, Katharine M., and Blake Sisk. 2013. Shifts in the employment outcomes among Mexican migrants to the United States, 1976–2009. *Research in Social Stratification and Mobility* 30 (1): 63–77.

Dunn, Timothy J. 1996. *The militarization of the U.S.-Mexico border, 1978–1992: Low-intensity conflict doctrine comes home*. Austin, TX: Center for Mexican American Studies, University of Texas at Austin.

Massey, Douglas S. 1987. Do undocumented migrants earn lower wages than legal immigrants? New evidence from Mexico. *International Migration Review* 21 (2): 236–74.

Massey, Douglas S. 2013. America's immigration policy fiasco: Learning from past mistakes. *Daedalus* 142 (3): 5–15.

Massey, Douglas S., Joaquín Arango, Graem Hugo, Ali Kouaouci, Adela Pellegrino, and J. Edward Taylor. 1998. *Worlds in motion: International migration at the end of the millennium*. Oxford: Oxford University Press.

Massey, Douglas S., and Chiara Capoferro. 2004. Measuring undocumented migration. *International Migration Review* 38 (3): 1075–1102.

Massey, Douglas S., Jorge Durand, and Nolan P. Malone. 2002. *Beyond smoke and mirrors: Mexican immigration in an age of economic integration*. New York, NY: Russell Sage Foundation.

Massey, Douglas S., Jorge Durand, and Karen A. Pren. 2015. Border enforcement and return migration by documented and undocumented Mexicans. *Journal of Ethnic and Migration Studies* 41 (7): 1015–40.

Massey, Douglas S., Jorge Durand, and Karen A. Pren. 2016. Why border enforcement backfired. *American Journal of Sociology* 121 (5): 1–44.

Massey, Douglas S., and Kerstin Gentsch. 2014. Undocumented migration and the wages of Mexican immigrants in the United States. *International Migration Review* 48 (2): 482–99.

Massey, Douglas S., and Karen A. Pren. 2012a. Origins of the new Latino underclass. *Race and Social Problems* 4 (1): 5–17.

Massey, Douglas S., and Karen A. Pren. 2012b. Unintended consequences of U.S. immigration policy: Explaining the post-1965 surge from Latin America. *Population and Development Review* 38 (1): 1–29.

Massey, Douglas S., and Audrey Singer. 1995. New estimates of undocumented Mexican migration and the probability of apprehension. *Demography* 32 (2): 203–13.

Massey, Douglas S., and René Zenteno. 2000. A validation of the ethnosurvey: The case of Mexico-U.S. migration. *International Migration Review* 34 (3): 765–92.

Nevins, Joseph. 2001. *Operation Gatekeeper: The rise of the "illegal alien" and the remaking of the U.S.-Mexico boundary*. New York, NY: Routledge.

Passel, Jeffrey S., Mark Hugo Lopez, and D'Vera Cohn. 2014. *As growth stalls, unauthorized immigrant population becomes settled*. Washington, DC: Pew Research Center.

Passel, Jeffrey S., and Paul Taylor. 2010. *Unauthorized immigrants and their U.S.-born children*. Washington, DC: Pew Research Center.

Phillips, Julie A., and Douglas S. Massey. 1999. The new labor market: Immigrants and wages after IRCA. *Demography* 36 (2): 233–46.

Piore, Michael J. 1979. *Birds of passage: Migrant labor in industrial societies*. New York, NY: Cambridge University Press.

Portes, Alejandro. 1987. The social origins of the Cuban enclave economy of Miami. *Sociological Perspectives* 30 (4): 340–72.

Portes, Alejandro, and Robert Bach. 1987. *Latin journey: Cuban and Mexican immigrants in the United States*. Berkeley, CA: University of California Press.

Santa Ana, Otto. 2002. *Brown tide rising: Metaphors of Latinos in contemporary American public discourse*. Austin, TX: University of Texas Press.

The Precarious Position of Latino Immigrants in the United States: A Comparative Analysis of Ethnosurvey Data

A majority of Mexican and Central Americans living in the United States today are undocumented or living in a marginal, temporary legal status. This article is a comparative analysis of how Mexican and non-Mexican Latino immigrants fare in the U.S. labor market. We show that despite higher levels of human capital and a higher class background among non-Mexican migrants, neither they nor Mexican migrants have fared very well in the United States. Over the past four decades, the real value of their wages has fallen across the board, and both Mexican and non-Mexican migrant workers experience wage penalties because they are in liminal legal categories. With Latinos now composing 17 percent of the U.S. population and 25 percent of births, the precariousness of their labor market position should be a great concern among those attending to the nation's future.

Keywords: immigration; undocumented migrants; liminal legality; wages; Mexicans; Central Americans

From 1970 through 2010, some 11.7 million legal Latin American immigrants arrived in the United States (U.S. Department of Homeland Security 2015); and over the same period, the undocumented population rose from around a half million to around 11 million,

Douglas S. Massey is the Henry G. Bryant Professor of Sociology and Public Affairs at Princeton University, where he directs the Office of Population Research in addition to serving as codirector of the Mexican Migration Project.

Jorge Durand is a senior research professor in the Department for the Study of Social Movements at the University of Guadalajara and codirector of the Mexican Migration Project. He is a member of the Mexican Academy of Sciences and a foreign associate of the U.S. National Academy of Sciences.

Karen A. Pren is the manager of the Mexican Migration Project and the Latin American Migration Project at Princeton University and the University of Guadalajara.

Correspondence: dmassey@princeton.edu

By
DOUGLAS S. MASSEY,
JORGE DURAND,
and
KAREN A. PREN

DOI: 10.1177/0002716216648999

about 80 percent of whom are from Latin America (Wasem 2011; Passel and Cohn 2011). Whereas in 1970 the U.S. population was just 4.7 percent Hispanic, by 2010 the figure had risen to 17.3 percent, making Latinos by far the nation's largest minority group. In addition to being a relatively small share of the population in the 1970s, Hispanics were also regionally isolated and divided into very distinct subgroups. Mexicans were the largest population, composing 59 percent of all Latinos at the time, and they were concentrated in the Southwest and were overwhelmingly native-born (Grebler, Moore, and Guzman 1970; Jaffe, Cullen, and Boswell 1980).

Hispanics in the Northeast consisted overwhelmingly of Puerto Rican migrants and their children, who had settled in and around New York City in the 25 years between 1945 and 1970, when mass migration effectively ended (Bean and Tienda 1987; Acosta-Belén and Santiago 2006). These migrants had come from the lower echelons of the island's socioeconomic distribution to take unskilled jobs in the manufacturing and service sectors. African ancestry was common among Puerto Rican migrants, making them subject to high levels of discrimination and exclusion (Massey and Bitterman 1985).

Cubans made up the last regional concentration of Hispanics present in the 1970s. They had arrived after 1959 as refugees from the left-wing regime of Fidel Castro (Portes and Bach 1985; Portes and Rumbaut 2014). Although Cubans arrived as refugees, asylum seekers, or in various irregular statuses, during the Cold War they were welcomed as exiles from Communism and quickly granted legal permanent residence. Whereas only 73,000 Cubans arrived from 1950 to 1959, the number increased to 202,000 in the 1960s and 256,000 in the 1970s (U.S. Department of Homeland Security 2015). The vast majority settled in the Miami metropolitan area, though smaller concentrations could be found in and around metropolitan New York (Bean and Tienda 1987). Unlike Mexicans and Puerto Ricans, however, Cuban migration to the United States began among socioeconomic elites, and African and mixed racial origins were not well represented in the early waves of arrivals (Portes and Bach 1985).

This status quo was upset by the emergence of new patterns of immigration that began in the 1970s but unfolded primarily after the 1980s. As we noted, the mass migration of Puerto Ricans ended around 1970 (Acosta-Belén and Santiago 2006). Cubans, however, continued to arrive in successive waves: 133,000 in the 1980s, 159,000 during the 1990s, and 305,000 from 2000 to 2010 (U.S. Department of Homeland Security 2015). These new migrants contained more persons of African origin, but like earlier arrivals, they settled overwhelmingly in South Florida. Beginning in 1965, Caribbean migrants from Cuba and Puerto Rico were joined by new flows from the Dominican Republic. Following the assassination of Rafael Trujillo in 1961, the Dominican Republic descended into political chaos, and in 1965, U.S. troops invaded to occupy the capital Santo Domingo.

NOTE: The authors thank the MacArthur Foundation (grant 12-102305-000-CFP) and the National Institute of Child Health and Human Development (grants R01 HD035643 and P2C HD047879-11) for support of this research.

To defuse political tensions, the U.S. Ambassador to the Dominican Republic was instructed to make U.S. resident visas freely available to qualified applicants, mostly middle-class students and intellectuals who had been agitating against the regime, thereby initiating a predominantly legal outflow that continues to the current day (Martin 1966; Grasmuck and Pessar 1991). Whereas only 10,000 Dominican immigrants entered the United States during the 1950s, the outflow of legal immigrants increased to 84,000 during the 1960s and expanded to 139,000 during the 1970s, 222,000 during the 1980s, and reached 360,000 during the 1990s before moderating slightly to 345,000 from 2000 to 2010 (U.S. Department of Homeland Security 2015). As of 2010, 78 percent of Dominicans lived in the northeastern United States, mainly in the Greater New York Area (Ennis, Ríos-Vargas, and Albert 2011).

Immigration from Central America began in the 1980s in response to a Cold War military and political intervention in the region by the United States. The success of the Sandinista Revolution in 1979 and the rise of left-wing insurgencies in Guatemala and Honduras prompted the Reagan administration to finance and train a covert military force known as the Contras, which operated from Honduras, in an effort to overthrow the Sandinistas in Nicaragua, all while supporting right-wing regimes and paramilitary militias in El Salvador and Guatemala (Lundquist and Massey 2005). As a result, during the 1980s, waves of violence swept through these four "frontline" nations and their economies shrank, sending streams of migrants northward to the United States (Massey, Durand, and Pren 2014).

From 1970 through 1979 only 78,000 legal immigrants had entered from these countries, but during the 1980s the number ballooned to 274,000. Although a regional peace accord was signed in 1987, the economies of the frontline states had been devastated, and civil violence continued for some time as gang violence increased. These factors led to an expansion of legal immigration from frontline nations during the 1990s (559,000) and from 2000 to 2010 (603,000; U.S. Department of Homeland Security 2015). As in the case of Cuba, Nicaraguans were welcomed as refugees from Communist tyranny and granted an easy path to permanent resident status, but those fleeing El Salvador, Guatemala, and Honduras were labeled as "economic" rather than "political" refugees and given few opportunities for legal entry, channeling these migrants into unauthorized migration. From 1980 to 2010, therefore, the number of undocumented migrants from these three nations rose from 93,000 to 1.5 million (Wasem 2011; Hoefer, Rytina, and Baker 2011).

Although emigration from South America can be tied to civil violence and political turmoil (beginning with Colombia during the 1960s and including Argentina and Chile in the 1970s, Peru in the 1980s and 1990s, and Venezuela in the 2000s), as import substitution industrialization gave way to neoliberalism Latin American economies were transformed, which in turn promoted emigration during the 1980s and 1990s (Massey, Behrman, and Sanchez 2006). Under the aegis of the "Washington Consensus" and in the wake of the 1982 debt crisis, structural adjustment packages were imposed on nations throughout Latin America, resulting in the privatization of state-owned companies, the downsizing of government bureaucracies, the termination of subsidies, the constriction of state transfers, and the opening of domestic markets to foreign investment.

These actions displaced a large number of workers who increasingly sought opportunities internationally (Donato et al. 2010). Whereas the number of legal immigrants entering the United States from South America was 246,000 and 235,000 during the 1960s and 1970s, it grew to 313,000 during the 1980s, 494,000 during the 1990s, and reached 863,000 from 2000 to 2010 (U.S. Department of Homeland Security 2015). Although the Ecuadorian undocumented population grew from 25,000 in 1980 to 180,000 in 2010, most immigrants from South America were legal. Rather than migrating to the United States without authorization, most undocumented migrants went to Spain or other countries in the European Union (Aysa-Lastra and Cachón 2015).

Despite the continuation of immigration from Cuba, and the addition of new flows from the Dominican Republic, Central America, and South America, by far the biggest influence on the size and structure of the Hispanic population in the United States was the resurgence of Mexican migration after 1965. This dramatically changed the size and composition of the Mexican-origin population, increasing it from 5.4 million in 1970 to 33.7 million in 2010 and raising the share of foreign-born among Hispanics from 14 percent to 35 percent while increasing the Mexican share among Hispanics from 59 percent to 63 percent (cf. Acosta and de la Cruz 2011; Ennis, Ríos-Vargas, and Albert 2011).

As of 2010, more than two-thirds of all people of Mexican origin in the United States were immigrants or the children of immigrants, and much of the growth in this population stemmed from unauthorized migration as the number of undocumented Mexicans in the United States swelled from around 225,000 to 6.4 million between 1970 and 2010 (cf. Warren and Passel 1987; Wasem 2011). As of 2010, nearly 60 percent of all Mexican immigrants in the United States lacked legal status and comprised more than a fifth of all persons of Mexican origin (cf. Hoefer, Rytina, and Baker 2011;Acosta and de la Cruz 2011; Ennis, Ríos-Vargas, and Albert 2011).

In addition, beginning in the 1980s and accelerating through the 1990s, Mexican immigration shifted from being a regional to a national phenomenon. Whereas 84 percent of all Mexican immigrants who arrived between 1965 and 1970 went to the border states of California, Texas, Arizona, and New Mexico (Durand, Massey, and Charvet 2000), among those who arrived between 1995 and 2000 the figure was 54 percent (Massey and Capoferro 2008). During the 1990s and 2000s, rapid Mexican population growth shifted into states of the South, Northeast, and Midwest (Durand and Massey 2003), a shift largely attributable to the militarization of the Mexico-U.S. border, which decreased rates of return migration among undocumented migrants and channeled Mexican migrants away from traditional crossing points and destinations, particularly in California (Massey, Durand, and Pren 2016).

To a lesser but still significant degree, the same geographic diversification occurred for Central Americans and, to a lesser extent, to South Americans. Whereas in 1980, 18 percent of Hispanics lived in the Northeast and 43 percent in the West, by 2010 these percentages fell to 14 percent and 41 percent, respectively; and while the share living in the Midwest remained roughly constant at around 9 percent, the share living in the South rose from 31 percent to 36 percent, putting Latinos in contact with people and regions with little or no prior experience of immigration (Massey 2008; Stepler and Brown 2015).

To a great extent, the Latino population boom occurred despite rather than because of shifts in U.S. immigration policies, which, starting in 1965, moved steadily to be more restrictive. In 1965, Congress canceled a long-standing temporary worker agreement with Mexico and imposed the first-ever numerical limits on immigration from the Americas. These limits were lowered even further to twenty thousand annual residence visas per country in 1976, accompanied by major expansions in immigration and border patrol policies, which took effect in 1986, 1990, 1996, and 2001 (Massey, Durand, and Malone 2002). These policies led to the expansion of undocumented migration (see Massey and Pren 2012; Massey, Durand, and Pren 2014).

Over time, undocumented status has increasingly come to predict negative labor market outcomes. The criminalization of undocumented hiring by the 1986 Immigration Reform and Control Act (IRCA), when combined with the massive increase in the number of undocumented migrants during the 1990s and 2000s, acted to put substantial downward pressure on immigrant wages throughout the nation. Whereas undocumented status had no effect on earnings prior to the IRCA, afterward it carried a 21 percent wage penalty (Phillips and Massey 1999). More recent work by Hall, Greenman, and Farkas (2010) estimated a 17 percent wage disparity between documented and undocumented Mexican immigrant men and a 9 percent wage disparity by legal status among Mexican immigrant women. Pena (2010b) found that undocumented migrants were also more likely to be paid piece rate than other workers and that they worked fewer hours and earned lower wages as a result. Undocumented agricultural workers experienced an average wage penalty of 5 to 6 percent (Pena 2010a).

The rising share of undocumented workers and the criminalization of undocumented hiring have undermined the wages not just of undocumented migrants but of all workers employed in the same labor markets (Massey and Gelatt 2010; Massey and Gentsch 2014). In their 2008 survey of low-wage workers in Chicago, Los Angeles, and New York, Bernhardt, Spiller, and Polson (2013, 725) found that "violations of employment and labor laws are pervasive across low-wage labor industries and occupations." According to their estimates, 31 percent of immigrant workers experienced a minimum wage violation compared with only 16 percent among native workers; and among those without documents, the figure was 37 percent compared with 21 percent among those with legal papers (Bernhardt et al. 2008). Another survey of immigrant workers in New Orleans found that 41 percent had experienced wage theft (Fussell 2011). Using data from the Current Population Survey, Orrenius and Zavodny (2009) documented a pronounced decline in employment, hours worked, and earnings among recent male Latin American immigrants that they attributed to harsher enforcement in the post-9/11 period. Hall and Greenman's (2014) research demonstrates that undocumented workers also face greater exposure to occupational hazards, such as physical strain, exposure to heights, and repetitive motions and that they are rewarded less for employment in hazardous settings.

Most prior work on legal status and wages has focused on Mexican immigrants; but as suggested above, the prevalence of undocumented migrants varies widely by region of origin. Puerto Ricans are U.S. citizens by birth, whether they are born on the island or the mainland; and virtually all Cubans in the United States are U.S. citizens or legal resident aliens, as are the large majority of Dominicans and South Americans present in the United States. In contrast, large shares of both Mexicans and Central Americans lack legal status. Among Mexican immigrants living in the United States in 2010, for example, 57 percent were undocumented, compared to 63 percent of both Guatemalans and Hondurans. Although the figure is only 52 percent for Salvadorans, when those in the legal limbo of Temporary Protected Status are added in, the percentage lacking a fully legal status probably approaches that of Guatemalans and Hondurans (cf. Acosta and de la Cruz 2011; Hoefer, Rytina, and Baker 2011).

In this article, we undertake a comparative analysis of how legal status affects wages among Mexicans and other Latin Americans, using data from the Mexican Migration Project together with comparable data collected under the aegis of the Latin American Migration Project. After describing our data and methods, we contrast the position of Mexican and non-Mexican Latin Americans in the U.S. labor market and move on to estimate wage regressions that assess the earnings penalties associated with undocumented and temporary legal statuses within each group. We conclude with an assessment of how precarious legal status undermines the economic status of Latino immigrants and constitutes a serious threat to the future of the United States.

Data and Methods

Given the success of the Mexican Migration Project (MMP), in 1998 the first two authors launched the Latin American Migration Project (LAMP) with a round of surveys in Puerto Rico. Their goal was to apply the ethnosurvey methods developed earlier by the MMP to gather data from successive rounds of surveys conducted in other countries of Latin America. The intention was to broaden the empirical base for testing theories and generalizing about patterns and processes of international migration. Since then, the LAMP investigators have collaborated with local researchers throughout the region to administer ethnosurveys in Puerto Rico, the Dominican Republic, Guatemala, El Salvador, Nicaragua, Costa Rica, Colombia, Ecuador, and Peru. In the current analysis, we draw upon these data to undertake a comparative examination of legal status and wages among Mexican and other Latin American immigrants.

Although ethnosurveys were also fielded in Haiti and Paraguay as part of the LAMP, we do not use those data here and instead rely on data gathered from samples of seven communities in Costa Rica, fourteen in Colombia, seven in the Dominican Republic, four in Ecuador, four in El Salvador, three in Guatemala, nine in Nicaragua, five in Peru, and five in Puerto Rico. Although the vast majority of Mexicans, Puerto Ricans, and Central Americans go to the United States, many and sometimes most international migrants from the other countries move elsewhere. A significant percentage of Dominican migrants go to Spain, for example, as do a large number of Ecuadorans and Colombians. Data collected in Peru revealed that its immigrants went to some twenty-five different nations around the world, including Japan, Australia, Canada, and many nations in Europe and Latin America, as well as the United States.

Rather than using a standard single semistructured interview schedule as is used in the MMP, LAMP interview schedules are adapted to reflect different social and cultural circumstances across nations. As in Mexico, the LAMP surveys enumerate the household head, spouse, and all children of the head in addition to any others present in the household; and in addition to compiling basic socio-economic and demographic information on each individual, interviewers also gather data on the first and most recent international trips, including location, occupation, hours worked, wages earned, and legal status. Household heads were also asked a detailed series of questions about their most recent international trip, which provides the bulk of the data for our analysis.

With 154 communities in the MMP dataset in contrast to 54 in the LAMP datafile, the Mexican sample size is necessarily much larger than that for non-Mexican nations. The Latin American sample size is also smaller because far more international migrants go to nations other than the United States. Thus the Mexican sample includes 4,250 observations once cases with missing data are excluded, whereas the Latin American sample has only 545 cases, yielding a large difference in the precision of our sample estimates. The LAMP-based estimates thus carry a greater risk of Type II errors compared to those based on MMP data, which makes it more difficult to identify true substantive relationships as statisti-cally significant.

We follow the standard method in labor force studies of estimating an earnings regression that expresses the natural log of the real hourly wage (in 2010 dollars) as a function of variables hypothesized to influence wage rates. Our leading vari-able is *legal status*, which is defined in terms of three categories. *Legal immi-grants* include U.S. permanent residents and naturalized citizens, *temporary migrants* hold legal visas authorizing temporary, term-limited periods of work or residence in the United States, and *undocumented migrants* include those who crossed the border without authorization or who entered on a tourist visa and then violated its terms by working for pay.

In assessing the effect of legal status on wages, we include controls for demo-graphic background (gender, age, marital status), human capital (education, U.S. experience, English ability, and occupational skill), social capital (whether par-ents or siblings had prior U.S. experience), how the job was obtained (by oneself or through a relative, acquaintance, or contractor), and degree of integration in the United States (whether the migrant had social relationships with Anglo Americans and whether he or she had a U.S. bank account). Both Mexican and non-Mexican models also control for period (in five-year intervals extending from 1970 to 2010); we also control for country fixed effects in the Latin American models. Unfortunately the questions necessary to measure sector of employment were not asked in all countries of the LAMP, so this variable is excluded from the analysis.

Mexicans and Latin Americans
in the U.S. Labor Market

Table 1 presents summary statistics for all variables in our wage regressions to contrast the labor market position of Mexicans and other Latin Americans in the United States. On average, non-Mexican Latin Americans earn about 23 percent more than Mexicans ($12.55 versus $10.21). This differential in earnings likely reflects the much more vulnerable status of Mexicans, owing to a variety of factors. First, whereas nearly three-quarters of Mexicans are undocumented (74 percent), the figure is less than half for Latin Americans (just 43 percent). Second, compared with Mexicans other Latin Americans have 3.4 more years of schooling (9.6 versus 6.2), are less likely to come from an agricultural occupational background (2 percent versus 25 percent among Mexicans), and are more likely to come from a skilled background (17 percent versus 4 percent). Finally, whereas 42 percent of Latin Americans reported that they spoke and understood much English, only 27 percent of Mexicans did so; and while Mexicans report more total trips to the United States (2.5 versus 0.5), they have less cumulative U.S. experience (77 months compared with 104 months), implying that their labor market experience was not only less but more fragmented across trips.

Although Guatemalans and Salvadorans share many of the characteristics of Mexicans, they make up a small share of the total Latin American sample. In general, then, non-Mexican Latin American migrants appear to come from a higher class background than Mexicans, have greater access to permanent resident visas, and bring more human capital to the labor market, thus enhancing their bargaining position. Indeed, whereas 34 percent of Latin Americans have bank accounts, only 16 percent of Mexicans do, suggesting that Latin American migration consists more of middle-class migration than unskilled worker migration. It also indicates a higher level of formal connection to U.S. social and economic institutions. Despite this difference in economic integration, Mexicans and non-Mexicans appear to be comparably integrated socially, with 35 percent of Mexicans reporting that they have social relationships with Anglo Americans compared to 36 percent among Latin Americans.

The costs of migrating to the United States are much greater for Central and South American migrants, who were mostly displaced from steady nonagrarian jobs by civil violence and economic restructuring and usually possessed the class resources to secure legal resident visas. Or, if that were not possible, they could more easily acquire a tourist visa to enter legally and only later lapse into illegal status rather than undertaking a clandestine border crossing from the start. Puerto Ricans are U.S. citizens, of course, and migration from the Dominican Republic from the outset was urban, middle class, and predominantly legal (see Riosmena 2010). In contrast, Mexicans generally fit the profile of unskilled labor migrants.

Mexican migrants, for example, are overwhelmingly male (95 percent compared to 76 percent for other Latin Americans), unmarried (with just 36 percent married compared with 58 percent of Latin Americans), heavily concentrated in

TABLE 1
Means and Standard Deviations of Variables Used in the Analysis of Wages
Earned by Mexicans and Other Latin Americans

Variable	Mexicans		Other Latin Americans	
	Mean	Standard Deviation	Mean	Standard Deviation
Earnings				
Hourly wage (2010 dollars)	10.21	5.62	12.55	7.18
Documentation				
Legal	0.207	0.405	0.505	0.500
Temporary	0.034	0.181	0.025	0.157
Undocumented	0.740	0.439	0.433	0.495
Demographic background				
Female	0.052	0.223	0.243	0.429
Age	33.17	11.95	33.61	11.89
Married or in union	0.362	0.481	0.581	0.494
Education				
School years completed	6.175	3.958	9.611	4.576
Occupation				
Agriculture	0.248	0.432	0.018	0.132
Unskilled	0.653	0.476	0.591	0.492
Skilled	0.041	0.198	0.169	0.375
U.S. experience				
Number of prior U.S. trips	2.491	4.902	0.531	1.721
Total months of U.S. experience	77.05	86.73	105.05	95.21
English ability				
Does not speak or understand English	0.335	0.472	0.119	0.324
Speaks and understands some English	0.368	0.482	0.298	0.458
Speaks and understands much English	0.271	0.445	0.423	0.494
Social capital				
Parent a migrant	0.192	0.394	0.120	0.325
Sibling a migrant	0.386	0.487	0.065	0.246
Community migration prevalence	22.45	15.54	14.41	12.81
How job obtained				
By oneself	0.260	0.439	0.236	0.425
Relative	0.311	0.463	0.192	0.394
Acquaintance	0.284	0.451	0.292	0.455
Contractor	0.009	0.092	0.010	0.101
Integration				
Relations with Anglos	0.349	0.477	0.362	0.481
Bank account	0.159	0.366	0.338	0.473

(continued)

TABLE 1 (CONTINUED)

Variable	Mexicans		Other Latin Americans	
	Mean	Standard Deviation	Mean	Standard Deviation
Period				
1970–1974	0.061	0.240	0.052	0.221
1975–1979	0.094	0.292	0.062	0.241
1980–1984	0.106	0.308	0.097	0.295
1985–1989	0.175	0.380	0.166	0.372
1990–1994	0.222	0.416	0.158	0.365
1995–1999	0.177	0.382	0.164	0.370
2000–2004	0.114	0.317	0.144	0.352
2005–2010	0.051	0.219	0.022	0.148

the secondary or enclave sectors of the labor market (see Durand, Massey, and Pren, this volume), and are more embedded within migrant networks than non-Mexican migrants. Some 19 percent of Mexicans report having U.S. migrant parents and 39 percent report having migrant siblings, and Mexican migrants report that they come from a community where an average of 22 percent of all adult residents have been to the United States, compared with respective figures of 12 percent, 7 percent, and 14 percent for non-Mexican Latin Americans.

Legal Status and Wages among Mexicans and Latin Americans

Table 2 presents separate wage regressions estimated for Mexican migrants surveyed by the MMP and non-Mexican Latin Americans surveyed by the LAMP. As noted earlier, the Latin American model was estimated using country fixed effects. Although not shown in the table, these estimates generally revealed the earnings of Caribbean and Central American migrants to lie below those from South America, with the sole exception of those from Costa Rica, which is a relatively prosperous egalitarian nation that was spared turmoil and violence during the U.S. Contra intervention. According to the fixed effects coefficients, wages were 33 percent greater for Costa Ricans, 26 percent greater for Colombians, 27 percent greater for Ecuadorians, and 30 percent greater for Peruvians, compared with migrants from the Caribbean and Central America generally.

The coefficient for undocumented status suggests that other Latin Americans lacking legal papers earn around 7 percent less than legal immigrants, compared with a 12 percent deficit among Mexicans. Although the former coefficient is not

TABLE 2
Regression of Logged U.S. Hourly Wages on Legal Status and Selected Other
Variables for Mexican and Latin American Migrants to the United States

Variable	Mexicans		Other Latin Americans	
	B	SE	B	SE
Documentation				
Legal	—	—	—	—
Temporary	−.115°°	.045	−.452°°	.151
Undocumented	−.123°°°	.021	−.069	.064
Demographic background				
Female	−.214°°°	.035	−.139°°	.046
Age	.010°°	.0003	−.009°°	.001
Age squared	−.0002°°°	.0001	.000	.001
Married or in union				
Education				
School years completed	.012°°°	.0021	.021°°°	.005
Occupation				
Agriculture	—	—	—	—
Unskilled	.101°°°	.017	.127	.094
Skilled	.224°°°	.037	.414°°°	.102
U.S. experience				
Number of prior U.S. trips	.006°°°	.002	−.005	.012
Total months of U.S. experience	.001	.001	.000	.000
English ability				
Does not speak or understand English	—	—	—	—
Speaks and understands some English	.046°°	.018	−.080	.069
Speaks and understands much English	.093°°°	.021	−.071	.073
Social capital				
Parent a migrant	.023	.018	.028	.055
Sibling a migrant	−.116°°°	.021	.335	.453
Community migration prevalence	.002°°	.001	.001	.002
How job obtained				
By oneself	—	—	—	—
Relative	−.011	.017	−.053	.054
Acquaintance	−.008	.017	−.107°°	.046
Contractor	.032	.074	.110	.164
Integration				
Relations with Anglos	.003	.015	.053	.042
Bank account	.200°°°	.021	.113°°	.048
Period				
1970–1974	—	—	—	—
1975–1979	−.230°°°	.036	−.199°	.107

(continued)

TABLE 2 (CONTINUED)

Variable	Mexicans		Other Latin Americans	
	B	SE	B	SE
1980–1984	−.219***	.035	−.449***	.103
1985–1989	−.309***	.033	−.456***	.098
1990–1994	−.355***	.033	−.405***	.103
1995–1999	−.378***	.035	−.483***	.108
2000–2004	−.310***	.039	−.433***	.119
2005–2010	−.342***	.048	−.346*	.199
Intercept	2.236***	0.073	2.555***	0.230
Adjusted R-squared	.171***		.276***	
Number of observations	4,250		545	

*p < .10. **p < .05. ***p < .001.

statistically significant, this likely owes to the fact that the smaller number of undocumented migrants in the non-Mexican sample yields a much less precise estimate. If the Latin American coefficient were measured with the same precision as the Mexican coefficient, it would be statistically significant. At the very least, we can state that the penalty for undocumented status is not as severe for non-Mexican Latin Americans as it is for Mexicans, but it is difficult to state with any accuracy the size of the gap or its significance.

When it comes to temporary legal status, however, the penalty is far more severe among the non-Mexicans than Mexicans. In the Latin American sample, those holding temporary visas earned a remarkable 45 percent lower wage than legal immigrants; whereas in the Mexican sample, the gap was only 11.5 percent. This huge gap between legal and temporary Latin American workers probably reflects the better bargaining position of legal immigrants in the non-Mexican sample, who, as we have already seen, boast relatively high educations, strong English abilities, and greater occupational skills than Mexicans and thus are better able to benefit from competition in open labor markets compared to migrants whose visas restrict job mobility. The gap probably also reflects the fact that other Latin Americans hold different kinds of temporary visas than Mexicans. Whereas the latter generally hold H-visas for temporary work in agriculture, food processing, and construction, many Central Americans, and to a lesser extent South Americans, languish in a category known as temporary protected status (TPS), one of the liminal legal statuses identified by Menjívar (2006).

Under the 1997 Nicaraguan Adjustment and Central American Relief Act, Nicaraguans were authorized to apply for legal permanent residence if they had been in the United States since December 1, 1995, irrespective of any prior lack of documentation. In contrast, Salvadorans and Guatemalans were only authorized to apply for a suspension of deportation or cancellation of removal, relief that was only temporary and never made permanent. TPS could be terminated at any time by Congress; and since its inception it has had to be renewed regularly, at a fee currently set at $380. Stranded in an uncertain legal limbo placed many Central Americans, especially Salvadorans, in a precarious position. That precariousness strained interpersonal relationships and fragmented social ties, which undermined the employment benefits of social capital enjoyed by Mexicans, thus undermining the position of TPS recipients in the labor force and American society generally (Menjívar 2000).

As shown in the right-hand columns of Table 2, social capital connections have no effect on earnings, getting a job through an acquaintance is associated with 11 percent lower wages, and there are no earnings returns to English language ability or U.S. experience for non-Mexicans. Only years of schooling and occupational skill have the expected positive effects. As can be seen at the bottom of the table, the intercepts of the wage regressions were quite similar, suggesting that the gap in average wages observed between Mexicans and non-Mexicans in Table 1 are largely explained by variables in the model.

A powerful pattern common to both groups of migrants, and one indicating the deteriorating labor market position of Latino immigrants generally in the United States, is the steady erosion of the real value wages over time. Compared to earnings during the early 1970s, the real value was 13 percent lower in the late 1970s and 22 percent lower in the early 1980s. Thereafter the gap increased, averaging 30 to 38 percent lower, reflecting the criminalization of undocumented hiring in 1986 and the growing share of undocumented migrants in the workforce thereafter (Massey and Gentsch 2014). Among Central Americans, wages were 20 percent lower in the late 1970s than during the early 1970s; and from 1980 onward wages were 40 to 48 percent lower, except for 2005 to 2010, when the negative differential dropped to 35 percent, matching the deficit of Mexicans. Although migrants with education and skills may be able to overcome depressed wages to some degree, it is very clear that the labor market has deteriorated markedly for all Latino immigrants since the 1970s and that they are now in very precarious circumstances economically.

Conclusion

Since 1970 the Hispanic population of the United States has grown from a small and regionally isolated population to become the nation's largest minority group with members dispersed widely throughout the nation. The boom in Latino immigration was led by Mexicans, who constituted the largest number among both documented and undocumented migrants from 1970 to 2010. The undocumented population grew slowly between 1965 and 1985, even as opportunities for legal entry were sharply reduced because cross-border movements were overwhelmingly circular and produced small annual net gains. The 1986 IRCA legalized around 2 million Mexicans, and these beneficiaries quickly began using the family reunification provisions of U.S. immigration law to sponsor the entry of relatives, without numerical limits on spouses, minor children, and parents of citizens (but subject to limitation if they were older children or siblings of citizens), thereby boosting the inflow of legal Mexican immigrants and sustaining it to the present day (Massey and Pren 2012). The most important effect of IRCA, however, was that it initiated a massive, decades-long militarization of the Mexico-U.S. border. The intensity of border enforcement dramatically increased the costs and risks of border crossing, prompting migrants to stop circulating back and forth and instead remain in the United States once they had achieved a successful crossing. The end result of the sharp drop in return migration by Mexican migrants was an increased net rate of undocumented migration and accelerated unauthorized population growth (Massey, Durand, and Pren 2016).

The growth of the Hispanic population was also bolstered by new immigration streams from the Caribbean, Central America, and South America. In the former two regions, the upsurge stemmed from Cold War policies that privileged persons fleeing left-wing regimes (which produced legal outflows from Cuba and Nicaragua) and stemmed from anti-leftist military interventions that produced a predominantly legal outflow in the Dominican Republic and generated even larger outflows of unwelcomed (undocumented) migrants from right-wing regimes in El Salvador, Guatemala, and Honduras. Although international migration was generated by civil violence in Colombia (Silva and Massey 2014) and a few other countries, in most South American nations it was more strongly associated with economic displacements stemming from the imposition of structural adjustment policies during the 1980s (Massey and Capoferro 2006).

Despite large increases in legal and temporary worker migration from Latin America, in the end a rather large share of Latino population growth over the past several decades has occurred through unauthorized migration. Undocumented migrants now constitute around 40 percent of the Latino immigrant population generally and 60 percent or more among Mexican and Central American immigrants. Mass illegality has thus come to be a prominent structural feature of America's Latino population and the most serious barrier to the integration of Latin American immigrants and their children (Waters and Pineau 2015).

Hence our current analysis of legal status and earnings among Latino immigrants is both timely and important. Our study drew upon data from the MMP (Durand and Massey 2004) and the LAMP (Donato et al. 2010), sibling projects directed by Jorge Durand and Douglas Massey designed to broaden the base of generalization about international migration by applying ethnosurvey methods developed in Mexico to other nations in Latin America. Using these data, we undertook a systematic comparison of Mexican and non-Mexican Latin American migrants to the United States to assess the wage penalties associated with undocumented and temporary legal status.

A descriptive analysis revealed that non-Mexican immigrants were more likely to be middle class than Mexican immigrants, with more schooling, greater occupational skills, and better English language abilities. These differences led to a larger relative number of documented as opposed to undocumented migrants, as well as more women and families as opposed to the single, unmarried men with low levels of education and poor English language skills who typified migrants from Mexico. Despite these advantages, however, Latin American immigrants have generally experienced a sharp decline in real wages over the past several decades, which has left them in precarious labor market circumstances. Real wages for both groups (Mexican and non-Mexican migrants) during 2005 to 2010 was around 35 percent below what they were in the early 1970s.

Beyond the overall erosion of wages over the past 40 years, migrants in liminal legal statuses generally experienced an additional wage penalty, with undocumented Mexicans earning about 12 percent less than legal immigrants and undocumented non-Mexicans possibly earning around 7 percent less. Likewise, temporary legal Mexican workers earned 11 percent lower wages, but temporary non-Mexican workers earned an impressive 45 percent less. Moreover, migrants in the Latin American sample experienced no wage returns to U.S. experience, English language ability, or social capital. In the end, while migrants in marginal legal status categories fared the worst, no Latin American migrants have fared well in U.S. labor markets since the passage of the 1986 IRCA, which simultaneously criminalized undocumented hiring and perversely accelerated undocumented population growth to put downward pressure on wages in markets where immigrants concentrated.

In 1994 the United States joined with Canada and Mexico to enact the North American Free Trade Agreement (NAFTA), which sought to create markets for capital, commodities, goods, land, and services but block the integration of markets for labor and human capital. Ironically, during the same year that NAFTA went into effect, the United States launched Operation Gatekeeper in San Diego to block the flow of Mexican migrants through the border's busiest corridor, which ultimately helped to transform what had been a circular flow of male undocumented workers traveling to three states into a settled population of undocumented families living in fifty states. This transformation produced mass illegality and precarious circumstances for workers in labor markets throughout the nation.

Widespread illegality has implications for the well-being of Latino immigrants beyond their position in the labor market. Greenman and Hall (2013) demonstrate, for example, that undocumented students are less likely than those with documents to graduate from high school and enroll in college. Hall and Stringfield (2014) show that Hispanic-white segregation rises as the estimated prevalence of undocumented migrants in the population increases, whereas Rugh and Massey (2014) document a strong connection between hostility toward illegal immigrants and higher levels of Hispanic segregation. Hall and Greenman (2013) find that undocumented householders are far less likely to be homeowners than documented migrants and non-Hispanic whites; and they also live in more crowded homes, report greater structural deficiencies with their dwellings, and express greater concern about the quality of public services and environmental conditions in their neighborhoods.

Given these findings, it is not surprising that studies have also documented the negative health effects of illegality. Although Mexican migrants are positively selected for good health when they leave for the United States, they display worse health than otherwise similar nonmigrants when they return (Ullmann, Goldman, and Massey 2011; Goldman et al. 2014). Illegal status not only undermines the well-being of undocumented migrants, but it also has negative consequences for the families and communities to which they belong. Undocumented immigrant children have limited access to health insurance and a consistent source of health-care, children with immigrant parents have poorer health than children with native parents, and children with undocumented parents have less access to a diagnosis from a doctor for common childhood ailments (Gelatt 2016).

The manifold negative consequences of mass illegality were created by U.S. policy actions, and U.S. policy actions are required to undo them. The two most critical actions are clearly the suspension of deportations for long-term undocu-mented residents and the authorization of a pathway to legal status for the 11 million such persons who currently reside in the United States. Undocumented migration rates have been zero or negative since 2008, and the population is no longer growing (Passel et al. 2014). As a result, most undocumented residents of the United States have been present for many years: 85 percent for five years or more, 63 percent for 10 years or more, and 35 percent for 15 years or more (Taylor et al. 2011). Moreover, around half now have U.S.-born children, thus tying the welfare of millions in the next generation of Americans to the fate of their undocumented parents (Center for Migration Studies 2015).

Unfortunately, no legalization program is likely to be enacted given the cur-rent composition of the U.S. House of Representatives, in which the Republican caucus to date has systematically blocked all attempts to consider immigration reform legislation. All 2016 Republican presidential candidates called for increased border enforcement and more deportations from the U.S. interior, despite the fact that undocumented migration rates have been at zero or negative for six years at the time of this writing. Barring a Republican loss of the House in the next three elections, reform legislation that creates a pathway to legal status for undocumented migrants is unlikely to get very far until after 2022.

A new census will be taken in 2020 and provide the basis for reapportioning a new House of Representatives in 2022, by which time the core Republican con-stituency (older white Americans) will have fallen to a much smaller share of the total population. According to Census Bureau projections, non-Hispanic whites will compose only 50 percent of the population in 2020, and older white Americans (aged 55+) will constitute just 21 percent, paving the way for a shift in the political control of Congress and thus opening up the possibility of significant movement toward immigration reform. Much will depend, however, on who controls the state legislatures in 2022 and the degree to which partisanship prevails. What is certain is that the longer a legalization program is postponed, the lower the earn-ings, the less the schooling, the poorer the health, and the more disadvantaged the neighborhoods of undocumented migrants and their children, and the higher the cost the United States will ultimately pay as a nation and a society.

References

Acosta, Yesenia D., and G. Patricia de la Cruz. 2011. *The foreign born from Latin America and the Caribbean: 2010*. Washington, DC: U.S. Census Bureau.

Acosta-Belén, Edna, and Carlos E. Santiago. 2006. *Puerto Ricans in the United States: A contemporary portrait*. Boulder, CO: Lynne Rienner Publishers.

Aysa-Lastra, María, and Lorenzo Cachón, eds. 2015. *Immigrant vulnerability and resilience: Comparative perspectives on Latin American immigrants during the Great Recession*. New York, NY: Springer.

Bean, Frank D., and Marta Tienda. 1987. *The Hispanic population of the United States*. New York, NY: Russell Sage Foundation.

Bernhardt, Annette, Heather Boushey, Laura Dresser, and Chris Tilly, eds. 2008. *The gloves-off economy: Workplace standards at the bottom of America's labor market*. Ithaca, NY: Cornell University Press.

Bernhardt, Annette, Michael W. Spiller, and Diana Polson. 2013. All work and no pay: Violations of employment and labor laws in Chicago, Los Angeles, and New York City. *Social Forces* 91 (3): 725–46.

Center for Migration Studies. 2015. *U.S.-born children of undocumented residents: Numbers and characteristics in 2013*. New York, NY: Center for Migration Studies.

Donato, Katharine, John Hiskey, Jorge Durand, and Douglas S. Massey, eds. 2010. *Continental divides: International migration in the Americas*. Thousand Oaks, CA: Sage Publications.

Durand, Jorge, and Douglas S. Massey. 2003. *Clandestinos: Migración México-Estados Unidos en los albores del siglo XXI*. México, DF: Editorial Porrúa.

Durand, Jorge, and Douglas S. Massey. 2004. *Crossing the border: Research from the Mexican Migration Project*. New York, NY: Russell Sage Foundation.

Durand, Jorge, Douglas S. Massey, and Fernando Charvet. 2000. The changing geography of Mexican immigration to the United States: 1910–1996. *Social Science Quarterly* 81 (1): 1–15.

Durand, Jorge, Douglas S. Massey, and Karen A. Pren. 2016. Double disadvantage: Unauthorized Mexicans in the U.S. labor market. *The ANNALS of the American Academy of Political and Social Science* (this volume).

Ennis, Sharon R., Merarys Ríos-Vargas, and Nora G. Albert. 2011. *The Hispanic population: 2010*. Washington, DC: U.S. Census Bureau.

Fussell, Elizabeth. 2011. The deportation threat dynamic and victimization of Latino migrants: Wage theft and robbery. *Sociological Quarterly* 52 (4): 593–613.

Gelatt, Julia. 2016. Immigration status and the healthcare access and health of children of immigrants. *Social Science Quarterly*. doi:10.1111/ssqu.12261.

Goldman, Noreen, Anne R. Pebley, Mathew J. Creighton, Graciela M. Terue, Luis N. Rubalcava, and Chang Chung. 2014. The consequences of migration to the United States for short-term changes in the health of Mexican immigrants. *Demography* 51 (4): 1159–73.

Grasmuck, Sherri, and Patricia R. Pessar. 1991. *Between two islands: Dominican international migration*. Berkeley, CA: University of California Press.

Grebler, Leo, Joan W. Moore, and Ralph C. Guzman. 1970. *The Mexican-American people: The nation's second largest minority*. New York, NY: Free Press.

Greenman, Emily, and Matthew Hall. 2013. Legal status and educational transitions among Mexican immigrant youth: Empirical patterns and policy implications. *Social Forces* 91 (4): 1475–98.

Hall, Matthew, and Emily Greenman. 2013. Neighborhood and housing quality among undocumented immigrants. *Social Science Research* 42 (6): 1712–25.

Hall, Matthew, and Emily Greenman. 2014. The occupational risk of being illegal in the United States: Legal status, job hazard, and compensating differentials. *International Migration Review* 49 (2): 406–42.

Hall, Matthew, Emily Greenman, and George Farkas. 2010. Legal status and wage disparities for Mexican immigrants. *Social Forces* 89 (2): 491–513.

Hall, Matthew, and Jonathan Stringfield. 2014. Undocumented migration and the residential segregation of Mexicans in new destinations. *Social Science Research* 47 (1): 61–78.

Hoefer, Michael, Nancy Rytina, and Bryan C. Baker. 2011. *Estimates of the unauthorized immigrant population residing in the United States: January 2010*. Washington, DC: U.S. Department of Homeland Security.

Jaffe, A. J., Ruth M. Cullen, and Thomas D. Boswell. 1980. *The changing demography of Spanish Americans*. New York, NY: Academic Press.

Lundquist, Jennifer H., and Douglas S. Massey. 2005. Politics or economics? International migration during the Nicaraguan Contra War. *Journal of Latin American Studies* 37 (1): 29–53.

Martin, John B. 1966. *Overtaken by events: The Dominican crisis from the fall of Trujillo to the civil war*. New York, NY: Doubleday.

Massey, Douglas S. 2008. Assimilation in a new geography. In *New faces in new places: The changing geography of American immigration*, ed. Douglas S. Massey, 343–54. New York, NY: Russell Sage Foundation.

Massey, Douglas S., Jere R. Behrman, and Magaly R. Sánchez, eds. 2006. *Chronicle of a myth foretold: The Washington Consensus in Latin America*. Thousand Oaks, CA: Sage Publications.

Massey, Douglas S., and Brooks Bitterman. 1985. Explaining the paradox of Puerto Rican segregation. *Social Forces* 64 (2): 306–31.

Massey, Douglas S., and Chiara Capoferro. 2006. The geographic diversification of U.S. immigration. In *New faces in new places: The changing geography of American immigration*, ed. Douglas S. Massey, 25–50. New York, NY: Russell Sage Foundation.

Massey, Douglas S., and Chiara Capoferro. 2008. Sálvese quien pueda: Structural adjustment and emigration from Lima. *The ANNALS of the American Academy of Political and Social Science* 606:116–27.

Massey, Douglas S., Jorge Durand, and Nolan J. Malone. 2002. *Beyond smoke and mirrors: Mexican immigration in an age of economic integration*. New York, NY: Russell Sage Foundation.

Massey, Douglas S., Jorge Durand, and Karen A. Pren. 2014. Explaining undocumented migration. *International Migration Review* 48 (4): 1028–61.

Massey, Douglas S., Jorge Durand, and Karen A. Pren. 2016. Why border enforcement backfired. *American Journal of Sociology* 121 (5): 1557–1600.

Massey, Douglas S., and Julia Gelatt. 2010. What happened to the wages of Mexican immigrants? Trends and interpretations. *Latino Studies* 8 (3): 328–54.

Massey, Douglas S., and Kirsten Gentsch. 2014. Undocumented migration and the wages of Mexican immigrants in the United States. *International Migration Review* 48 (2): 482–99.

Massey, Douglas S., and Karen A. Pren. 2012. Unintended consequences of U.S. immigration policy: Explaining the post-1965 surge from Latin America. *Population and Development Review* 38 (1): 1–29.

Menjívar, Cecilia. 2000. *Fragmented ties: Salvadoran immigrant networks in America*. Berkeley, CA: University of California Press.

Menjívar, Cecilia. 2006. Liminal legality: Salvadoran and Guatemalan immigrants' lives in the United States. *American Journal of Sociology* 111 (4): 999–1037.

Orrenius, Pia M., and Madeline Zavodny. 2009. The effects of tougher enforcement on the job prospects of recent Latin American immigrants. *Journal of Policy Analysis and Management* 28 (2): 239–57.

Passel, Jeffrey, and D'Vera Cohn. 2011. *Unauthorized immigrant population: National and state trends, 2010*. Washington, DC: Pew Research Center.

Passel, Jeffrey S., D'Vera Cohn, Jens Manuel Krogstad, and Ana Gonzalez-Barrera. 2014. *As growth stalls, unauthorized immigrant population becomes more settled*. Washington, DC: Pew Research Center.

Pena, Anita Alves. 2010a. Legalization and immigrants in agriculture. *B.E. Journal of Economic Analysis and Policy* 10 (1): 1–22.

Pena, Anita Alves. 2010b. Poverty, legal status, and pay basis: The case of U.S. agriculture. *Industrial Relations* 49 (3): 429–56.

Phillips, Julie A., and Douglas S. Massey. 1999. The new labor market: Immigrants and wages after IRCA. *Demography* 36 (2): 233–46.

Portes, Alejandro, and Robert L. Bach. 1985. *Latin journey: Cuban and Mexican immigrants in the United States*. Berkeley, CA: University of California Press.

Portes, Alejandro, and Rubén G. Rumbaut. 2014. *Immigrant America: A portrait*. 4th ed. Berkeley, CA: University of California Press.

Riosmena, Fernando. 2010. Policy shocks: On the legal auspices of Latin America–U.S. migration. *The ANNALS of the American Academy of Political and Social Science* 630:270–93.

Rugh, Jacob S., and Douglas S. Massey. 2014. Segregation in post-civil rights America: Stalled integration or end of the segregated century? *DuBois Review: Social Science Research on Race* 11 (2): 202–32.

Silva, Carolina, and Douglas S. Massey. 2014. Violence, networks, and international migration from Colombia. *International Migration* 54 (5): 162–78.

Stepler, Renee, and Anna Brown. 2015. *Statistical portrait of Hispanics in the United States, 1980–2013*. Washington, DC: Pew Research Center.

Taylor, Paul, Mark Hugo Lopez, Jeffrey S. Passel, and Seth Motel. 2011. *Unauthorized immigrants: Length of residency, patterns of parenthood*. Washington, DC: Pew Research Center.

Ullmann, Norbis, Noreen Goldman, and Douglas S. Massey. 2011. Healthier before they migrate, less healthy when they return? The health of returned migrants in Mexico. *Social Science & Medicine* 73 (3): 421–28.

U.S. Department of Homeland Security. 2015. Website of the Office of Immigration Statistics. Available from http://www.dhs.gov/immigration-statistics-publications.

Warren, Robert, and Jeffrey S. Passel. 1987. A count of the uncountable: Estimates of undocumented aliens counted in the 1980 United States Census. *Demography* 24 (3): 375–93.

Wasem, Ruth E. 2011. *Unauthorized aliens residing in the United States: Estimates since 1986.* Washington, DC: Congressional Research Service.

Waters, Mary C., and Marisa G. Pineau, eds. 2015. *The integration of immigrants into American society.* Washington, DC: National Academies Press.

Shadow Labor: Work and Wages among Immigrant Hispanic Women in Durham, North Carolina

By
CHENOA A. FLIPPEN

This article examines the forces shaping the labor supply and wages of immigrant Hispanic women in new destinations. The analysis draws on data collected in Durham, North Carolina, and evaluates how labor market outcomes are influenced by variables including human capital, immigration characteristics (including legal status), family structure, and immigrant-specific labor market conditions such as subcontracting. Findings indicate that the main determinants of labor supply among immigrant Hispanic women in Durham relate to family structure, with human capital playing a relatively minor role. Important variation is observed in the degree of work-family conflict across occupations. For wages, human capital and immigration characteristics (including documentation) are more important than family structure. Results show that the position of immigrant Hispanic women in Durham's low-wage labor market is extremely precarious, with multiple, overlapping sources of disadvantage, particularly related to legal status and family structure.

Keywords: Hispanic; female labor force participation; wages; immigrant; new destinations

Over the past 20 years, three key trends have transformed the U.S. Hispanic population: a massive increase in immigration that swelled the number of foreign-born from 8.4 million in 1990 to 21.2 million in 2010, a sharp rise in both the absolute and relative size of the undocumented population, and the dramatic dispersal of this population outside of traditional receiving areas to "new destinations" across the

Chenoa A. Flippen is an associate professor of sociology at the University of Pennsylvania. Her research addresses diverse topics in racial and ethnic stratification, including minority aging and retirement security, the impact of residential segregation on minority housing wealth, the social mobility consequences of internal migration, and Hispanic immigrant adaptation.

NOTE: This research was supported by grant #NR 08052-05 from NINR/NIH.

Correspondence: chenoa@sas.upenn.edu

DOI: 10.1177/0002716216644423

country. The prospect for the successful incorporation of recent, particularly undocumented, immigrants into the labor market looms large in both academic and public debate on the subject. The more pessimistic voices in this debate point to the marked deterioration that has occurred in recent decades in the work conditions of the low-skill labor market as a critical challenge to immigrant adaptation. Hispanic immigrants in particular are disproportionately concentrated in the low-wage sector, registering some of the lowest earnings and highest rates of working poverty in the country (Hauan, Landale, and Leicht 2000).

Within this larger debate, there is also growing interest in the particular labor market experiences of immigrant women. High rates of family poverty among immigrant Hispanics suggest the urgent need for female labor force participation among this group, and yet their paid employment trails far behind that of native women. Moreover, even though nearly 45 percent of adult Hispanic immigrants are women, the common presumption that they are secondary migrants joining husbands already in the United States has contributed to their relative neglect in labor market research (Donato et al. 2008). Their high rates of employment instability and part-time and informal work likewise make it difficult both to measure their employment position and to accommodate their experiences within theories of incorporation based on the male experience. And finally, while a number of qualitative ethnographic studies have highlighted the complex interplay between gender and immigration and provided a nuanced portrayal of the constraints on paid work among immigrant Hispanic women, these studies have to date focused exclusively on traditional areas of settlement, leaving open the question of how women are faring in new destinations.

Thus an immigrant- and women-centered analysis of the variation in employment outcomes among Hispanics in new destinations holds the potential to significantly add to our understanding of immigrant women's work. Here I draw on original data collected in Durham, North Carolina, to provide a detailed account of the labor market position of immigrant Hispanic women. The analysis focuses on two critical aspects of economic incorporation: labor supply (the decision to work, in which occupations, and how many hours per week) and wages; and the human capital, immigration, and family characteristics that structure variation in outcomes. This analysis is particularly concerned with whether immigrant Hispanic women in Durham are able to convert greater human capital and U.S. experience into better wages and employment outcomes and with the extent to which they are able to balance paid work and family obligations. Results highlight the extremely precarious position of immigrant Hispanic women in Durham's low-wage labor market and multiple, overlapping sources of disadvantage, particularly relating to legal status and family structure.

Background

The growing emphasis on free trade, reduced regulation, and heightened flexibility (including the greatly diminished strength of labor unions) has transformed the U.S. employment structure in recent decades, contributing to rising inequality by skill and the erosion of wages and work conditions in the lower segment of the employment hierarchy (Kopczuk, Saez, and Song 2010). Nonstandard work arrangements, such as on-call work, temporary help agencies, subcontracting, independent contracting/contingent work, and part-time employment in conventional jobs, have grown dramatically, increasing their dominance in industries where they were already common and spreading to numerous other areas of the economy, with negative implications for both wages and job quality (Ferber and Waldfogel 1998; Kalleberg 2011).

As conditions in the low-wage labor market worsened, the share of workers in this sector who were foreign-born rose appreciably, from a mere 12 percent in 1980 (Enchautegui 1998) to 50 percent in 2010 (Bureau of Labor Statistics 2011). The concentration of undocumented workers has been especially dramatic; for 2005, it was estimated that they made up a full 23 percent of low-skill workers (Capps, Fortuny, and Fix 2007). Indeed, recent immigration policies, such as the 1986 Immigration Reform and Control Act (IRCA) and 1996 Illegal Immigration Reform and Immigrant Responsibility Act (IIRIRA), which imposed and then heightened employer sanctions for the hiring of undocumented labor, have contributed to marginalizing undocumented workers, particularly by hastening the shift to subcontracting in immigrant-intensive areas (Gentsch and Massey 2011). The end result is that citizenship and legal status increasingly drive labor market outcomes, including the sorting of workers into the least desirable jobs (Donato and Massey 1993; Donato and Sisk 2013; Hudson 2007; Phillips and Massey 1999).

Gender also figures prominently at the intersection of economic restructuring and immigration. First, women in general have long been disproportionately concentrated in low-wage and nonstandard employment, and they are also less likely than their male counterparts to receive employer-sponsored health insurance and retirement benefits. Moreover, their employment patterns are shaped by family characteristics to a far greater degree than is the case for men (Donato, Piya, and Jacobs 2014). It is telling that while parenthood is often unrelated to job quality for men, women having children increases their exposure to adverse work conditions, and having children may also depress wage growth for women (Kalleberg 2011).

Second, structural changes in the U.S. economy in recent decades have substantially increased the demand for low-skill female labor. While innumerable manufacturing jobs have left the United States for lower-wage countries, those that remained have tended to be downgraded, with lower rates of unionization and wages. This, in tandem with the explosive growth of "caring" jobs in childcare and health fields, has dramatically increased the demand for women's low-skill labor. As native women have gained greater access to a wider range of better jobs, it is increasingly immigrant women who meet this rise in demand (Gonzalez Baker 1998; Myers and Cranford 1998).

Despite growing demand for their labor, there is ample evidence that Hispanic immigrant women are disadvantaged in the U.S. labor market. Their concentration in a handful of highly disadvantaged occupational niches is extreme, making it difficult to maximize the returns on human capital (Catanzarite and Aguilera

2002; Cobb-Clark and Kossoudji 1999). Indeed, immigrant Hispanic women are more likely to work part time; average lower starting wages and wage growth; and receive a lesser payoff for factors such as education and labor market experience than non-Hispanic white women, native Hispanic women, and immigrant Hispanic men (Blau and Kahn 2007; Capps, Fortuny, and Fix 2007; De Jong and Madamba 2001; Hall, Greenman, and Farkas 2010; Rivera-Batiz 1999; Valenzuela and Gonzalez 2000).

While prior studies have made important strides in outlining the labor market position of immigrant Hispanic women, a number of gaps remain. First, studies that compare immigrant Hispanic women to their native counterparts generally lack data on such factors as time in the United States, documentation, subcontracting, and other structural aspects of the immigration experience. Thus, while they give a sense of Hispanic immigrant women's disadvantage relative to others, they are far less able to assess key sources of variation in outcomes within the immigrant population. At the same time, immigrant-oriented data sources, such as the Legalized Population Survey or the New Immigrant Survey, tend to focus on legal immigrants, necessarily excluding the vast majority of recently arrived entrants to the low-skill labor market. Many of these studies are also male-centric, in that they compare men and women along the dimensions that they have in common, such as hourly wages and the return on education, to the relative neglect of factors more pertinent to women, such as variation in labor supply and the constraints imposed on paid labor by family life. Our deepest understanding of the complex interplay between gender, legal status, and labor market incorporation among immigrant women comes from ethnographic accounts (Hondagneu-Sotelo 2003). However, these studies rely on relatively small and nonrandom samples and to date have overwhelmingly focused on traditional areas of immigrant settlement in the West and Southwest. The extent to which their observations are generalizable, particularly to new destinations, remains an open question.

Accordingly, the main objective of this article is to provide a deeper understanding of the economic position of immigrant Hispanic women in new destinations and the social forces that shape variation in their outcomes. Integrating the literatures on gender, immigrant adaptation, and low-wage labor markets, we take a broad view of economic incorporation, considering both labor supply and wages. As a first step, we elaborate on the labor supply of immigrant Hispanic women, with a focus on explaining who works and in which occupations, as well as variation in hours worked among the employed. We also consider variation in immigrant Hispanic women's wages, considering both hourly and weekly pay. The primary motivation in both sets of analyses is to understand the extent to which human capital, migration, and family considerations explain variation in women's labor market outcomes. We also elaborate on the role of employment characteristics in shaping hours worked and wages, both in terms of their direct impact and the extent to which they mediate the effect of human capital and immigration characteristics (particularly legal status) on outcomes, as the channeling of immigrant women into particular occupational niches is likely to translate into differential returns on work.

Data and Methods

The analysis draws on original and locally representative ethnosurvey data collected among Hispanic immigrants during 2006 and early 2007 in the Durham/Chapel Hill, North Carolina, metropolitan area (for the sake of parsimony, referred to simply as Durham, where the vast majority of respondents live). Durham represents a valuable vantage point to study Hispanic immigrant incorporation. The area has been growing rapidly, as part of the national shift in this population from Rustbelt to Sunbelt states. The influx of highly educated workers attracted to growing job opportunities in the nearby Research Triangle Park, universities, and other large employers generated an intense demand for low-skill service and construction labor. Some employers responded by recruiting Hispanic immigrant laborers from more traditional receiving areas or even directly from Latin America, and a cycle of chain migration began that saw the Hispanic population explode from a mere 1 percent of the total population of Durham in 1990 to nearly 9 percent by 2000 and 11.9 percent by 2007 (Flippen and Parrado 2012). The Hispanic population of Durham is primarily of Mexican origins (70 percent), though there are also a sizable number of Hondurans (17.5 percent), Salvadorans (5.5 percent), and Guatemalans (4.5 percent).

The precarious position of Hispanic immigrants in Durham presented unique challenges for approximating a locally representative sample. Our study relied on a combination of community-based participatory research (CBPR) and targeted random sampling to overcome these difficulties. CBPR is an approach to research that incorporates members of the target community in all phases of the research process (Israel et al. 2005). In our case, a group of fourteen community members assisted in the planning phase of the study, survey construction and revision, and devising strategies to boost response rates and data quality. In addition, CBPR members were trained in research methods and conducted all surveys. Finally, through ongoing collaborative meetings, the CBPR group was also influential in the interpretation of survey results.

At the same time, the relatively recent nature of the Hispanic community in Durham rendered simple random sampling prohibitively expensive. We therefore employed targeted random sampling techniques (Watters and Biernacki 1989). Based on CBPR insights and field work in the community, we identified forty-nine apartment complexes and blocks that housed a large number of immigrant Hispanics. We then collected a census of all the apartments in these areas and randomly selected individual units to be visited by interviewers. Using community members as interviewers helped to achieve a refusal rate of only 9 percent, and a response rate, which also discounted randomly selected units in which contact was not made after numerous attempts, of over 72 percent. A total of 882 and 1,299 interviews were conducted with immigrant Hispanics women and men, respectively, between the ages of 18 and 49. All interviews were conducted in Spanish, usually in the homes of respondents, with interviewers filling out paper surveys that included a mix of close-ended and open-ended questions. A main advantage of the collaborative data collection approach was the ability to develop a questionnaire specifically tailored to assess the experience of immigrants in the low-wage labor market (for a more detailed project description, see Parrado, McQuiston, and Flippen 2005).

Our main outcomes of interest relate to labor supply and compensation among Durham's immigrant Hispanic women. Labor supply is captured by three dependent variables. The first is simply a dummy variable indicating whether the respondent was working at the time of the survey. The second dependent variable combines labor force participation with type of occupation and comprises seven categories: not working, working in food preparation, cleaning, childcare, laundry, factory, or other jobs. The multinomial approach assesses not only the impact of human capital, family obligations, and immigration characteristics on employment probabilities, but also whether the social factors shaping labor force participation differ across occupations. The final dependent variable critical to understanding women's labor supply is hours worked per week (logged). Immigrant women, in particular, often work less than full time, including a considerable number who work very few or erratic hours. This may be particularly common among women with greater family obligations.

Assessing working immigrant women's compensation is somewhat more complex. Because women's labor supply is highly variable, it is difficult to construct a single measure of wages that gives a comprehensive view of earnings. Focusing on hourly wages alone overstates the incomes and living standards for women who work relatively few hours per week. And focusing on weekly wages alone fails to capture the experience of women who achieve modest weekly incomes only by working very long hours. The analysis therefore includes both hourly and weekly wages as dependent variables, the latter of which reflects both labor supply and compensation.

Independent variables fall into three broad categories: human capital and immigration characteristics, family structure, and mediating employment characteristics (in the models of hours and wages). First, theorists have long debated whether the monetary returns on human capital are suppressed in low-wage segments of the economy, which is characterized by instability and limited prospects for upward mobility (Hall and Farkas 2008; Piore 1970). While factors such as age, education, length of U.S. work experience, and English language ability have been found to predict wages even among low-skill immigrant workers (Bleakley and Chin 2004; Catanzarite 2000; Chiswick 1984; Hall, Greenman, and Farkas 2010; Kossoudji 1988; Phillips and Massey 1999), there is evidence that immigrants' return on human capital and experience are substantially lower among both women and undocumented workers (Blau and Kahn 2007; Hall, Greenman, and Farkas 2010). Thus, their impact on both wages and labor supply in new destinations such as Durham remains open to question. Likewise, while a number of studies have found a direct negative effect of undocumented status on wages, net of differences among immigrants in human capital considerations (Donato et al. 2008; Hall, Greenman, and Farkas 2010; Phillips and Massey 1999; Orrenius and Zavodny 2009; Rivera-Batiz 1999), the impact of documentation on women's labor supply and wages in new destinations has yet to be established.

Accordingly, we include both age (including a squared term to capture nonlinear effects) and educational attainment as rough measures of human capital.

Educational attainment is measured by a set of dummy variables distinguishing between those with 6 or fewer years, 7 to 9 years, and 10 or more years of completed schooling. These distinctions correspond to primary, secondary, and above secondary education in Mexico. Immigration-related characteristics include a variable capturing self-reported number of years of residence in the Durham area, and English ability, which is measured by a dummy variable indicating whether the respondent reported being able to speak English well or very well (as opposed to "more or less" or "not at all").[1] A dummy variable for undocumented status reflects the response from a direct question on legal status.

The second set of independent variables included in the analyses relates to family structure. Previous research suggests that women's family obligations undermine labor force participation. While the negative impact of children on women's paid work is lower today than in previous generations, mothers remain more often responsible for childcare than fathers and, thus, must replace their own reproductive work with paid help in order to be employed. Children thus effectively raise the wages needed to make work pay (England, Garcia-Beaulieu, and Ross 2004). The relationship between marriage and employment is less uniform, though at least for Hispanic women there is evidence of a negative effect even in the absence of children (Greenlees and Saenz 1999; Menjivar 2000; Kahn and Whittington 1996). Likewise, a substantial body of work documents a significant earnings penalty to motherhood among the general population (Anderson, Binder, and Krause 2003), though studies that examine the issue among low-skill Hispanic immigrants are scant.

To examine the potential conflict between work and family obligations among the women in our sample, we account for both marital status and presence of children in the household. Specifically, a set of four mutually exclusive dummy variables indicate whether a woman is married and living with children, married and not living with children, unmarried and living with children, or unmarried and not living with children. Married women include both those who report a formal, legal marriage and those who report being in a consensual union.

And finally, the models of hours worked and wages among working women also include a number of mediating employment characteristics as independent variables. Nonstandard work arrangements, particularly subcontracting, are both very common in the low-wage labor market and often associated with lower wages among both the general population (Kalleberg 2011) and immigrants (Massey 2010). Hispanic immigrants are also disproportionately employed in small firms and job sites where other Hispanics predominate, which has been shown to undermine wages among Hispanic men (Catanzarite and Aguilera 2002). We expect the same to be true for women. As such, we also consider five mediating employment characteristics in our models of hours worked and wages among working women: occupation/industry (described above), firm size (a dummy indicator of whether a person is working in a firm with ten or fewer workers at all locations), Hispanic work sites (a dummy variable indicating whether the respondent reported working mostly with other Hispanics), and exposure to nonstandard work arrangements (measured through a dummy indicator of working for a subcontractor).

The statistical estimation varies according to the distribution of the dependent variables. For the analysis of being employed where the dependent variable is a dummy indicator, we estimate logistic regression models. For the analysis of working in a particular type of occupation where the dependent variable comprises seven mutually exclusive categories we estimate multinomial logit models with the reference group being women who were not working. For the continuous dependent variables, i.e. hours worked per week, hourly wages, and weekly wages, we report results from standard ordinary least squares (OLS) models.[2]

Descriptive Results

Table 1 presents descriptive results for the dependent variables in the analysis, providing results for men as a counterpoint for assessing the unique position of immigrant Hispanic women. While the overwhelming majority of men (96.0 percent) were working at the time of interview, among women 61.8 percent reported working for pay. Moreover, as previous studies have documented, the occupational concentration of immigrant Hispanics in Durham is extreme, with considerable differences by sex. A stunning 88.5 percent of all men in the sample were working in construction, yard work, or food preparation (68.1, 7.4, and 13.0 percent, respectively). Among women, just more than two-thirds worked in one of three areas: cleaning (32.9 percent, which includes both private house cleaning and offices or hotels), food preparation (30.7 percent) or factory work (10.2 percent). An additional 5.9 and 5.5 percent of women worked in childcare and laundry, respectively. Finally, while virtually all men were working at least 40 hours in a typical week, women's work hours were much more variable. The average work week was 35.7 hours for women (compared to 41.6 for men), but ranged from a mere 5 hours to 60 hours per week. Only 68.3 percent of working women reported working at least 35 hours during a typical week, while 21.5 percent reported working between 20 and 35 hours weekly, and an additional 10.2 percent reported working fewer than 20 hours per week.

Average hourly wages were also markedly lower for women than for men, $8.03 relative to $10.90. Not only were average hourly wages lower, but the distributions also varied in important ways, as seen in Figure 1. There is a sizable subset of women, close to 5 percent, who earned very low wages—some as little as $2 per hour. There is no male equivalent of this phenomenon. Likewise, the modal earnings categories for men were $10–12 and $12–15 an hour, and a nontrivial number, close to 8 percent, earned in excess of $15 an hour. For women, the most common categories were $6–7 and $7–8 an hour, and a scant 10 percent earned more than even $10 an hour.

Table 1 also presents human capital, immigration, family status, and mediating employment characteristics for the women in our sample, again providing data on men for comparison. Our sample is in many ways typical of immigrants in new destinations: the women are relatively young, with an average age of 30.1 years, and poorly educated. Averaging just under 8 years of schooling, 43.5 percent of immigrant Hispanic women in Durham did not advance beyond primary school,

TABLE 1
Descriptive Results by Sex

	Women	(SE)	Men	(SE)
Dependent variables				
Employment outcomes				
Labor supply				
Working (%)	61.8		96.0	
Type of occupation (%)				
Construction	4.7		68.1	
Yard	0.0		7.4	
Food	30.7		13.0	
Childcare	5.9		0.0	
Retail	4.1		0.6	
Cleaning	32.9		0.9	
Laundry	5.5		0.6	
Factory	10.2		0.9	
Other	6.1		7.4	
Hours worked per week (mean)	35.7	(9.8)	41.6	(7.7)
Compensation				
Hourly wages (mean)	$8.0	($3.7)	$10.9	($3.1)
Weekly wages (mean)	$286.7	($35.9)	$454.7	($166.8)
Explanatory variables				
Human capital				
Age (mean)	30.1	(7.8)	30.3	(8.3)
Education (%)	7.8	(3.6)	7.8	(3.3)
6 or less	43.2		41.4	
7–9	26.3		31.3	
10 or more	30.2		27.3	
Immigration characteristics				
Years in Durham (mean)	4.2	(3.6)	4.5	(3.9)
Good English (%)	6.8		9.2	
Undocumented (%)	90.1		91.1	
Family obligations				
Marriage and childbearing (%)				
Married, living with children	62.8		35.1	
Married, no coresident children	17.9		29.7	
Unmarried, living with children	10.8		2.0	
Unmarried, no coresident children	8.5		33.1	
Mediating employment conditions (%)				
Subcontractor	14.5		25.8	
Hispanic worksite	60.1		67.7	
Small firm	54.8		44.6	
N	882		1,299	

FIGURE 1
Hourly Wages by Sex

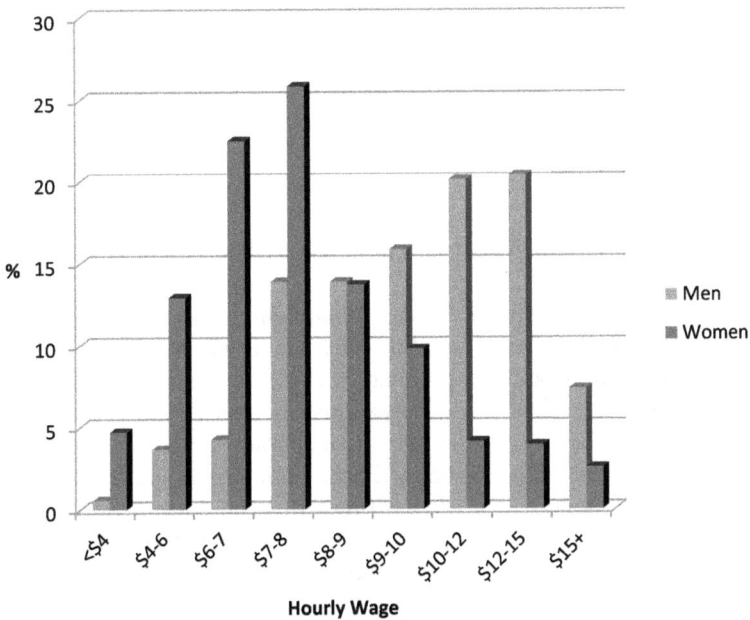

an additional 26.3 percent finished between 7 and 9 years of education, and just under one-third (30.2 percent) completed 10 or more years of schooling. Respondents were also recently arrived, averaging a mere 4.2 years in Durham. Reflecting this recent arrival, only 6.8 percent of women reported speaking English well or very well; and an overwhelming majority, fully 90 percent, were undocumented at the time of interview. While the men in the sample averaged slightly better English skills and longer residence in Durham, overall sex differences in human capital and immigration characteristics were remarkably modest.

The main factor that distinguished women from men relates to family structure. Just over 62 percent of women in the sample were married and living with children at the time of survey, and an additional 17.9 percent were married with no coresident children (the majority were childless, though a small share had children in their home communities). The greater incidence of men migrating without their families meant that only 35.1 percent of men were married with children in Durham, and an additional 30 percent were married and without coresident children. Women were also far more likely than men to be single parents (10.8 vs. 2.0 percent). Thus, overall, a very small share of immigrant Hispanic women were free of work-family conflict in Durham; only 25 percent were not raising children, and less than 9 percent were neither married nor residing with children.

Finally, women exhibited a number of mediating employment characteristics that also differed from men and have been shown to negatively impact wages

(Flippen 2012). In addition to their occupational concentration described above, a sizable number of women were paid via a subcontractor (14.5 percent), though this figure is nearly half the number exhibited among men (25.8 percent). Women were also less likely than men to work in a predominantly Hispanic work site, though the number was large for immigrants of both sexes (60.1 vs. 67.7 percent). However, more than half of all women (54.8 percent) worked for a firm of ten or fewer employees, a figure that is higher than that reported by men (44.6 percent).

Multivariate Results

While the overall pattern described above highlights many elements of disadvantage associated with the secondary labor market, there is considerable variation in employment outcomes and work characteristics among Hispanic immigrant women in Durham. The next set of analyses investigates the dimensions undergirding this variation and how various employment characteristics relate to one another. We first investigate the factors associated with labor supply. Table 2 reports results from logit and multinomial logit models predicting the odds of working as well as of being in one of six employment categories, relative to not working. As described above, these models give us a sense for both what kinds of factors predict employment among these women and for whether the conflict between work and family is lower for some occupations than for others. Results demonstrate relatively modest effects of human capital on the labor supply and occupational choices of immigrant Hispanic women. While age is positively associated with employment both overall and in most occupations relative to not working, the impact of education is more complex and in many ways departs from human capital theory. Specifically, Table 2 shows considerable nonlinearity in the effect of education on labor force participation; while women with intermediate levels of education are only 0.73 times ($\exp[-0.32]$) as likely to work as those with 10 or more years of education, the least educated women are no less likely to work than the most educated. It is only in childcare that the least educated are also least likely to work, possibly due to the greater interpersonal skills required to find work as a nanny.

The impact of immigration characteristics on employment is likewise limited and mixed. Longer periods of residence in the Durham area are associated with higher likelihoods of working overall, and the positive effect is particularly significant for factory and non-niche "other" occupations, relative to not working. Similarly, speaking English well significantly expands employment opportunities. Women with good English skills are 1.79 times ($\exp[0.58]$) more likely to work than women with more limited English ability. The positive connection between English and working is likely to be mutually reinforcing but appears to be particularly strong for jobs that require personal interactions such as childcare and non-niche occupations. The effect of lack of documentation, though negative, is not a significant constraint on women's employment propensities. However, there is important variation across occupations with undocumented women significantly more likely to work in childcare (1.61).

Binomial and Multinomial Logit Models Predicting Employment in a Particular Type of Occupation.

	Working	Food	Childcare	Cleaning	Laundry	Factory	Other
			Working in Particular Type of Occupation				
Human capital							
Age	0.28**	0.25**	0.44**	0.31**	0.34*	0.21	0.30**
	(0.07)	(0.09)	(0.20)	(0.09)	(0.20)	(0.14)	(0.12)
Age squared	0.00**	0.00**	-0.01*	0.00**	0.00	0.00	0.00**
	(0.00)	(0.00)	(0.00)	(0.00)	(0.00)	(0.00)	(0.00)
Education (ref = 10 years or more)							
6 years or less	-0.19	-0.15	-0.79*	-0.06	-0.09	-0.20	-0.33
	(0.18)	(0.24)	(0.49)	(0.24)	(0.47)	(0.37)	(0.34)
7–9 years	-0.32*	-0.51*	-0.34	-0.07	-0.64	-0.50	-0.22
	(0.20)	(0.27)	(0.49)	(0.26)	(0.58)	(0.43)	(0.35)
Immigration characteristics							
Time in Durham	0.04*	0.04	-0.07	0.03	-0.04	0.08*	0.09**
	(0.02)	(0.03)	(0.06)	(0.03)	(0.06)	(0.04)	(0.04)
Good English	0.58**	0.39	1.59**	0.58	-0.46	-1.07	1.27**
	(0.34)	(0.44)	(0.68)	(0.44)	(1.13)	(1.08)	(0.48)
Undocumented	-0.23	-0.21	1.61*	-0.16	-0.82	-0.37	-0.50
	(0.27)	(0.37)	(1.10)	(0.35)	(0.63)	(0.52)	(0.40)
Family obligations							
Marital status (ref = married, with coresident children)							
Married, no coresident children	0.83**	0.88**	0.50	0.71**	0.60	0.86**	1.26**
	(0.20)	(0.27)	(0.51)	(0.27)	(0.52)	(0.42)	(0.36)
Unmarried, coresident children	1.34**	1.55**	-0.40	1.10**	0.94	1.73**	1.70**
	(0.28)	(0.35)	(1.07)	(0.35)	(0.69)	(0.45)	(0.41)
Unmarried, no coresident children	1.91**	2.17**	1.29*	1.84**	0.47	1.27*	2.42**
	(0.34)	(0.39)	(0.73)	(0.40)	(1.09)	(0.69)	(0.48)
Intercept	-4.82**	-5.18**	-11.71**	-6.63**	-7.35**	-5.82**	-7.57**
	(1.10)	(1.53)	(3.48)	(1.50)	(3.31)	(2.34)	(2.00)
R-squared	.09			.06			

NOTE: Reference category = not working. Standard errors in parentheses.

*$p < .10$. **$p < .05$.

Instead, the key determinants of labor supply relate to family structure. Overall, women who are married and living with children are significantly less likely to work than other women. Unmarried women not living with children are the most likely to work relative to married women with children, followed by unmarried women with children and married women without coresident children. Thus, from a simple comparison of the size of the coefficients across categories, it would seem that being married alone is at least as large an impediment to working as is having children, if not larger. Indeed, additional models (not shown), which control for marital status and children separately, show that marriage exerts an independent and significant negative effect on working even after accounting for the presence of children. It is important to note, however, that for two occupations, namely, childcare and laundry work, there are few differences between women who are married with children and others with respect to employment probabilities. This suggests that the conflict between work and family is lower in these occupations.

Of course, immigrant women's labor supply is not adequately described by the distinction between working and not working alone, as 32 percent of all working women do not work full time. Table 3 therefore reports results from OLS models predicting the log of hours women work in a typical week, among working women. Once again we see relatively little effect of human capital and immigration characteristics on this dimension of women's labor supply. Women with greater time in Durham work significantly longer hours than those who are more recently arrived, though substantively the effects are modest; each additional year in Durham increases the number of hours worked by a mere 1 percent. Neither education nor English skills promote longer hours among the employed.

Legal status, on the other hand, does exert a significant influence over hours worked. While the undocumented were no less likely than their peers with legal status to work, among the employed they average a significantly shorter (10 percent) work week. Interestingly, the effect loses statistical significance in model 2 when we control for mediating employment characteristics. Additional models (available upon request) show that undocumented women are more likely to work for a subcontractor, at predominantly Hispanic work sites, and for small firms, the latter of which is also associated with a shorter work week. It is thus the funneling of women into disadvantaged, mediating work that accounts for the shorter work week of undocumented respondents.

Regardless, as was the case for the models predicting employment, the primary determinant of work hours among immigrant Hispanic women is family structure. And there is again evidence that both marriage and the presence of children exert independent, negative effects on work hours. For instance, unmarried women with and without coresident children are both significantly more likely to work than married women with children, and the size of the coefficient is roughly comparable for the two groups, suggesting that children do not pose an additional barrier to longer work hours among employed nonmarried mothers. Married women without coresident children, on the other hand, are only marginally more likely to work longer hours than their counterparts with children, suggesting that marriage itself is an important impediment to work among these

TABLE 3
OLS Models of Log of Hours Worked per Week among Working Women

	Model 1		Model 2	
Human capital				
Age	0.00	(0.016)	0.01	(0.015)
Age squared	0.00	(0.000)	0.00	(0.000)
Education (ref = 10 years or more)				
6 years or less	−0.02	(0.040)	−0.01	(0.039)
7–9 years	0.00	(0.044)	0.00	(0.044)
Immigration characteristics				
Time in Durham	0.01°°	(0.005)	0.01°	(0.005)
Good English	−0.05	(0.063)	−0.03	(0.063)
Undocumented	−0.10°	(0.053)	−0.08	(0.053)
Family obligations				
Marital status (ref = married, with coresident children)				
Married, no coresident children	0.08°	(0.044)	0.07°	(0.044)
Unmarried, coresident children	0.13°°	(0.048)	0.12°°	(0.048)
Unmarried, no coresident children	0.11°°	(0.053)	0.12°°	(0.052)
Mediating employment conditions				
Occupation (ref = food preparation)				
Other			0.04	(0.051)
Childcare			0.04	(0.073)
Cleaning			−0.01	(0.042)
Laundry			0.05	(0.080)
Factory			0.15°°	(0.059)
Labor market position				
Subcontractor			−0.02	(0.047)
Hispanic worksite			0.02	(0.035)
Small firm			−0.09°°	(0.036)
Intercept	3.50°°	(0.260)	3.48°°	(0.258)
R-squared	.040		.07	

NOTE: Standard errors in parentheses.
°p < .10. °°p < .05.

women, irrespective of childrearing. Once again, these impressions are confirmed in models measuring marriage and childrearing separately (not shown).
And finally, of the remaining mediating employment characteristics introduced
in model 2, factory employment offers women the greatest access to longer work
hours, as this is the only occupation that averages a significantly longer work week
(15 percent) than food preparation. Employment in small firms, in contrast, is
associated with 9 percent fewer weekly hours worked.

Turning to compensation outcomes, Table 4 presents results from OLS models predicting both hourly and weekly wages (logged). Across models the effect

TABLE 4
OLS Models Predicting Log of Hourly and Weekly Wages

	Log of Hourly Wage				Log of Weekly Wage			
Human capital								
Age	0.01	(0.02)	0.02	(0.01)	0.02	(0.02)	0.02	(0.02)
Age squared	0.00	(0.00)	0.00	(0.00)	0.00	(0.00)	0.00	(0.00)
Education (ref = 10 years or more)								
6 years or less	-0.04	(0.04)	-0.06*	(0.04)	-0.06	(0.05)	-0.07*	(0.04)
7–9 years	-0.06	(0.04)	-0.08*	(0.04)	-0.06	(0.05)	-0.07*	(0.05)
Immigration characteristics								
Time in Durham	0.01**	(0.00)	0.01**	(0.00)	0.02	(0.01)	0.02**	(0.00)
Good English	0.16**	(0.06)	0.17**	(0.06)	0.11	(0.07)	0.14**	(0.07)
Undocumented	-0.12**	(0.05)	-0.08*	(0.05)	-0.22	(0.06)	-0.16**	(0.06)
Family obligations								
Married no coresident children	0.01	(0.04)	-0.01	(0.04)	0.09	(0.05)	0.07	(0.05)
Unmarried, coresident children	0.01	(0.05)	-0.02	(0.05)	0.14**	(0.06)	0.11**	(0.05)
Unmarried, no coresident children	0.01	(0.05)	0.00	(0.05)	0.12**	(0.06)	0.12**	(0.06)
Mediating employment conditions								
Occupation (ref = food preparation)								
Other			0.11**	(0.05)			0.15**	(0.06)
Childcare			-0.46**	(0.07)			-0.43**	(0.08)
Cleaning			0.14**	(0.04)			0.12**	(0.05)
Laundry			0.02	(0.08)			0.07	(0.09)
Factory			0.02	(0.05)			0.17**	(0.06)
Subcontractor			0.05	(0.04)			0.04	(0.05)
Hispanic worksite			-0.06*	(0.03)			-0.04	(0.04)
Small firm			0.00	(0.03)			-0.09**	(0.04)
Intercept	1.90**	(0.26)	1.79**	(0.24)	5.39	(0.30)	5.26**	(0.28)
R-squared	.06		.21		.10		.22	

NOTE: Standard errors in parentheses.
*p < .10. **p < .05.

of human capital on wages is weak. Only after controlling for mediating employment characteristics do we find that lower levels of education negatively affect wages. Results show that compared to women with 10 or more years of education, both the hourly and weekly wages of women with lower levels of education are 7 percent lower. Immigration characteristics, on the other hand, are among the most important determinants of wages among the women in our sample. The effect of time in Durham is statistically significant, though substantively small; every additional year in Durham increases hourly and weekly wages by 1 and 2 percent, respectively. English language ability, in contrast, has a more sizable effect; women with good English skills average 17 and 14 percent higher hourly and weekly wages, respectively. Thus, part of the effect of education on wages is no doubt mediated by its association with English fluency. Once again, undocumented status significantly undermines immigrant women's labor market position. Results show that undocumented women earn 16 percent lower hourly wages than their documented counterparts. Since lack of documentation also undermines the hours that women work, when we measure the compounded effect on weekly wages undocumented women earn a full 22 percent less than documented immigrants. The negative effect of undocumented status is reduced, but not eliminated, once mediating labor market characteristics are taken into account. Specifically, results for the full model show that lack of documentation reduces women's hourly and weekly earnings by 8 and 16 percent, respectively. It is worth noting that this figure is considerably higher than the negative effect of being undocumented among men in Durham (self-identifying reference).

While family structure was by far the most important determinant of immigrant Hispanic women's labor supply, it has very little effect on the wages of working women. Among women who work, neither marriage nor childrearing significantly predicts hourly wages. Thus, the effect of family structure on weekly wages is completely driven by its impact on hours worked per week. Differences in weekly earnings by family status are nonetheless dramatic, as unmarried women with and without children earn 12 and 14 percent higher weekly wages, respectively, than married women with children.

Not surprisingly, wages vary considerably according to our mediating employment characteristics. With respect to occupation, women engaged in both cleaning and non-niche occupations earn significantly more per hour and per week than those in food preparation, while those in childcare earn significantly less. Factory employment is also associated with higher weekly wages, but the effect mainly stems from the larger number of hours that factory women work since there is no positive effect on hourly wages. While these differences across occupations are telling, they mask important variation within categories. To illustrate these differences, Figure 2 shows the wage distribution for women employed in childcare, cleaning, and food occupations in relation to the federal minimum wage ($7.25 per hour).

Virtually no women working in cleaning and food preparation earn less than the official minimum hourly wage. The wages for those employed in food preparation tend to concentrate around the minimum wage and decline rapidly at higher levels. Cleaning also tends to concentrate around the minimum wage,

FIGURE 2
Distribution of Hourly Wages in Relation to Minimum Wage within
Childcare, Cleaning, and Food Occupations

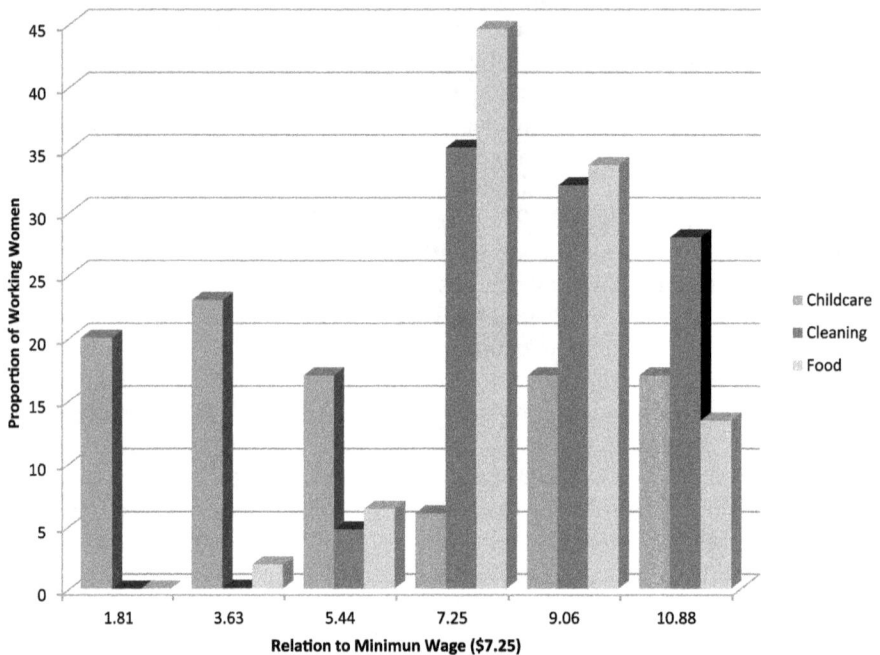

though the likelihood of higher wages is much greater than in food occupations. Virtually all of the higher-earning women in cleaning are independent house cleaners, while most of the lower-earning women either clean hotels or offices, or work for a house-cleaning subcontractor. In sharp contrast to both food and cleaning workers, women engaged in childcare show a clearly bimodal distribution, with a large number earning substantially below minimum wage.

In fact, almost 45 percent of women in childcare earned less than 75 percent of the established minimum wage (or $5.44 an hour). At the same time, only 6 percent earned around minimum wage, and a full 34 percent earned more than 1.25 times the minimum wage (or $9.06 an hour). Without exception, the higher-earning women in childcare are nannies for families outside of immigrant communities, while the very low wage earners are uniformly women who care for the children of other immigrant women out of their own homes. These women, who often cannot earn enough to pay for childcare themselves, are forced to accept as little as $60 to $80 a week for full-time childcare.

Finally, returning to Table 4, contrary to expectations, subcontracting is not negatively associated with wages. Working in a Hispanic work site, on the other hand, significantly reduces women's hourly wages. The effect on weekly wages, while negative, fails to reach statistical significance. Finally, working for a small firm reduces weekly wages by 9 percent. It is important to note that these effects closely correlate with lack of documentation. Small firm employment is the main factor mediating the negative effect of documentation on wages. Rather than acting independently, these dimensions intersect in a manner that compounds the vulnerabilities of immigrant women.

Conclusion

The low-wage labor market, which has experienced a sharp deterioration in work conditions in recent decades, has grown increasingly reliant on immigrant labor. Hispanic immigrants, including a large number of women, have stepped in to meet this growing demand. Still, we know less than we should about the economic incorporation of immigrant women, particularly in new destinations. This article draws on original data that are specifically tailored to capture the employment dynamics of low-skill immigrants and examines the forces shaping both labor supply (the decision to work, in which occupations, and how many hours per week) and wages (hourly and weekly) among immigrant Hispanic women in Durham.

Results indicate that when it comes to labor supply, it is primarily family status and not human capital that shapes outcomes among Durham's immigrant Hispanic women. Both marriage and childrearing exert an independent effect, dampening the likelihood of working and reducing the number of hours worked in a typical week among those who are employed. The negative effect of marriage and childrearing holds across occupations, with the notable exceptions in childcare and laundry work, where the conflict between work and family is dramatically reduced. Human capital characteristics such as education, English language ability, and years in Durham all exert a far more modest influence on women's labor supply than expected.

Results for models predicting wages, on the other hand, show the opposite pattern. Among women who work, it is human capital and immigration characteristics, and not family structure, that are the primary determinants of wages. Women who are more educated, speak English well, and with longer periods of residence in Durham all earn higher hourly and weekly wages than their less advantaged peers. Marriage and childrearing, on the other hand, have no effect on hourly wages and lower weekly wages only because women who are married or with children tend to work shorter hours.

One of the most consistent and troubling findings relates to the impact of legal status on women's work. While documentation did not predict women's ability to find employment, it funneled them into childcare, small firms, subcontractors, and predominantly Hispanic work sites. Many of these characteristics, in turn, were associated with shorter average work weeks or lower wages. Moreover, even when we account for the disadvantaged mediating employment characteristics associated with lack of legal status, undocumented women still earn significantly lower hourly and weekly wages than other women. The size of the effect is also substantively large. Our estimates show that the combination of lack of documentation and concentration in small firms that are characteristic of immigrant Hispanic women in Durham reduces their weekly wages by 25 percent.

Our study also highlights the extremely marginal position of immigrant Hispanic women's occupational niches in the U.S. economy. While a handful of women, most working outside of areas of immigrant concentration or independently employed as housecleaners, earn a decent hourly wage, the majority earn close to the official minimum wage. Moreover, nearly 40 percent of our sample earned less than the minimum wage; and a nontrivial number, roughly 5 percent, earned less than $4 an hour. These women, who consist almost entirely of women who provide childcare services to other immigrant women out of their homes, represent the most precarious of an already highly vulnerable population.

These findings, together with the previous literature, suggest serious impediments to the labor market incorporation of low-skill immigrant Hispanic women that extend far beyond their human capital characteristics. The current anti-immigrant atmosphere and emphasis on employer sanctions have resulted in an extremely precarious labor market position for both legal and undocumented Hispanic immigrants, who suffer from multiple, overlapping elements of disadvantage. The meager impact of classic aspects of assimilation (e.g., time in the United States) on employment outcomes suggests that without policy changes, contemporary immigrants in the low-wage labor market may face a lifetime of low wages. Such a prospect undermines immigrants' ability to provide for their old-age security and to contribute to their children's education, and undermines the potential for intergenerational social mobility.

While a large and growing body of work examines work-family balance among professional and white women, there is growing interest in how it shapes employment and earnings among low-skill and minority women. More work on how work-family issues play out among immigrants is clearly in order. Results also confirm the importance of considering multiple dimensions of immigrant Hispanic women's work simultaneously, to gain a more accurate sense for the forces shaping economic integration. It is not sufficient to examine only the factors predicting whether women work; different occupations vary in the extent of work-family conflict, and there is wide variation in the number of hours worked among working women. Extending studies based on immigrant men to include women (i.e., focusing largely on hourly wages) misses critical aspects of women's economic disadvantage.

Moreover, while these findings were obtained from a case study of Durham, North Carolina, there is ample reason to believe that they may be widely applicable. Other new destinations, particularly southeastern cities such as Charlotte, North Carolina, and Atlanta, Georgia, differ somewhat in their industrial compositions from Durham. They nevertheless share the pattern of dramatic growth in their native populations, with attendant increases in demand for low-skill labor and a sharp rise in Hispanic immigrant populations after 1990. The large share of undocumented migrants across new destinations bodes poorly for women's successful labor market integration across the region. The situation could be even more precarious in traditional immigrant gateways, where labor markets are saturated with immigrant labor and new arrivals face intense competition with coethnics, including a large number with legal authorization to work.

Notes

1. In separate analyses we explored differences in employment patterns by national origin and between those in formal and consensual unions. As no significant differences were noted, these distinctions were not included in the final models. Likewise, multiple specifications of English language ability were tested, and the cut-off with the greatest statistical significance was reported in the article.

2. One concern in models of compensation outcomes is the potential selectivity bias arising from restricting the sample only to working women. We tested for this potential effect by estimating sample selection models following variations of Heckman's proposed methods. Results (available upon request) indicate that the selectivity correction was statistically insignificant in all cases and did not affect other parameter estimates.

References

Anderson, Doborah, Melissa Binder, and Kate Krause. 2003. The motherhood wage penalty revisited: Experience, heterogeneity, work effort, and work-schedule flexibility. *Industrial and Labor Relations Review* 56:273–94.

Blau, Francine D., and Lawrence M. Kahn. 2007. Gender and assimilation among Mexican Americans. In *Mexican immigration to the United States*, ed. George J. Borjas. 57–106. Washington, DC: National Bureau of Economic Research.

Bleakley, Hoyt, and Aimee Chin. 2004. Language skills and earnings: Evidence from childhood immigrants. *Review of Economics and Statistics* 86 (2): 481–96.

Bureau of Labor Statistics. 2011. Employment status of the foreign-born and native-born populations by selected characteristics, 2009–10. Economic release: Table 1. Available from http://www.bls.gov/news.release/forbrn.t01.htm.

Capps, Randy, Karina Fortuny, and Michael Fix. 2007. *Trends in the low-wage immigrant labor force, 2000–2005*. Washington, DC: The Urban Institute Migration Policy Institute.

Catanzarite, Lisa. 2000. Brown-collar jobs: Occupational segregation and earnings of recent-immigrant Latinos. *Sociological Perspectives* 43:45–75.

Catanzarite, Lisa, and Michael B. Aguilera. 2002. Working with co-ethnics: Earnings penalties for Latino immigrants at Latino jobsites. *Social Problems* 49 (1): 101–27.

Chiswick, Barry R. 1984. Illegal aliens in the United States labor market: An analysis of occupational attainment and earnings. *International Migration Review* 18 (3): 714–32.

Cobb-Clark, Deborah, and Sherrie Kossoudji. 1999. Did legalization matter for women? Amnesty and the wage determinants of formerly unauthorized Latina workers. *Gender Issues* 17 (4): 3–14.

De Jong, Gordon, and Anna Madamba. 2001. A double disadvantage? Minority group, immigrant status, and underemployment in the United States. *Social Science Quarterly* 82 (1): 117–30.

Donato, Katharine M., and Douglas S. Massey. 1993. Effects of the Immigration Reform Act on the wages of Mexican migrants. *Social Science Quarterly* 74 (3): 523–41.

Donato, Katharine M., Bhumika Piya, and Anna Jacobs. 2014. The double disadvantage reconsidered: Gender, immigration, marital status, and global labor force participation in the 21st century. *International Migration Review* S1 (Fall): S335–S376.

Donato, Katharine M., and Blake Sisk. 2013. Shifts in the employment outcomes among Mexican migrants to the United States, 1976–2009. *Research in Social Stratification and Mobility* 30 (1): 63–77.

Donato, Katharine, Chizuko Wakabayashi, Shirin Hakimzadeh, and Amada Armenta. 2008. Shifts in the employment conditions of Mexican immigrant men and women: The effects of U.S. immigration policy. *Work and Occupations* 35 (4): 462–95.

Enchautegui, Maria. 1998. Low-skilled immigrants and the changing American labor market. *Population and Development Review* 24 (4): 811–24.

England, Paula, Carmen Garcia-Beaulieu, and Mary Ross. 2004. Women's employment among blacks, whites, and three groups of Latinas: Do more privileged women have higher employment? *Gender and Society* 18 (4): 494–509.

Ferber, Marianne, and Jane Waldfogel. 1998. The long-term consequences of nontraditional employment. *Monthly Labor Review* 121 (5): 3–12.

Flippen, Chenoa A. 2012. Laboring underground: The employment patterns of Hispanic immigrant men in Durham, NC. *Social Problems* 59 (1): 21–42.

Flippen, Chenoa, and Emilio Parrado. 2012. The formation and evolution of Hispanic neighborhoods in new destinations: A case study of Durham, NC. *City and Community* 11 (1): 1–30.

Gentsch, Kerstin, and Douglas Massey. 2011. Labor market outcomes for legal Mexican immigrants under the new regime of immigrant enforcement. *Social Science Quarterly* 92 (3): 875–93.

Gonzalez Baker, Susan. 1998. Mexican-origin women in southwestern labor markets. In *Latinas and African American women at work: Race, gender, and economic inequality*, ed. Irene Browne, 244–69. New York, NY: Russell Sage Foundation.

Greenlees, Clyde, and Rogelio Saenz. 1999. Determinants of employment of recently arrived Mexican immigrant wives. *International Migration Review* 33:354–77.

Hall, Matthew, and George Farkas. 2008. Does human capital raise earnings for immigrants in the low-skill labor market? *Demography* 45:619–39.

Hall, Matthew, Emily Greenman, and George Farkas. 2010. Legal status and wage disparities for Mexican immigrants. *Social Forces* 89 (2): 491–514.

Hauan, Susan, Nancy Landale, and Kevin Leicht. 2000. Poverty and work effort among urban Latino men. *Work and Occupations* 27 (2): 188–222.

Hondagneu-Sotelo, Pierrette, ed. 2003. *Gender and U.S. immigration: Contemporary trends*. Berkeley, CA: University of California Press.

Hudson, Kenneth. 2007. The new labor market segmentation: Labor market dualism in the new economy. *Social Science Research* 36 (1): 286–312.

Israel, Barbara, Eugenia Eng, Amy Schulz, and Edith Parker, eds. 2005. *Methods in community-based participatory research for health*. San Francisco, CA: Jossey-Bass.

Kahn, Joan, and Leslie Whittington. 1996. The labor supply of Latinas in the USA: Comparing labor force participation, wages, and hours worked with Anglo and black women. *Population Research and Policy Review* 15 (1): 45–73.

Kalleberg, Arne. 2011. *Good jobs, bad jobs: The rise of polarized and precarious employment systems in the United States, 1970s–2000s*. New York, NY: Russell Sage Foundation.

Kopczuk, Wojciech, Emmanuel Saez, and Jae Song. 2010. Earnings inequality and mobility in the United States: Evidence from Social Security data since 1937. *Quarterly Journal of Economics* 125 (1): 91–128.

Kossoudji, Sherrie. 1988. English language ability and the labor market outcomes of Hispanic and East Asian immigrant men. *Journal of Labor Economics* 6 (2): 205–28.

Massey, Douglas S., ed. 2010. *New faces in new places: The changing geography of American immigration*. New York, NY: Russell Sage Foundation.

Menjívar, Cecilia. 2000. *Fragmented ties: Salvadoran immigrant networks in America*. Berkeley, CA: University of California Press.

Myers, Dowell, and Cynthia Cranford. 1998. Temporal differentiation in the occupational mobility of immigrant and native-born Latina workers. *American Sociological Review* 63 (1): 68–93.

Orrenius, Pia, and Maeline Zavodny. 2009. The effects of tougher enforcement on the job prospects of recent Latin American immigrants. *Journal of Policy Analysis and Management* 28 (2): 239–57.

Parrado, Emilio, Chris McQuiston, and Chenoa Flippen. 2005. Participatory survey research: Integrating community collaboration and quantitative methods for the study of gender and HIV risks among Hispanic migrants. *Sociological Methods and Research* 34:204–39.

Phillips, Julie, and Douglas S. Massey. 1999. The new labor market: Immigrants and wages after IRCA. *Demography* 36 (2): 233–46.

Piore, Michael. 1970. The dual labor market: Theory and implications. In *The state and the poor*, eds. Samuel H. Beer and Richard E. Barringer. Cambridge, MA: Winthrop Publishers.

Rivera-Batiz, Francisco. 1999. Undocumented workers in the labor market: An analysis of the earnings of legal and illegal Mexican immigrants in the United States. *Journal of Population Economy* 12 (1): 91–116.

Valenzuela, Abel, and Elizabeth Gonzalez. 2000. Latino earnings inequality: Immigrant and native born differences. In *Prismatic metropolis: Inequality in Los Angeles*, eds. Lawrence Bobo, Melvin Oliver, James Johnson, and Abel Valenzuela, 249–79. New York, NY: Russell Sage Foundation.

Watters, John, and Patrick Biernacki. 1989. Targeted sampling: Options for the study of hidden populations. *Social Problems* 36 (4): 416–30.

The Departed: Deportations and Out-Migration among Latino Immigrants in North Carolina after the Great Recession

EMILIO A. PARRADO
and
CHENOA A. FLIPPEN

This article explores the impact of the 2007 recession and immigration enforcement policies on Latin American immigrants' out-migration from the Durham, North Carolina, area—a new immigrant destination. Drawing on an original ethnosurvey collected in 2011, the analysis assesses the extent of out-migration over time, what precipitated the move, and whether individuals returned to their country of origin or migrated within the United States. We find that out-migration more than doubled after the 2007 recession and that migrants overwhelmingly returned to their home countries. While family considerations and accidents accounted for most of the departures before the recession, economic considerations became the dominant drivers of out-migration after 2007. Deportations also grew in number but accounted for a negligible share of all out-migration. Departures were more prevalent among immigrants from Mexico and those with lower educational attainment. Latin American migration, especially from Mexico, continues to be circular, and deportation is a relatively ineffective strategy for immigrant population control when compared to voluntary returns.

Keywords: immigration; recession; deportation; Hispanic

B etween 1990 and 2000, Latin American migration to the United States was characterized by two trends: a substantial increase

Emilio A. Parrado is a professor in and chair of the Department of Sociology at the University of Pennsylvania. His research focuses on issues of stratification, development, and social change in Latin America and among the Latino population of the United States. He is currently principal investigator of an NIH-funded project investigating the connection between fertility and immigration.

Chenoa A. Flippen is an associate professor of sociology at the University of Pennsylvania. Her research addresses diverse topics in racial and ethnic stratification, including minority aging and retirement security, the impact of residential segregation on minority housing wealth, the social mobility consequences of internal migration, and Hispanic immigrant adaptation.

NOTE: This research was supported by NIH/Fogarty grant #TW008704-03.

Correspondence: eparrado@upenn.edu

DOI: 10.1177/0002716216646563

in the volume of the flow, which more than doubled over the period; and the dramatic dispersion of the Latino immigrant population away from traditional receiving gateways such as Los Angeles, Chicago, and Miami and toward new destinations, especially in the Southeast (Massey 2008; Parrado and Kandel 2008). Both of these trends were disrupted by the combination of the 2007 economic recession and the continuous escalation of enforcement efforts both at the border and in the U.S. interior. Mounting evidence suggests that the volume of in-flows from Latin America fell sharply and that a record number of migrants have returned to their sending countries, both voluntarily and via deportation (Passell, Cohn, and Gonzalez-Barrera 2012). Mexico is a case in point; estimates from the Mexican census indicate that the population returning from the United States increased from 92,000 in 1990 to 267,000 in 2000 to a record 825,000 in 2010 (Parrado and Gutiérrez 2015).

Several studies have investigated the phenomenon of return migration from within sending countries (Campos-Vazquez and Lara 2012; Cuecuecha and Rendon 2012; Lindstrom 1996; Masferrer and Roberts 2012; Reyes 1997). Less is known, however, about how economic conditions and immigration enforcement policies, primarily deportations, shape return migration from U.S. receiving areas (Parrado 2012). The issue is relevant for several reasons. First, it is important to assess the relative significance of forced removals versus voluntary returns. While official statistics are available regarding the number of annual deportations, voluntary returns to sending countries can be assessed only indirectly, from Latin American censuses and other sources, which cannot capture the extent of internal migration within the United States. Second, migration in all forms tends to be highly selective, and it is important to ascertain the individual and family characteristics of those most affected by out-migration to assess the implications for well-being and adaptation. Finally, a better understanding of the magnitude and nature of out-migration might be particularly salient in new destinations, where the population dynamics are strongly influenced by the migration patterns of immigrants and natives alike.

Accordingly, this article investigates the extent, timing, motivation, and destination of Latino immigrant out-migration from Durham, North Carolina. Drawing on an original ethnosurvey administered in 2011, the analysis applies multiplicity sampling techniques that rely on respondents' answers to queries regarding the mobility of siblings to assess the extent of out-migration over time, what precipitated the move (i.e., whether an accident, family demands, economic conditions, or deportation), and whether individuals returned to their country of origin or migrated within the United States. In addition, we model the correlates of these behaviors according to respondents' characteristics to assess who is affected by out-migration and what the traits of these movers are. Together, these analyses provide a unique perspective on the dynamics of out-migration and its relation to the economic recession and immigration enforcement policies in a new Latino immigrant destination.

New Destinations and Out-Migration
by Latino Immigrants

New immigrant destinations have been the subject of much research in recent years. Scores of books and articles have begun to paint a portrait of how these communities formed and key differences between these areas and more traditional immigrant gateways (Flippen and Parrado 2012; Massey 2008). However, the relative newness of the phenomenon has prevented the study of how these communities evolve over time, including how they respond to changing economic and policy conditions. While the forces drawing immigrants to new destinations are as diverse as the destinations themselves (Flippen and Kim 2015; Parrado and Kandel 2008), many immigrants were driven locally by an influx of businesses and native workers and the boom in residential and commercial construction that they engendered. As such, they were hit particularly hard by the 2007 economic recession, which began in the housing sector and resulted in massive losses in construction employment (Hadi 2011).

The implicit assumption in much of the work on new destinations was that these communities would continue to grow and mature into more established immigrant destinations. However, a number of features of the immigrant populations in these areas call this assumption into question. Specifically, compared to those in more traditional gateway areas, immigrants in new destinations are disproportionately more recently arrived to the United States, undocumented, and less established in families (i.e., a higher share of men are either unmarried or unaccompanied by wives, who remain in countries of origin) (Flippen and Parrado 2012). In other words, they are precisely those who are most mobile and most able to relocate in response to changing economic conditions. Whether and how new destinations endure over time thus remains an open question.

Our understanding of international migrants' mobility patterns after initial entry is limited. While return migration to sending countries has received theoretical and empirical attention, far less is known about relocation within receiving countries. Moreover, most research has focused on the impact of return migration on sending communities, to the relative neglect of how out-migration impacts receiving communities, and the implications of exits for understanding processes of settlement and adaptation.

The departure of international migrants, especially those who return to sending countries, has also been inconsistently incorporated into theories of migration and settlement (Cassarino 2004). The dominant neoclassical economic framework regards migration as a form of investment in human capital. According to this view, individuals migrate when the expected benefits to employment and wages resulting from mobility exceed the expected costs (Sjasstad 1962). As an investment in long-term, lifetime earnings, migration is not generally expected to involve returns. In the absence of substantial reversal in the wage or the opening of employment gaps across locations, return migration from this perspective is in many ways an anomaly and most likely signals return migrants' failure to achieve their expected labor market gains from relocation.

Alternative perspectives, in contrast, have highlighted that in many situations, circularity and return migration are very much part and parcel of the process of international migration. Piore's seminal book *Birds of Passage* (1979), for instance, argued that many international migrants are target earners who engage in circular migration in response to financial needs at home. The circularity of the flow together with capital accumulation abroad were thought to foster the transfer of new skills and entrepreneurial activities to sending communities. Likewise, the new economics of labor migration framed migration as a household risk-diversification strategy to protect against uncertain and unstable economic conditions by providing alternative sources of income (Stark 1982). Under this model, migration was also argued to respond not only to absolute wage differentials but also to relative socioeconomic position and mobility prospects at home (Stark and Taylor 1989). The latter viewpoint directly connects the remittances and savings of migrants, especially return migrants, to business formation in sending areas (Massey and Parrado 1994; Papail 2002; Woodruff and Zenteno 2007).

For both perspectives, return migration is not framed as an anomalous failure to achieve expected lifetime labor market gains. On the contrary, it represents an expression of migrants' successful capital accumulation at destination that is then translated into absolute or relative social mobility upon return. More recently, scholars have also pointed out that processes of transnationalism lead to sustained connections between migrants and their sending communities, spurring business enterprises that transcend national borders (Portes, Guarnizo, and Haller 2002). Taken together, these perspectives invite a more systematic consideration of the forces and patterns shaping return migration and the selectivity of return migrants and the patterns of settlement that they display.

A more dynamic view of return migration is particularly relevant for the case of Latin American migration to the United States. Massey and colleagues have long described Mexican migration to the United States not as a single event but, rather, as a social process that develops over the life course of individuals (Massey et al. 1987; Massey, Durand, and Malone 2002). The process is described as a sequence of stages that include initial departure, return, recurrent migration, and ultimately settlement or final return. From this view, then, return migration and circularity are defining characteristics of Latin American migration. In addition, a dynamic perspective explicitly recognizes that the fluidity of population movements is significantly affected by macrolevel conditions in the economic and political spheres. It is well documented that immigrant inflows and outflows closely mirror cycles of labor demand in the United States, with immigrants arriving when employment opportunities are plentiful and returning to their home countries during periods of economic slowdown (Angelucci 2012; Mandelman and Zlate 2012). Moreover, immigration policy can also exert a direct effect on the social process of migration, changing not only the legal standing of labor migrants but also the dynamism of the movement (Massey, Durand, and Pren 2015).

The impact of immigration policies on Latin America–U.S. migration patterns can be traced to the unintended consequences of changes to immigration legislation in the mid-1960s. Massey and Pren (2012) argue that the elimination of the Bracero program, which served as a critical mechanism for satisfying the temporary and seasonal labor demands in the United States, and the imposition of numerical caps on immigration from the Western Hemisphere in the Hart-Celler Immigration and Nationality Act of 1965, effectively transformed a long-standing, deeply institutionalized, circular and legal migration flow into an undocumented one. The practical consequences of this transformation became particularly detrimental as restrictive immigration legislation and increased border enforcement disrupted the circularity of the flow. Starting with the passage of the Immigration Reform and Control Act (IRCA) in 1986, the criminalization of unauthorized entry significantly increased the costs of circular migration for the vast majority of low-skill labor migrants. With no legal channels to reenter the United States, voluntary returns became less prominent.

The passage of the 1996 Illegal Immigration Reform and Immigrant Responsibility Act (IIRIRA), and the enhanced measures to enforce immigration restrictions it entailed, marked another turning point in Latin American migration. As a result of programs such as Secure Communities, which created partnerships among federal, state, and local law enforcement agencies to promote the interior enforcement of immigration law, the deportation of labor migrants increased considerably post-1996. The number of annual deportations grew steeply over time, from 70,000 in 1996 to more than 420,000 by 2012. More than 70 percent of deportations were Mexican nationals, with the cumulative number of deportations of Mexicans between 2000 and 2012 exceeding 2.7 million (Parrado 2012).

From the perspective of local areas, these changing economic conditions and immigration policies raise many questions related to return migration and out-mobility. There are no estimates of the actual extent of out-migration and whether the departed are returning to their countries of origin or moving to another area within the United States. In addition, the reasons for the move remain unclear, making it difficult to separate responses to changing economic and family conditions from deportations. Finally, we know very little about the socioeconomic background of those departing, limiting our understanding of the implications of out-migration for the adaptation trajectories of those settling in the United States.

Data and Methods

Data for the analysis come from the Gender, Migration, and Health among Hispanics study (for more detail, see Parrado, McQuiston, and Flippen 2005), an original ethnosurvey collected in repeated cross-sections in 2001, 2006, and 2011 in the Durham, Chapel Hill, and Carrboro metropolitan areas of North Carolina (for the sake of expediency simply referred to as "Durham," where the majority of respondents lived). The current analysis focuses on the 2011 data, which capture conditions during and after the Great Recession, though figures from the 2006 data are also used as points of comparison. Since the relatively recent nature of the Latino community in Durham rendered simple random sampling prohibitively expensive, the project employed targeted random sampling techniques to approximate a representative sample of the Durham Latino immigrant community.

Through Community Based Participatory Research (CBPR) that involves a partnership between academics and community members at all stages of the research process, we identified forty-nine apartment complexes and blocks that housed a large number of immigrant Latinos. We then collected a census of all the apartments in these areas and randomly selected individual units to be visited by interviewers. CBPR members were trained as interviewers and collected all the data. Although our survey may have been less likely to capture established immigrants, the targeted design and community involvement method was more effective than nonrandom methods of recruitment such as snowball or convenience sampling.

In addition to information about the employment and immigration histories of respondents, the 2011 survey included a battery of questions specifically designed to capture out-migration from Durham. Out-migrants are by definition no longer residing locally, so they are impossible to observe at the time of the survey. Building on multiplicity sampling techniques (Sirken 1970), however, we queried respondents about the mobility of prior Durham residents. Multiplicity sampling is a data collection strategy in which a respondent is asked to report on the occurrence of a rare event among a set of individuals known to them (Laumann et al. 1993). A specific multiplicity rule defines the set of individuals respondents are asked to report about. The rule typically follows consanguine or spatial relationships. Respondents are also asked to report on the overall size of the individuals they know within the set defined by the multiplicity rule, which is then used to weigh the number exposed to the event. This strategy has been shown to provide an unbiased estimate of the number of persons experiencing otherwise impossible-to-measure events (Laumann et al. 1993).

In our case, respondents were probed in depth about how many brothers, sisters, and other close family members had ever lived in Durham, how many were still residing in the area, and how many had left. For each person identified as ever having lived in Durham, their current location was ascertained. For those who had left the area, the year of departure; city, state, and country of destination; and reason for departure (including deportation) were obtained. We also asked the same set of questions for all blood relatives, other than siblings, who were in Durham at some point and departed. While substantive patterns are similar for siblings and other relatives, we focus our analysis on the former mainly because the socioeconomic correlates in our analysis include household background characteristics that are strongly correlated among siblings of the same household. The correlation across households in background characteristics is likely considerably weaker.

Based on the respondents' information, we expanded the dataset to construct a siblings file that listed all the siblings who had ever lived in Durham, whether they had left the area, year of departure, reason for the move, and destination. The survey also collected information about the socioeconomic characteristics of the respondents, including country of origin, gender, educational attainment, size of community of origin (rural area, town, or city), how well they speak English, whether they migrated to Durham directly from abroad or via another area within the United States, and current occupation. The multivariate analysis correlates respondents' socioeconomic characteristics with the likelihood of reporting a sibling leaving the area, reason for the move, and destination. Ideally the survey would have collected detailed information on the human capital, family structure, and migration and employment history of departed siblings. However, that was not feasible within the constraints of the project and also would have been subject to significant recall and other errors.

As such, we use respondent characteristics to model the departure behaviors of their siblings. This serves two purposes. First, because some characteristics were set before migration, they are likely to be strongly correlated among siblings (particularly country of origin, rural origins, and educational attainment). Thus, they provide a proxy for the socioeconomic selectivity of the departed. Second, while we do not directly model individual behaviors, the analyses identify the socioeconomic background of the immigrants exposed to the loss of family members through out-migration, adding to our understanding of the changes in the Durham Latino immigrant community.

We collected a total of 517 surveys in 2011, with 339 and 178 adult male and female respondents, respectively. More than half of the respondents, 60 percent, were of Mexican origin; and 37 percent were from Central America, primarily Honduras (17 percent), with a small portion (2.3 percent) from other Latin American countries. In terms of their educational attainment, the majority of respondents (42 percent) had achieved 6 or fewer years of education, 28 percent reported 7 to 9 years of schooling, 21 percent completed 10 to 12 years of school, and 7 percent reported 13 or more years of education. Respondents were evenly distributed in terms of the size of their community of origin, with 28, 37, and 35 percent reporting growing up in a city, town, and rural area, respectively. Almost 11 percent of the sample reported speaking English well, and 46 percent were internal U.S. migrants prior to arriving in Durham. At the time of the survey, the vast majority of respondents were working in construction (35 percent), landscaping (7 percent), food services (14 percent), and cleaning/babysitting services (14 percent). On average, respondents reported having had 1.33 siblings in the area. Expanding the dataset to create a siblings file produced a total of 1,199 siblings.

We first describe the likelihood of siblings departing Durham over time, the reasons for the move (distinguishing among accidents or illnesses, family considerations, economic concerns, and deportation), and whether it involved return migration to the county of origin or migration within the United States. We then use logistic regression techniques to model the likelihood of a sibling leaving Durham according to respondent characteristics. Finally, we extend the multivariate analysis by modeling, conditional on reporting a sibling departing Durham, whether the move was for family or economic reasons and whether it was a return to their countries of origin or internal U.S. migration.

The Setting

Durham offers a valuable vantage point from which to explore migration dynamics. Growth of the high-tech sector during the 1990s spurred a boom in business and residential construction, heightening demand for construction and other semiskilled laborers, as well as for domestic workers and other service employees for the growing class of professionals in the area. The result of this combination of forces was dramatic. In 1990, fewer than two thousand foreign-born Latin Americans resided in the area; but by 2010, the number had reached close to forty thousand, or 12 percent of the total population.

The Great Recession, which began in December 2007, significantly altered economic conditions in the area. In North Carolina, payroll employment levels fell in every private industrial sector with the exception of education, health services, and professional and business services; and contraction in the construction and manufacturing sectors was particularly pronounced. Between December 2007 and June 2012, construction and manufacturing employment in the state declined 32.1 and 17.9 percent, respectively, and the unemployment rate increased from 5 to more than 10 percent. The unemployment rate for North Carolina Latinos in 2010 reached 12.1 percent (Gitterman, Coclanis, and Quintero 2012).

One of the most striking features of new Latino destinations such as Durham is the degree to which Latinos were concentrated in precisely those industries that were most strongly affected by the recession. As a result, Latino unemployment in Durham more than doubled, from 4 to 10 percent, between 2006 and 2010. The change in economic fortunes was clearly evident in our data as well, at least among men. In 2006, a mere 4 percent of Latino immigrant men reported being out of work at interview (Flippen 2012), compared to more than 13 percent in 2011. Among women, however, roughly 42 percent were not working at interview in both periods, though the share reporting unemployment (as opposed to more voluntary reasons for nonparticipation) rose over time (Flippen 2013). Like other new destinations, moreover, Durham tends to attract segments of the immigrant population that are the most likely to be mobile geographically: new arrivals to the United States, undocumented migrants, and unaccompanied men.

The sharp deterioration in the city's economic conditions and the significant changes in its immigration enforcement policies make Durham an interesting vantage point to evaluate the out-migration of Latin American immigrants. In February 2008, the Durham police department initiated the 287(g) program. The 287(g) is an umbrella program in which Immigration and Customs Enforcement (ICE), a federal entity in the Department of Homeland Security (DHS), provides assistance and information to local police officers enforcing immigration laws.

In its Memorandum of Agreement with ICE, the Durham police department followed the more stringent "field model" of enforcement, which included officers who work in the field, rather than the alternative "detention model," which limited training in the 287(g) program to officers who work in jails. The region's entry into the Securities Communities Program further enhanced immigration enforcement in the area. Wake County, which includes the capital city of Raleigh, was the first in the state to join Secure Communities, which it did in November 2008. Orange County, which includes Carrboro and Chapel Hill, followed suit in January 2009; and Durham County did so in February 2009.

Secure Communities is a DHS program designed to identify immigrants in U.S. jails who are deportable under immigration law. Under Secure Communities, participating jails submit arrestees' fingerprints not only to criminal databases but to immigration databases as well, allowing ICE access to this information. By 2015, the Secure Communities program in Durham and Orange counties had produced 701 removals and returns (ICE 2015).

Descriptive Results

Figure 1 reports the share of siblings reported as having departed the Durham area by year of the move. Overall, 14.4 percent of siblings who had ever lived in Durham moved out of the area between 1995 and 2011. However, only 2.8 percent did so prior to the 2007 recession, compared to 11.6 percent afterward. Moreover, the increased prevalence of out-migration was already evident in 2006, suggesting that migrants were responding to deteriorating employment conditions even before the official start of the recession. This pattern also suggests that out-migration was already increasing before the application of the 287(g) and Secure Communities programs in 2008 and 2009, respectively. By 2009, the share of siblings departing Durham had increased to five times the level reported for 2006, reaching 3.3 percent. The prevalence of sibling out-migration remained high in 2010 (2.9 percent) and 2011 (1.7 percent, which, due to the timing of data collection, reflects departures occurring during the first six months of the year).

The coincidence between the timing of the economic recession and the introduction of enhanced immigration enforcement policies makes it difficult to disentangle the forces causing the increase in out-migration. To explore this issue, Figure 2 presents the share of departed siblings who left Durham according to the reported reason for the move, separating departures before and after the recession. Before 2007, out-migration from Durham was dominated by personal considerations, particularly family concerns and injury from accidents, which constituted 55.1 and 12.2 percent of all departures, respectively. At 28.5 percent of all departures, lack of employment was another important impetus behind out-migration from Durham even prior to 2007. However, there were relatively few cases of deportations, which represented only 4 percent of all departures before 2007.

After 2007, however, we see an important shift in the motivation behind departures from Durham. While family concerns remain an important reason for out-migration (26.3 percent), both economic considerations and, to a lesser extent, deportations gain considerably in significance. It is particularly striking that the share of out-migrants perceived as having left due to lack of employment more than doubled after the recession, reaching 63.4 percent of all departing siblings. Likewise, the share leaving Durham due to deportations also increased to 9 percent of departures. Even with this increase, however, the likelihood of out-migration due to deportation remained only 0.15 and 0.37 times as likely as departing due to economic or family reasons, respectively.

Figure 3 presents results from the queries regarding the destination of departing siblings. Results show that respondents overwhelmingly reported that their

FIGURE 1
Percentage of Siblings Reported as Leaving Durham by Year

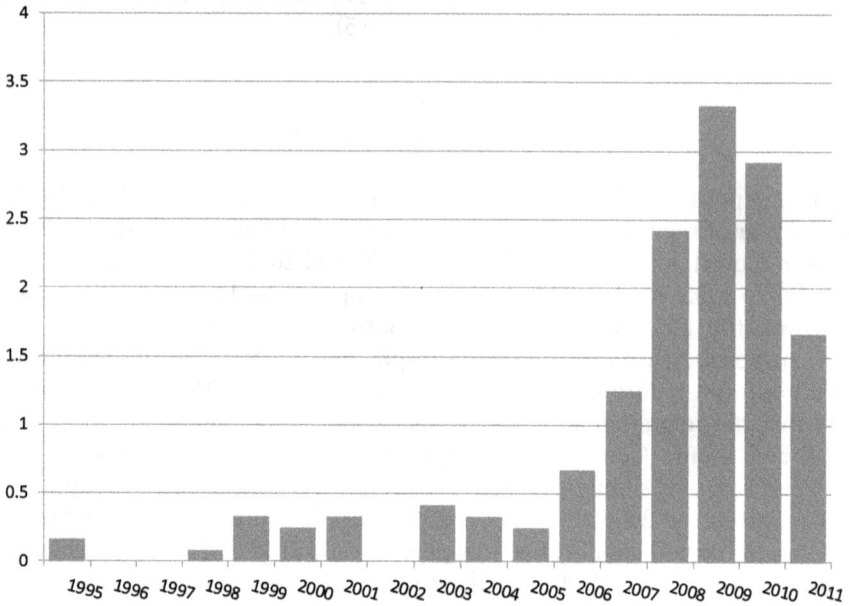

FIGURE 2
Reported Reasons for Migration Pre- and Post-2007

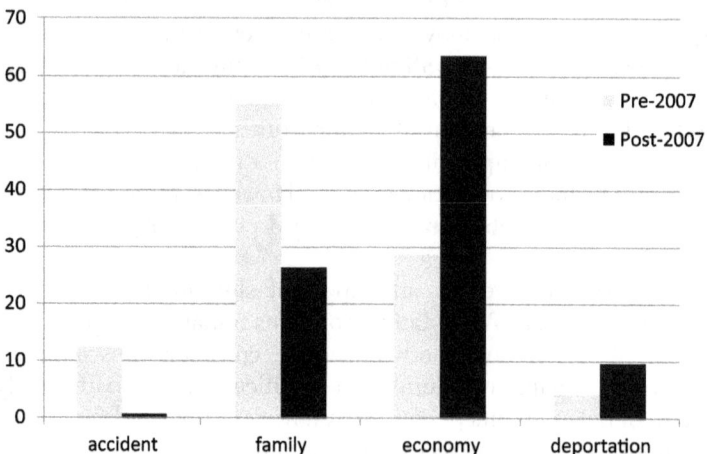

sibling returned to their countries of origin rather than relocating within the United States. The pattern is very similar before and after the recession with 77.5 and 78.4 percent of siblings voluntarily returning to their home countries before and after 2007, respectively. If anything, the prevalence of internal migration

FIGURE 3
Destination Pre- and Post-2007

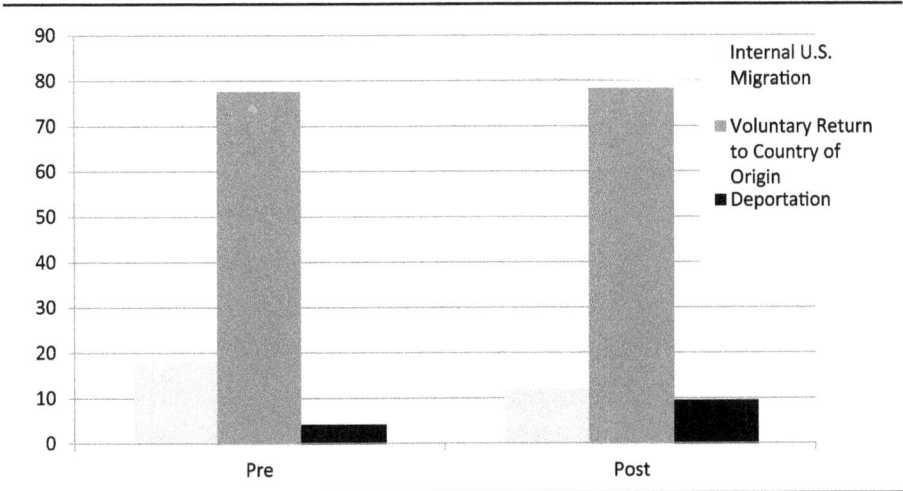

actually declined after the recession from 18.4 to 11.9 percent. The combination of dim economic prospects in other states and rising salience of deportations likely combined to heighten return migration over time.

Multivariate Results

While the descriptive statistics document important shifts in the magnitude, motivation, and destination of out-migration over time, it is also important to explore potential selectivity in the flow and its implications for those left behind. Table 1 shows results from logistic regression equations estimated to predict sibling out-migration patterns from respondents' socioeconomic characteristics. To the extent that the socioeconomic characteristics of siblings are correlated, multivariate results can help us to assess the socioeconomic selectivity of out-migration flows, as many sibling traits are household characteristics acquired before migration.

The first model reports the coefficients predicting the likelihood of out-migration. Results show that relative to Mexicans, Central American respondents are only 0.762 (exp[−0.271]) as likely to report having had a sibling depart the Durham area. The result is likely a function of both the fact that Central Americans benefited from specific immigration policies, such as Temporary Protected Status (TPS) that afforded them legal status and that the greater distance and difficulty involved in Central American migration discourages exit and circularity relative to Mexicans.

The coefficients for educational attainment show that the likelihood of reporting sibling departure from the Durham area decreases consistently with higher levels of education. Residents with 10 to 12 and those with 13 or more years of

TABLE 1
Coefficients from Multivariate Logit Models Predicting the Likelihood of Sibling
Out-Migration from Durham and Reason for and Destination of the Move

	Out-Migration		Economic vs. Family Reason		Return vs. Internal U.S. Move	
Intercept	−1.586**	(0.269)	−0.207	(0.496)	3.182**	(0.887)
Country of origin (Ref: Mexico)						
Central America	−0.271*	(0.186)	0.853**	(0.362)	−0.427	(0.465)
Other nationality	0.339	(0.792)	0.175	(1.745)	−0.416	(1.738)
Survey respondent characteristics						
Male	−0.081	(0.258)	−0.830	(0.620)	0.203	(0.793)
Educational attainment (Ref: 0–6 years of education)						
7–9 years	−0.028	(0.192)	0.446	(0.377)	−0.201	(0.499)
10–12 years	−0.499*	(0.273)	1.183**	(0.581)	0.654	(0.810)
13+ years	−1.025**	(0.502)			−0.622	(1.130)
Region of origin (Ref: City)						
Pueblo	0.006	(0.203)	−0.282	(0.391)	−0.469	(0.562)
Rancho	−0.370**	(0.226)	0.227	(0.446)	−0.772	(0.580)
U.S. characteristics						
Speaks good English	0.196	(0.308)	−0.216	(0.636)	−0.107	(0.786)
Internal migrant	−0.047	(0.175)	−0.190	(0.352)	−0.771**	(0.443)
Occupation (Ref: Not working)						
Construction	0.535**	(0.279)	0.562	(0.616)	−0.846	(0.698)
Landscaping	0.081	(0.384)	0.778	(0.788)		
Restaurant	0.045	(0.313)	−0.039	(0.688)	−1.416	(0.811)
Cleaning/babysitting	−0.095	(0.284)	0.034	(0.600)	−1.233	(0.850)
N	1,199		173		173	
Likelihood ratio	24.7**		15.7		13.4	

NOTE: Standard errors in parenthesis.
*$p < .10$. **$p < .05$.

education are 0.607 (exp[−0.499]) and 0.359 (exp[−1.025]) as likely, respectively, to report a sibling departing than residents with 6 or fewer years of education. To the extent that siblings' level of education is correlated, results suggest negative selectivity in the out-migration flow. After controlling for other socioeconomic characteristics, those who grew up in rural areas are also less likely (−0.370) to report a sibling departure than those raised in cities. Again, assuming that sibling places of origin are highly correlated and that return migrants often settle in their communities of origin, the limited economic opportunities in rural areas in Latin America will discourage out-migration from Durham, once other characteristics are taken into account.

Interestingly, results show that respondents employed in construction are 1.708 (exp[0.535]) times more likely than nonworking residents to report a sibling departing Durham. Again, the construction industry was not only the main employer of Latino immigrants in the Durham area but also the sector most adversely affected by the recession. Given the importance of social networks to the process of securing a job among immigrants, the likely correlation in sibling industry renders this pattern at least suggestive of greater out-migration among workers in the construction industry. At a minimum, it demonstrates that working in construction is associated with greater exposure to experiencing the out-migration of siblings, a key source of social support in migrant communities.

The next two models report the coefficients from logistic regression models predicting the likelihood of out-migration due to economic circumstances versus family reasons, and whether the move entailed a return migration to the country of origin versus an internal move to another U.S. destination. The models are conditional on a respondent having reported a sibling departure from Durham. The restricted sample size ($N = 173$) reduces the statistical significance of many of the estimates. However, some patterns still emerge. Even though Central American siblings were less likely to depart the Durham area than Mexicans, they are more likely to do so due to economic rather than family reasons. Again, we attribute this pattern to distance and cost. Returning to home communities to visit or care for family members is less costly for Mexican migrants than it is for Central American migrants, who tend to return only when economic conditions are seriously untenable. We also find that even though higher educational levels are negatively associated with sibling out-migration, conditional on sibling depar-ture, better-educated residents are more likely to report economic than family motivations for exit. Again, we speculate that more educated respondents gener-ally come from families with more advantaged socioeconomic backgrounds, who are likely to be less dependent on others for their support. In these families, it is only when the economic position seriously deteriorates that members return to sending communities.

The final model reports coefficients from logistic regression models predicting the likelihood of returning to sending countries versus moving to another area in the United States. We find that those residents with prior migration experience in the United States are more likely to report a sibling moving internally rather than returning to their home countries. If internal migration reflects family con-nections in other areas of the United States, it appears that those extended con-nections reduce return migration to sending communities.

Conclusion

This article investigates the prevalence and motivation of out-migration, and destination of out-migrants among Latin American immigrants in the Durham-Chapel Hill-Carrboro metropolitan area of North Carolina, a new Latino immi-grant destination. Most studies of immigrant out-migration tend to focus on return migration to sending countries and are primarily conducted in receiving areas. Relying on an original survey and multiplicity sampling techniques, our study constructed a dataset of respondents' siblings ever residing in Durham and assessed their out-migration propensities; whether they left the area due to accidents, family considerations, economic conditions, or deportations; and whether they moved internally within the United States or returned to their home countries. We then modeled these outcomes according to respondents' socioeconomic characteristics to assess the socioeconomic background of those most affected by siblings' out-migration and to tentatively explore the selectivity of immigrants departing the area.

Durham provides a unique setting to investigate these issues. As an emerging area of destination, it experienced exponential growth in its Latino immigrant population in conjunction with the expansion of the construction and low-skilled service sector industries. Employment in the construction industry was particularly hard hit by the 2007 economic recession. The community, like many others in the nation, also participated in enhanced interior immigration enforcement policies. Specifically, Durham and Orange counties, which coincide with the area under consideration, activated the 287(g) and Secure Communities programs in 2008 and 2009, resulting in more than seven hundred deportations by early 2015 (ICE 2015). Thus, the area provides an ideal setting to investigate the relative role of voluntary versus involuntary departures among Latino immigrant residents.

The analysis documents a dramatic increase in departures from Durham coinciding with the 2007 recession. As many as 14.4 percent of siblings who had ever lived in the Durham area had departed by 2011, and 80.3 percent of those departing did so after 2007. The prevalence of departures was already high in 2007 and 2008, before the activation of programs incorporating local police departments into immigration enforcement policies. We find that before the recession, family considerations and accidents accounted for 77.3 percent of all sibling departures. After 2007, economic considerations increased to represent 63.4 of the reasons given for leaving the area. Deportations rose from 4.1 and 9.7 percent of the reasons for departures before and after 2007, respectively. Overwhelmingly, those departing returned to their home countries (close to 80 percent), with little change before and after the recession.

Central Americans were less exposed to sibling departures than Mexicans, though out-migration was more often attributed to economic rather than family considerations for the former. The greater difficultly involved in reaching the United States from Central America likely contributes to both of these patterns. An examination of the human capital and migration histories of respondents with out-migrating siblings also hints at the selectivity of the departing flow. Respondents who herald from rural areas are less likely to report out-migrant siblings, as are those with higher levels of education. Those employed in construction, in contrast, are more likely to report out-migrant siblings. There is some evidence that prior experience with internal U.S. migration is associated with movements within the United States rather than the return to countries of origin.

Taken together, these patterns are supportive of the argument that immigrants' characteristics interact with conditions in both sending and receiving areas to shape patterns of return migration. Those whose easiest option is to return to underperforming rural areas are less likely to leave Durham than those who grew up in cities. Those with higher levels of education are better able to weather economic downturns in the United States and are particularly unlikely to leave for family-related reasons. Finally, leaving Durham for another U.S. location is more likely among those whose family networks include internal migrants, as opposed to those more likely to have migrated directly to the Durham area from abroad.

The analysis has important implications for the literature on immigrant adaptation and incorporation. Return migration and other forms of out-migration are often neglected in accounts of the socioeconomic mobility of immigrant origin populations, including both contemporary flows from Latin America and Asia and also historical flows from Europe. The issue has received some attention in the health literature where the Latino advantage in some health and mortality indicators has been attributed to the negative selectivity of those departing the United States (Palloni and Arias 2004). Our analysis highlights that return migration and other forms of out-migration are an important factor affecting the settlement and development of Latino immigrant communities in the United States. The concentration of the most mobile immigrants, particularly the newly arrived, undocumented, and unaccompanied men, in new destinations could make their immigrant populations especially vulnerable to sizable shifts in composition in response to changing conditions.

As such, research that seeks to examine the process of immigrant incorporation over time or across generations must take into consideration the complex dynamics of in- and out-migration. Not only do processes of selection shape both types of movements, but these processes also likely differ for in- and out-migration, as well as for different national origin groups. Our results show, for example, that the considerable out-migration in response to the recession is an indicator that efforts to assess the impact of macroeconomic change in the United States that rely on unemployment and nonparticipation figures understate the true magnitude of job loss for Latino immigrants.

Our analysis also adds to our understanding of contemporary migration from Latin America. While the militarization of the border and enhanced enforcement of immigration restrictions throughout the United States have discouraged circular migration and tipped the scales in favor of settlement, the flow is far from unidirectional, particularly for Mexicans. Even though departures increased dramatically after 2007, they were also an important feature of the Durham Latino immigrant community even during a period of booming employment in immigrant-intensive industries. The large share of migrants who return to their home countries for family and other noneconomic reasons, in good times and bad, strongly suggests that were immigration policies to shift away from blocking entry toward the approach taken in earlier generations, a sizable segment of the Latino migrant population would return to the more fluid and circular pattern that predominated in the pre-IRCA era. The fact that considerable return migration is evident even from a metropolitan area were immigrants are concentrated in relatively well-paid fields outside of agriculture indicates that temporary legal worker programs could be efficacious in the contemporary service-driven economy.

Another important implication of the analysis is that despite the massive investment in financial and human resources to enforce immigration control in local areas, and the tremendous hardship that these policies impose on immigrant communities and families (Brabeck, Lykes, and Hunter 2014), deportations had a surprisingly small impact on return migration. The vast majority of Latino immigrants leaving Durham returned to their home countries on their own. While the majority of returns were in response to deteriorating economic conditions in Durham, it is noteworthy that more migrants voluntarily returned to attend to family matters than were deported. To the extent that the objective of immigration policy is to regulate the labor market so that it is in line with economic opportunities, relying on the natural forces of circularity and adaptation to changing economic conditions appears as a much more effective mechanism to maintain well-functioning local labor markets than forced removal. For deportations to reach the same level as voluntary returns, they would have to increase more than tenfold. Our findings indicate that given the tremendous costs associated with interior immigration enforcement, relying on deportations to regulate the size of immigrant communities is an untenable, ineffective, and unnecessary strategy.

References

Angelucci, Manuela. 2012. U.S. border enforcement and the net flow of Mexican illegal migration. *Economic Development and Cultural Change* 60 (2): 311–57.

Brabeck, Kalina M., M. Brinton Lykes, and Cristina Hunter. 2014. The psychosocial impact of detention and deportation on U.S. Migrant children and families. *American Journal of Orthopsychiatry* 84 (5): 496–505.

Campos-Vazquez, Raymundo, and Jaime Lara. 2012. Self-selection patterns among return migrants: Mexico 1990-2010. *IZA Journal of Migration* 1 (1): 1–18.

Cassarino, Jean-Pierre. 2004. Theorising return migration: The conceptual approach to return migrants revisited. *IJMS: International Journal on Multicultural Societies* 6 (2): 253–79.

Cuecuecha, Alfredo, and Silvio Rendon. 2012. Mexicans in and out of the United States: Facts on job search and international migration. In *Migration and remittances from Mexico: Trends, impacts, and new challenges*, eds. Alfredo Cuecuecha and Carla Pederzini, 119–42. Plymouth, UK: Lexington Books.

Flippen, Chenoa A. 2012. Laboring underground: The employment patterns of Hispanic immigrant men in Durham, NC. *Social Problems* 59 (1): 21–42.

Flippen, Chenoa A. 2013. Intersectionality at work: Determinants of labor supply among immigrant Hispanic women in Durham, NC. *Gender and Society* 20:1–31.

Flippen, Chenoa A., and Eubni Kim. 2015. Immigrant context and opportunity: New destinations and socioeconomic attainment among Asians in the United States. *The ANNALS of the American Academy of Political and Social Science* 660:175–98.

Flippen, Chenoa A., and Emilio A. Parrado. 2012. Forging Hispanic communities in new destinations: A case study of Durham, NC. *City & Community* 11 (1): 1–30.

Gitterman, Daniel P., Peter A. Coclanis, and John Quintero. 2012. *Recession and recovery in North Carolina: A data snapshot, 2007–12.* Chapel Hill, NC: Global Research Institute, University of North Carolina.

Hadi, Adam. 2011. Construction employment peaks before the recession and falls sharply throughout it. *Monthly Labor Review* 134 (4): 24–27. Available from http://www.bls.gov/opub/mlr/2011/04/art4full.pdf.

Immigration and Custom Enforcement Agency (ICE). 2015. *ICE's use of IDENT/IAFIS interoperability.* Available from https://www.ice.gov/sites/default/files/documents/FOIA/2015/sc_stats_YTD2015.pdf.

Laumann, Edward O., John H. Gagnon, Stuart Michaels, Robert T. Michael, and L. Philip Schumm. 1993. Monitoring AIDS and other rare population events: A network approach. *Journal of Health and Social Behavior* 34 (1): 7–22.

Lindstrom, David P. 1996. Economic opportunity in Mexico and return migration from the United States. *Demography* 33 (3): 357–74.

Mandelman, Federico S., and Andrei Zlate. 2012. Immigration, remittances, and business cycles. *Journal of Monetary Economics* 59 (2): 196–13.

Masferrer, Claudia, and Bryan R. Roberts. 2012. Going back home? Changing demography and geography of Mexican return migration. *Population Research and Policy Review* 31 (4): 465–96.

Massey, Douglas S., ed. 2008. *New faces in new places: The changing geography of American immigration.* New York, NY: Russell Sage Foundation.

Massey, Douglas S., Rafael Alarcón, Jorge Durand, and Humberto González. 1987. *Return to Aztlan: The social process of international migration from western Mexico.* Berkeley, CA: University of California Press.

Massey, Douglas S., Jorge Durand, and Nola Malone. 2002. *Beyond smoke and mirrors: Mexican immigration in an age of economic integration.* New York, NY: Russell Sage Foundation.

Massey, Douglas S., Jorge Durand, and Karen A. Pren. 2015. Border enforcement and return migration by documented and undocumented Mexicans. *Journal of Ethnic and Migration Studies* 41 (7): 1015–40.

Massey, Douglas S., and Emilio A. Parrado. 1994. Migradollars: The remittances and savings of Mexican migrants to the United States. *Population Research and Policy Review* 13 (1): 3–30.

Massey, Douglas S., and Karen A. Pren. 2012. Unintended consequences of U.S. immigration policy: Explaining the post-1965 surge from Latin America. *Population and Development Review* 38 (1): 1–29.

Palloni, Alberto, and Elizabeth Arias. 2004. Paradox lost: Explaining the Hispanic adult mortality advantage. *Demography* 41 (3): 385–415.

Papail, Jean. 2002. De asalariado a empresario: la reinserción laboral de los migrantes internacionales en la región centro-occidente de México. *Migraciones Internacionales* 1 (3): 79–102.

Parrado, Emilio A. 2012. Immigration enforcement policies, the economic recession, and the size of local Mexican immigrant populations. *The ANNALS of the American Academy of Political and Social Science* 641:16–37.

Parrado, Emilio A., and Edith Gutiérrez. 2015. The changing nature of return migration to Mexico, 1990–2010: Implications for labor market incorporation and development. Working Paper, Population Studies Center, University of Pennsylvania, Philadelphia.

Parrado, Emilio A., and William Kandel. 2008. New Hispanic migrant destinations: A tale of two industries. In *New faces in new places: The changing geography of American immigration,* ed. Douglas S. Massey, 99–123. New York, NY: Russell Sage Foundation.

Parrado, Emilio A., Chris McQuiston, and Chenoa Flippen. 2005. Participatory survey research: Integrating community collaboration and quantitative methods for the study of gender and HIV risks among Hispanic migrants. *Sociological Methods and Research* 34 (2): 204–39.

Passel, Jeffrey S., D'Vera Cohn, and Anna Gonzalez-Barrera. 2012. *Net migration from Mexico falls to zero—and perhaps less.* Washington, DC: Pew Research Center.

Piore, Michael. 1979. *Birds of passage: Migrant labor in industrial societies.* Cambridge: Cambridge University Press.

Portes, Alejandro, Luis Eduardo Guarnizo, and William J. Haller. 2002. Transnational entrepreneurs: An alternative form of immigrant economic adaptation. *American Sociological Review* 67 (2): 278–98.

Reyes, Belinda I. 1997. *Dynamics of immigration: Return migration to western Mexico.* San Francisco, CA: Public Policy Institute of California.

Sirken, Monroe G. 1970. Household surveys with multiplicity. *Journal of the American Statistical Association* 65:257–66.

Sjaastad, Larry. 1962. The costs and returns of human migration. *Journal of Political Economy* 70 (5): 80–93.

Stark, Oded. 1982. On migration and risk in LDCs. *Economic Development and Cultural Change* 31 (1): 191–96.

Stark, Oded, and J. Edward Taylor. 1989. Relative deprivation and international migration. *Demography* 26 (1): 1–14.

Woodruff, Christopher, and René Zenteno. 2007. Migration networks and microenterprises in Mexico. *Journal of Development Economics* 82 (2): 509–28.

Undocumented Others: Bangladeshis, Africans, and Chinese

The Effects of Legal Status on Employment and Health Outcomes among Low-Skilled Chinese Immigrants in New York City

By
ZAI LIANG
and
BO ZHOU

Using a 2004 survey done in New York City's Chinese community, we explore the extent to which legal status affects immigrants' labor market performance and health status. We focus on five issues related to legal status of immigrants: wages, weekly working hours, employment location, self-rated health, and health care utilization. Our results show that undocumented immigrants are more likely to work for exceptionally long hours and are less likely to see a doctor when they get sick. However, we also find that current legal status does not have a significant effect on current health status. This work contributes to a growing literature on how legal status is linked to labor market and health consequences.

Keywords: undocumented; Chinese immigrants; health; work hours

In this article, we explore linkages between undocumented immigration status and employment and health outcomes. In so doing, we seek to increase the public understanding of the potential negative effects of illegal status on immigrants. In November 2014, President Obama issued an executive order for Deferred Action for Parents of Americans and Lawful Permanent Residents (DAPA), which would allow undocumented immigrants meeting certain criteria to stay and work legally in the

Zai Liang is a professor of sociology at the University at Albany, SUNY. He studies processes and consequences of internal and international migration. His current projects include the new spatial settlement pattern among low-skilled Chinese immigrants in the United States and a National Science Foundation–funded project on education and health of children left behind in China.

Bo Zhou is a PhD candidate in the Department of Sociology at the University at Albany, SUNY. His research interests include health outcomes of migrant children and left-behind children in China and the assimilation of Asian immigrants in the United States.

Correspondence: zliang@albany.edu

DOI: 10.1177/0002716216650632

United States for three years—an action that could potentially benefit about 3.7 million undocumented immigrants. In December 2014, however, twenty-six U.S. states filed a lawsuit to block DAPA, which led to the issuance of a temporary injunction blocking the executive order. Since then, millions of immigrants have been forced either to cease working or have continued to work illegally.

This article builds on and expands the existing research on the topic of immigrant health and employment. Studies of immigrants in the labor market often focus on wages, but we move beyond wages to study the impact of illegal status on immigrants' health and hours of work. The effects of illegal status have not been studied extensively, mostly due to a lack of adequate data. For obvious reasons, questions about immigrant status are not included in government censuses and surveys. Prior studies have also focused mainly on Latino immigrants. We present results using Chinese immigrants in the United States, providing a new case study of the effect of legal status on immigrants' labor market and health issues. A major advantage of our dataset is that it contains information on legal status and the job history of immigrants. From these data, we can measure, for example, the duration of immigrants' time spent in the United States and assess its long-term effects on immigrants' health and labor market performance.

Background

Previous studies on the influence of legal status on immigrant well-being have focused on labor market outcomes such as wages and occupational status. This orientation stems from interest in the labor market effects of immigrants and whether they have the potential to drive down wages for native workers, a concern that has figured prominently in U.S. immigration policy debates. Using data from the Mexican Migration Project (MMP), Massey (1987) examined the effect of legal status on hourly wages earned by Mexican migrants. A unique feature of the MMP's research design is its inclusion of Mexican migrants from both migrant-sending and migrant-receiving communities, thereby avoiding potential selection bias. In his original study, Massey (1987) did not find significant wage differentials by legal status. The data for that article, however, were gathered before the passage of the Immigration Reform and Control Act, which criminalized undocumented hiring. Later analyses using MMP data have found a growing wage gap between documented and undocumented workers (Phillips and Massey 1999; Massey and Gentsch 2014).

NOTE: The Survey of Chinese Immigrants in the U.S. used in this article was supported by grants from the National Institutes of Child Health and Human Development (1R01 HD39720-01) and the Ford Foundation (1025-1056). We thank UAlbany's Center for Social and Demographic Analysis with funding from Eunice Kennedy Shriver National Institutes of Child Health and Human Development (R24HD044943). We also thank Katherine M. Donato, Douglas S. Massey, and Emily Babson for comments and suggestions on earlier versions of the article.

Using data from the Survey of Income and Program Participation, Hall, Greenman, and Farkas (2010) also found a sizable difference in wages earned by documented and undocumented Mexican workers. However, they used an approach to infer "undocumented" status rather than measuring it directly. Though the procedure was innovative in its indirect derivation of legal status in a national survey dataset, its accuracy remains unclear. Hall and Greenman (2015) used a similar strategy to study the occupational cost of being undocumented and found that workers lacking legal status faced more dangerous work conditions than native-born workers. In earlier work, however, Kandel and Donato (2009) found that undocumented Mexican workers were less likely to work on jobs that handle pesticides. Like earlier studies, we assess the effect of legal status on wages, but we also examine how legal status is linked to working hours, location of employment, self-rated health, and health care utilization. Below, we review relevant literature covering these topics.

Hours of work and health

Meta-analyses of twenty-one studies indicate a significant correlation between poor health symptoms and hours of work (Sparks et al. 1997). The fatigue associated with overtime work has been found to produce chronic impairments to physical health (Dembe et al. 2005), and studies from a variety of countries reveal that working long hours increases heart attacks and other cardiovascular problems (Uehata 1991; Starrin et al. 1990). Long hours of work also lead to negative effects on mental health, producing depression and other forms of psychological distress (Michie and Williams 2003; Baldwin, Dodd, and Wrate 1997; Shields 1999). Suicide rates also tend to increase in the population as rates of overtime work increase (Starrin et al. 1990). Studies have also found a link between overtime work and poor health habits, with people who work long hours being more likely to smoke and drink frequently (Maruyama and Morimoto 1996).

To the extent that undocumented migrants work longer hours than other workers, they can be expected to experience worse health outcomes. In addition, studies have found that excessive overtime and extended work hours increase the rate of occupational injury. Data from the National Longitudinal Survey of Youth (NLSY) showed, for example, that working at least 12 hours per day was associated with a 37 percent greater hazard rate, and working at least 60 hours per week was associated with a 23 percent greater hazard rate (Dembe et al. 2005).

Therefore, we hypothesize that undocumented immigrants work longer hours than legal immigrants and, thus, put their health at a higher risk. For the purposes of our study, two factors are important in understanding the long hours that undocumented immigrants often work. First, undocumented Chinese immigrants in most cases have paid high fees to come to the United States, and consequently, they need to make money quickly to pay off their debts. Second, undocumented status carries with it a lot of uncertainty. Those without documents fear that they will be deported at any moment and, therefore, feel they need to make the most of their time to make money.

Location of work and health

Most immigrant groups are concentrated in a few large cities, such as New York, Los Angeles, and Houston; but in recent years a growing number of immigrants have chosen to work in new destination areas. As these immigrants leave gateway cities, they also lose connections to friendship and kinship networks, thereby reducing the ethnic solidarity and support systems that typically prevail in larger gateway cities. Support from family and friends (Oppedal and Røysamb 2004; Draganovic 2014) and ethnic networks (Jasinskaja-Lahti et al. 2006) have been shown to have significant positive effects on immigrants' mental health, which leads us to hypothesize that immigrants working outside of gateway cities are more likely to suffer from mental illness because of the relative lack of social support in new destinations.

Living in an ethnic enclave can have both negative and positive effects on the physical health of immigrants. On one hand, high concentrations of disadvantaged minorities and neighborhood poverty may lead to lower health among immigrants (Do and Finch 2008). On the other hand, for immigrants who need health care, such as those who are elderly or pregnant, neighborhoods with high concentrations of immigrants may provide easier access to health-related information and support (Eschbach et al. 2004; Korinek and Smith 2011). Jobs in nongateway destinations often provide higher wages and sometimes include lodging, thus yielding financial gains to the immigrants in these new destinations. Since undocumented Chinese generally pay large fees to come to the United States, they often take on jobs regardless of working conditions to pay off their debts; therefore, we expect the undocumented immigrants in our sample to be more likely to work outside of New York City.

Legal status and health care utilization

As shown by prior research, immigrants face many challenges in making use of health care facilities in the United States (Hacker et al. 2011; Korinek and Smith 2011; Ransford, Carrillo, and Rivera 2010). Beyond economic and language barriers, the lack of familiarity with U.S. administrative systems and policies makes it difficult for the foreign-born to access medical care (Maldonado et al. 2013). In addition, many undocumented migrants choose not to go to hospitals or clinics either because they believe the staff might report them to legal authorities or because they fear they might be treated poorly because of their immigration status (Berk and Schur 2001; Maldonado et al. 2013). We hypothesize, then, that undocumented immigrants are less likely to go to a hospital or clinic when they become ill.

Data and Methods

This article relies on migration data collected by Liang and colleagues in New York City in 2004 (Liang et al. 2008). Liang and his research team carried out surveys in both migrant-sending areas in China and in New York City. The survey used three different questionnaires: a household questionnaire used in China, a household questionnaire used in the United States, and a community-level questionnaire for migrant-sending communities in China. For this article, we draw upon data from the New York City portion of the survey, collected using the U.S. household questionnaire, which included questions on basic sociodemographic characteristics, migration histories, marital histories, fertility histories, labor histories, consumption patterns, remittances, property ownership, and housing conditions. It also asked detailed questions about specific migration trips, including the date of travel, duration of the trip, smuggling fees paid, knowledge of the snakehead or smuggler, and the number of people on the trip. Given life history data, we measure legal status as time-varying, which allows us to do much more analysis than would be possible with cross-sectional data only.

Within the northeastern Fujian province, investigators selected eight towns known to send a large number of migrants to the United States and to the New York City region in particular. In each town, we gathered a sample of forty to fifty immigrants with migratory experience in the New York area, yielding information on 410 immigrants and their families. To study labor supply, the data provide us with a continuous variable for hours worked per week on U.S. jobs. Using the locational information from the survey, we generated a dichotomous variable to consider the effect of place of employment, creating a variable labeled "NYC," where 1 equaled "living in New York City" and 0 equaled "living outside of New York City." To measure health, we draw upon an ordinal variable on self-rated health, which varies from 1 to 5 (where 1 = *bad*, 2 = *not good*, 3 = *average*, 4 = *fairly good*, and 5 = *excellent*). It should be noted that self-rated health has been used in many previous studies as a variable to measure current and future health conditions (Jylhä 2009; Lundberg and Manderbacka 1996).

To derive our final outcome variable, we asked respondents what they would do if they or their family members became ill, offering them a choice of three options: go to a doctor's office or clinic, buy some medicine, or do nothing. Using the answers to this question, we generated a dichotomous variable "doctor" to measure the likelihood of health care utilization by immigrants, where 1 equaled "going to a doctor's office" and 0 equaled "either buy some medicine or do nothing."

We examine the effect of legal status on employment and health outcomes using ordinary least squares (OLS) regression, logistic regression, and ordered logistic regression, as appropriate, regressing each outcome on legal status (documented versus undocumented) and duration of time spent in the United States, and adding controls for demographic characteristics and education.

Results

Table 1 provides descriptive statistics for our dependent and independent variables tabulated separately for those with and without documents, and all immigrants combined. It is immediately clear that there is not a big difference in

TABLE 1

Descriptive Statistics for Sample of Immigrants from China to the United States

Variables	Documented Migrants	Undocumented Migrants	All Migrants
Work			
Hourly wage	7.983	7.459	7.707
Log of hourly wage	1.928	1.913	1.920
Hours of work per week	55.806	65.839	61.082
Personal background			
Age	41.066	34.791	37.844
Education: High school or beyond	0.210	0.215	0.212
Male	0.503	0.702	0.605
Married	0.884	0.607	0.742
Number of children	1.955	1.089	1.511
Working in NYC	0.845	0.775	0.809
Can't speak and/or can't understand English	0.583	0.632	0.608
Can speak and understand English a bit	0.339	0.326	0.332
Can speak and understand English well	0.078	0.042	0.059
Health			
Self-rated health: Very poor	0.017	0.000	0.008
Self-rated health: Poor	0.181	0.076	0.127
Self-rated health: Average	0.241	0.244	0.236
Self-rated health: Good	0.500	0.557	0.537
Self-rated health: Very Good	0.060	0.122	0.093
Seeing a doctor when ill	0.724	0.497	0.608
Migration background			
Currently has legal status	—	—	0.487
Years in United States	9.353	6.952	8.121

NOTE: For most variables, the n for all migrants is 372; variables related to work have 348 observations; the self-rated health variable has 247 valid observations.

wages by legal status, with undocumented migrants reporting a wage of $7.46 per hour compared with $7.98 for documented migrants, both well above the 2004 minimum wage of $5.15 in New York State. The muted difference may reflect the fact that undocumented immigrants are more likely to be male (70 percent; 50 percent among documented migrants), and among immigrants, as in the workforce generally, men earn more than women.

Initial results also seem to suggest that a higher proportion of undocumented immigrants report good or very good health. Among documented migrants, only 6 percent report excellent health and 50 percent report fairly good health, compared with figures of 12 percent and 56 percent, respectively, for undocumented migrants. At the other end of the scale, 18 percent of documented migrants report health that is not good and 2 percent report bad health, whereas among undocumented migrants the same figures are 8 percent and 0 percent, respectively. On average, the health rating for legal migrants was 3.4 on the 5-point scale compared with 3.7 for their undocumented counterparts. In the end, some 93 percent of undocumented immigrants considered their health to be average or better than average, while about 80 percent of legal immigrants did so. Undocumented migrants tend to be younger (around 35 years on average) than those with documents (around 41 years). Since younger migrants report more favorable health conditions, it is not surprising that self-reported health for undocumented (younger) migrants is better than for documented migrants.

Another major difference between the two groups is that undocumented immigrants work much longer hours with a mean around 66 hours per week compared with 56 hours for documented migrants. Indeed, some 57 percent of undocumented immigrants work more than 70 hours per week, and many reported working six days a week and 12 hours a day, suggesting that undocumented immigrants are likely to suffer more from the negative effects of working long hours. The largest difference between undocumented immigrants and documented immigrants is in the share who report that they would see a doctor if they or their family members fell ill. While 72 percent of documented immigrants said they would see a doctor when sick, only 50 percent of undocumented immigrants did so. In terms of sociodemographic background, undocumented Chinese immigrants tend to be younger, more frequently male, unmarried, have shorter stays in the United States, and have lower levels of English ability (both in terms of speaking and understanding).

Next we consider the wages of immigrants and present results in Table 2 from OLS models regressing logged hourly wages on legal status and other variables. Basic human capital variables such as age, education, and duration in the United States are all significant in expected directions. According to the estimates of model 2, wages rise up to the age of 40 before declining, are 32 percent greater for men than women, and rise by 1 percent for every additional year spent in the United States. We also observe a substantial wage premium for English language ability. Compared with immigrants who cannot speak or understand English, those who can speak and understand a bit earn 20 percent more per hour, and those who can speak and understand English well earn 42 percent more per hour. However, consistent with earlier research (Massey 1987), legal status does not have a significant effect on hourly wages. Our recent fieldwork in the Chinese immigrant community indicates that most of these low-skilled Chinese workers are employed in restaurants or other service industries, and interviews with employers suggest that employers care more about filling these jobs and retaining workers than offering lower wages to those without documents.

Table 3 presents an OLS regression of weekly work hours on legal status and selected other independent variables. The results show that gender, age, and legal status have significant effects on working hours of immigrants. According to model 2, men work almost 11 hours more per week than women; work declines

TABLE 2
Coefficients from OLS Regression Predicting Logged Hourly Wage

	(1)		(2)	
	B	t	B	t
Age	0.04	2.67**	0.04	2.48*
Age squared	−0.0004	−2.89**	−0.0005	−2.88**
Education: High school or beyond	−0.02	−0.31	−0.004	−0.08
Male	0.37	8.92***	0.32	6.89***
Married	0.02	0.32	0.01	0.19
Number of children	0.02	0.69	0.01	0.38
Living in NYC	0.02	0.4	−0.02	−0.39
English proficiency[a]				
Can speak and understand English a bit	0.26	5.65***	0.20	4.08***
Can speak and understand English well	0.44	4.93***	0.42	4.06***
Documented			0.03	0.61
Years in United States			0.01	2.27*
Constant	0.84	3.25***	0.85	2.92**
Adjusted R^2	.255		.262	

NOTE: $N = 346$.
*$p < .05$. **$p < .01$. ***$p < .001$.
a. Can't speak English and/or can't understand English is the reference category.

TABLE 3
Coefficients from OLS Regression Predicting Hours of Work per Week

	(1)		(2)	
	B	t	B	t
Age	−0.29	−2.94**	−0.31	−2.77**
Education: High school or beyond	−2.66	−1.50	−1.13	−0.61
Male	10.53	7.21***	10.93	6.64***
Married	−0.63	−0.30	−0.03	−0.01
Number of children	−1.83	−1.96*	−1.02	−1.00
Living in NYC	0.91	0.49	0.93	0.49
Currently has legal status			−5.58	−3.51***
Years in United States			0.03	0.13
Constant	68.76	20.78***	69.32	19.83***
Adjusted R^2	.222		.261	

NOTE: $N = 348$.
*$p < .05$. **$p < .01$. ***$p < .001$.

TABLE 4
Coefficients from Logistic Regression Predicting Employment in NYC

	(1)		(2)	
	B	t	B	t
Age	0.08	3.24°°°	0.07	2.66°°
Education: High school or beyond	−0.75	−2.36°	−0.74	−2.31°
Male	−0.45	−1.46	−0.58	−1.77
Married	0.16	0.36	0.19	0.44
Number of children	−0.19	−0.90	−0.23	−1.04
Currently has legal status			−0.01	−0.02
Years in United States			0.06	1.45
Constant	−0.63	−0.96	−0.58	−0.88
Pseudo R^2	.104		.110	

NOTE: N = 372; log likelihood = −161.466.
°p < .05. °°p < .01. °°°p < .001.

by around 2.8 hours per week with each additional year of age; and undocumented migrants work around 5.6 more hours per week than documented migrants, enabling them to accumulate greater weekly earnings (around $45 more assuming an hourly wage of $8). Marital status, number of children, education, and number of years in the United States do not show significant effects on working hours.

Table 4 reveals a typical story of migration: immigrants who choose to work outside of New York City tend to be younger and better educated. According to the estimates shown in model 2, each year of age raises the odds of working in New York City by around 7 percent (exp[0.07] = 1.072), and those who have a high school or greater education are 48 percent more likely to work outside the city (exp[−0.74] = 0.478). Although earlier descriptive statistics indicated that undocumented immigrants had a higher proportion working outside of New York City, results presented in Table 4 show that legal status of immigrants does not have a significant impact on job location once individual-level characteristics are taken into account.

Turning to the relationship between legal status and health, we caution readers that there is a high proportion of missing data for the self-rated health variable. Although the descriptive statistics indicate that undocumented migrants generally rated their health better than legal immigrants, we should not jump to the conclusion that being documented has a negative effect on health. Differences in other independent variables between the two groups of immigrants might have led to this result. Indeed, as indicated by the ordered logistic regression model shown in Table 5, the only statistically significant effect on self-rated health is location of employment. The ordered logit coefficient indicates that moving from outside to inside New York City would reduce the ordered log-odds of being in a higher health category by a sizable 1.24 units, holding constant the influence of other variables in the model. Of course, we cannot exclude the possibility of

TABLE 5
Coefficients from Ordered Logistic Regression Predicting Self-Rated Health

	(1)		(2)	
	B	t	B	t
Age	−0.03	−1.61	−0.02	−1.21
Education: High school or beyond	−0.61	−1.90	−0.57	−1.76
Male	0.39	1.48	0.43	1.53
Married	−0.05	−0.13	−0.03	−0.07
Number of children	−0.04	−0.22	0.02	0.10
Living in NYC	−1.28	−3.4***	−1.24	−3.25***
Currently has legal status			−0.28	−0.99
Years in U.S.			−0.03	−0.92
Intercept 1	−7.13	−7.37***	−7.12	−7.33***
Intercept 2	−4.13	−6.13***	−4.11	−6.07***
Intercept 3	−2.68	−4.16***	−2.65	−4.09***
Intercept 4	0.36	0.58	0.40	0.64
Pseudo R^2	.048		.052	

NOTE: N = 247; log likelihood = −281.282.
***$p < .001$.

reverse causation if immigrants who are in worse health prefer to live in New York City to take advantage of stronger support networks and easier access to health care.

Table 6 shows a logistic regression equation predicting the likelihood of going to see a doctor when illness strikes one's self or one's family. The significant determinants here are legal status and time spent in the United States. The logistic regression coefficient of 0.66 for documented migrants means that the odds of going to a doctor are almost two times greater for those with legal papers than for those without ($\exp[0.66] = 1.93$). This is consistent with previous studies that find that undocumented immigrants tend to avoid formal organizations out of fear (Yoshikawa 2011). Immigrants who have lived in the United States for a longer period of time are also significantly more likely to see a doctor when they or their family members are ill, with the odds of seeing a doctor rising by 16 percent with each additional year of U.S. residence ($\exp[.0.15] = 1.16$). Gender, marital status, and education level do not have significant effects. These results support the hypothesis that undocumented immigrants are less likely to see a doctor when sick because they are not familiar with the U.S. medical system and policies and are worried about being identified by the authorities.

To illustrate the effect that legal status has on hours of work and the likelihood of seeing a doctor, we use the equation estimates in Tables 3 and 6 to generate predicted values, assuming average values of independent variables observed for documented and undocumented migrants (see Table 1). The comparison is thus between a typical undocumented immigrant and a typical documented immigrant in our sample. This exercise reveals that the typical undocumented

TABLE 6
Coefficients from Logistic Regression Predicting Seeing a Doctor When Ill

	(1)		(2)	
	B	t	B	t
Age	0.02	(1.12)	−0.02	(−0.93)
Education: High school or beyond	−0.12	(−0.41)	−0.02	(−0.05)
Male	0.12	(0.50)	−0.16	(−0.59)
Married	0.66	(1.930)	0.59	(1.66)
Number of children	0.05	(0.31)	−0.06	(−0.38)
Living in NYC	0.66	(2.25)°	0.55	(1.83)
English proficiency[a]				
Can speak and understand English a bit	0.26	(0.98)	−0.22	(−0.77)
Can speak and understand English well	1.25	(2.23)°	0.29	(0.46)
Currently with legal status			0.66	(2.58)°°
Years in U.S.			0.15	(4.18)°°°
Constant	−1.55	(−2.6)°°	−0.99	(−1.57)
Pseudo R^2		.058		.116

NOTE: N = 370; log likelihood = −233.815.
°$p < .05$. °°$p < .01$. °°°$p < .001$.
a. Can't speak English and/or can't understand English is the reference category.

immigrant will work for 70 hours per week compared to 56 hours per week for documented migrants. In addition, a typical documented immigrant is predicted to have a probability of .90 to see a doctor when ill compared to a probability of .64 for undocumented immigrants.

Conclusion

Understanding how undocumented status affects labor market and health outcomes is not only important for immigration policy but also for the well-being of millions of undocumented immigrants in the United States. Our analysis moves beyond the usual focus on wages alone by studying other aspects of employment and health, including hours of work, spatial location of job, self-rated health, and health care utilization. Our study of Chinese immigrants is also novel, inasmuch as most of the prior work on the effects of legal status draws on surveys of Mexican and Latino immigrants.

Appreciating the contribution of this research means understanding its limitations. Our research is cross-sectional and not well suited for making causal inferences. Legal status is a process, not an event. Ideally we would have modeled immigrant's legalization process, given that research (Jasso et al. 2008) shows that about 30 percent of new green card holders have prior undocumented experience. Treating all currently documented immigrants as "legal" does not allow us to take into account the likelihood that many were once undocumented. Our data do contain detailed job histories and legal status of immigrants at each job, but given the large number of jobs and memory, there are many missing values. We plan to develop procedures to deal with missing data issues in future work. Another possibility is to treat legal status as an "exposure" variable measured as time spent in undocumented status to assess cumulative effects on immigrant health.

Notwithstanding these drawbacks, our study provides some important findings for immigration research. One such major finding is that undocumented immigrants and their family members are less likely to see a doctor when someone gets sick, for fear of being identified by the authorities. This behavior could lead to long-term consequences for this population. For migrants themselves, going to see a doctor can lead to earlier detection and treatment of diseases (such as cancer). In addition, as Yoshikawa (2011) argues, the health of undocumented immigrants, especially mental health, also affects the development of their children (often children who are U.S. citizens). Perhaps the most important finding from our current study is that undocumented immigrants work much longer hours than do documented immigrants. This is important because previous studies have linked working long hours to higher incidences of heart attacks and a significantly greater chance of suffering from mental illness (Michie and Williams 2003; Sparks et al. 1997; Uehata 1991). Several recent tragedies in the immigrant community illustrate this reality. In 2011, 18-year-old Joaquin Luna committed suicide because he felt his undocumented status limited his options for the future (Fernandez 2011). In 2013, an undocumented Chinese immigrant killed his cousin's wife and four children in Brooklyn because he felt everyone around him was more successful (Schweber 2015). Millions of undocumented immigrants struggle with anxiety and depression in the U.S. labor market, making the plight of undocumented migrant workers important for policymakers and immigration scholars (American Psychological Association 2013; Sullivan and Rebm 2005).

References

American Psychological Association (APA). 2013. *Working with immigrant-origin clients: An update for mental health professionals*. Washington, DC: APA.

Baldwin, P. J., M. Dodd, and R. M. Wrate. 1997. Young doctors' health? How do working conditions affect attitudes, health and performance. *Social Science and Medicine* 45 (1): 35–40.

Berk, Marc L., and Claudia L. Schur. 2001. The effect of fear on access to care among undocumented Latino immigrants. *Journal of Immigrant Health* 3 (1): 151–56.

Dembe, A. E., J. B. Erickson, R. G. Delbos, and S. M. Banks. 2005. The impact of overtime and long work hours on occupational injuries and illnesses: New evidence from the United States. *Occupational and Environmental Medicine* 62 (9): 588–97.

Do, D. Phong, and Brian K. Finch. 2008. The link between neighborhood poverty and health: Context or composition? *American Journal of Epidemiology* 168 (6): 611–19.

Draganovic, Selvira. 2014. Reaching out: Social support and mental health problems of Bosnian immigrants in Switzerland. *Epiphany* 7 (1): 199–217.

Eschbach, Karl, Glenn V. Ostir, Kushang V. Patel, Kyriakos Markides, and James S. Goodwin. 2004. Neighborhood context and mortality among older Mexican Americans: Is there a barrio advantage? *American Journal of Public Health* 94 (10): 1807–12.

Fernandez, Manny. 11 December 2011. Disillusioned young immigrant kills himself, starting an emotional debate. *New York Times*.

Hacker, Karen, Jocelyn Chu, Carolyn Leung, Robert Marra, Alex Pirie, Mohamed Brahimi, Margaret English, Joshua Beckmann, Dolores Acevedo-Garcia, and Robert P. Marlin. 2011. The impact of immigration and customs enforcement on immigrant health: Perceptions of immigrants in Everett, Massachusetts, USA. *Social Science & Medicine* 73 (4): 586–94.

Hall, Matthew, and Emily Greenman. 2015. The occupational cost of being illegal in the United States: Legal status, job hazards, and compensating differentials. *International Migration Review* 49 (2): 406–42.

Hall, Matthew, Emily Greenman, and George Farkas. 2010. Legal status and wage disparities for Mexican immigrants. *Social Forces* 89 (2): 491–513.

Jasinskaja-Lahti, Inga, Karmela Liebkind, Magdalena Jaakkola, and Anni Reuter. 2006. Perceived discrimination, social support networks, and psychological well-being among three immigrant groups. *Journal of Cross-Cultural Psychology* 37 (3): 293–311.

Jasso, Guillermina, Douglas S. Massey, James P. Smith, and Mark Rosenzweig. 2008. From illegal to legal: Estimating previous illegal experience among immigrants in the United States. *International Migration Review* 42 (4): 803–42.

Jylhä, Marja. 2009. What is self-rated health and why does it predict mortality? Towards a unified conceptual model. *Social Science & Medicine* 69 (3): 307–16.

Kandel, William A., and Katherine M. Donato. 2009. Does unauthorized status reduce exposure to pesticides? Evidence from the National Agricultural Workers Survey. *Work and Occupations* 36 (4): 367–99.

Korinek, Kim, and Ken R. Smith. 2011. Prenatal care among immigrant and racial-ethnic minority women in a new immigrant destination: Exploring the impact of immigrant legal status. *Social Science & Medicine* 72 (10): 1695–1703.

Liang, Zai, Miao David Chunyu, Guotu Zhuang, and Wenzhen Ye. 2008. Cumulative causation, market transition, and emigration from China. *American Journal of Sociology* 114 (3): 706–37.

Lundberg, Olle, and Kristiina Manderbacka. 1996. Assessing reliability of a measure of self-rated health. *Scandinavian Journal of Public Health* 24 (3): 218–24.

Maldonado, Cynthia Z., Robert M. Rodriguez, Jesus R. Torres, Yvette S. Flores, and Luis M. Lovato. 2013. Fear of discovery among Latino immigrants presenting to the emergency department. *Academic Emergency Medicine* 20 (2): 155–61.

Maruyama, Soichiro, and Kanehisa Morimoto. 1996. Effects of long working hours on lifestyles, stress and quality of life among intermediate Japanese managers. *Scandinavian Journal of Work, Environment and Health* 22 (5): 353–59.

Massey, Douglas S. 1987. Do undocumented migrants earn lower wages than legal immigrants? New evidence from Mexico. *International Migration Review* 21 (2): 236–74.

Massey, Douglas S., and Kerstin Gentsch. 2014. Undocumented migration and the wages of Mexican immigrants in the United States. *International Migration Review* 48 (2): 482–99.

Michie, Susan, and Steve Williams. 2003. Reducing work related psychological ill health and sickness absence: A systematic literature review. *Occupational and Environmental Medicine* 60 (1): 3–9.

Oppedal, Brit, and Espen Røysamb. 2004. Mental health, life stress and social support among young Norwegian adolescents with immigrant and host national background. *Scandinavian Journal of Psychology* 45 (1): 131–44.

Phillips, Julie A., and Douglas S. Massey. 1999. The new labor market: Immigrants and wages after IRCA. *Demography* 36 (2): 233–46.

Ransford, H. Edward, Frank R. Carrillo, and Yessenia Rivera. 2010. Health care-seeking among Latino immigrants: Blocked access, use of traditional medicine, and the role of religion. *Journal of Health Care for the Poor and Underserved* 21 (3): 862–78.

Shields, Margot. 1999. Long working hours and health. *Health Reports* 11 (2): 33–48.

Schweber, Nate. 7 October 2015. Brooklyn man pleads guilty of killing cousin's wife and four children. *New York Times*.

Sparks, Kate, Cary Cooper, Yitzhak Fried, and Arie Shirom. 1997. The effects of hours of work on health: A meta-analytic review. *Journal of Occupational & Organizational Psychology* 70 (4): 391–408.

Sullivan, Margaret M., and Roberta Rebm. 2005. Mental health of undocumented Mexican immigrants: A review of the literature. *Advances in Nursing Science* 28:240–51.

Starrin, Bengt, Gerry Larsson, Sten-Olof Brenner, Lennart Levi, and Inga-Lill Petterson. 1990. Structural changes, ill-health, and mortality in Sweden, 1963–1983. A macroaggregated study. *International Journal of Health Services* 20 (1): 27–42.

Uehata, Tetsunojo. 1991. Long working hours and occupational stress-related cardiovascular attacks among middle-aged workers in Japan. *Journal of Human Ergology* 20 (2): 147–53.

Yoshikawa, Hirokazu. 2011. *Immigrants raising citizens*. New York, NY: Russell Sage Foundation.

Legal Status, Gender, and Labor Market Participation of Senegalese Migrants in France, Italy, and Spain

By
ERIK R. VICKSTROM
and
AMPARO GONZÁLEZ-
FERRER

Policymakers are understandably concerned about the integration of migrants into labor markets. This article draws on retrospective data from the MAFE-Senegal (Migration between Africa and Europe) survey to show that the effect of legal status on Senegalese migrants' labor market participation in France, Italy, and Spain differs for men and women because of gendered immigration policies. We find that there is little association between Senegalese men's legal status and their labor force participation. For Senegalese women, however, those who legally migrate to these countries for family reunification are more likely to be economically inactive upon arrival than women with other legal statuses. Family reunification does not preclude labor market participation entirely, however, as some of these women eventually transition into economic activity.

Keywords: immigration; Europe; legal status; labor market integration; Senegal

The labor market integration of migrants is a major concern for policymakers, as is the legal status of immigrants in the labor market. Immigration-control legislation that confers residence and work authorization should theoretically mediate migrants' access to the labor force, but the presence and economic activity of millions of undocumented migrants in different receiving countries indicates that irregular legal status[1] is often not a barrier to work. Indeed,

Erik R. Vickstrom is a research associate with IZA-Institute for the Study of Labor. His research has been published in International Migration Review, The Annual Review of Sociology, and Ethnic and Racial Studies.

Amparo González-Ferrer is a senior research fellow at the Spanish National Research Council (CSIC) and a member of the Research Group on Demographic Dynamics. She is currently coordinating an EU project titled TEMPER-Temporary versus Permanent Migration (http://temperproject.eu/) and was main investigator of the Spanish team of MAFE-Migration between Africa and Europe, both funded by the VII Framework Program of the EU Commission.

Correspondence: erikvickstrom@gmail.com

DOI: 10.1177/0002716216643555

some research suggests that immigrants are able to find work precisely because of their irregular legal status, which removes most legal recourse against exploitation by unscrupulous employers (Portes 1978). Most migrants are thus assumed to have economic motivations for their migration and to work in the destination economy regardless of their legal status.

Perceptions of the link between migrants' legal status and economic incorporation, though, often fail to consider the role of gender. While postwar labor migrants to the United States and Western Europe were mostly male, flows of immigrants since the 1970s have seen an increasing share of women. Many of these women have entered through legal channels of family reunification (Kofman 1999). Although research has underlined the heterogeneity of these migrant women's legal and economic situations, family-reunification policies have been highly gendered and have largely consigned women to economic and administrative dependency on their male sponsors. In addition, different countries award different authorizations to reunified family members, thus creating different forms of dependency (González-Ferrer 2011b).

These policies have created a gendered asymmetry between legal status and work for migrant men and women: migrant women enter their destination countries through legal channels more frequently than men, but restrictions on work access often attached to their authorization may imply that they are initially less likely to work than their male counterparts, even when men are in an irregular administrative situation. While migrant women's lower likelihood of work has provoked concerns about the growing number of inactive and "unproductive" migrants in some countries (Constant and Zimmermann 2005), the initial gendered asymmetry of migrant work may obscure the subsequent mobility of women into the labor market. The impact of legal status on labor market integration thus seems to depend on gendered channels created by immigration policies.

This article draws on the literature on the gendering of immigration policies to examine the link between legal status and economic incorporation of Senegalese migrants in France, Italy, and Spain. We argue that the effect of legal status on Senegalese migrant's labor market participation will differ for men and women because of gendered immigration policies. The next section of the article reviews the literature on gendered immigration policies and the creation of migrant women's economic and administrative dependency. The third section lays out the article's hypotheses. The fourth section reviews the data and presents the methods. We draw on a unique multisite survey of Senegalese migrants that has detailed and time-varying information on economic activity and legal status but lacks explicit information about migrants' "category of admission" (i.e., whether people used legal family reunification channels). The fifth section presents the results, and the sixth discusses the findings and conclusions.

Literature Review

Gendered channels of migration

Research since the 1980s has increasingly focused on the exclusion of women from studies of the economic incorporation of migrants (Kofman 1999, 2004a).

One of the main insights of this body of research is that immigration policies, while officially gender neutral, have differential impacts on the mobility and subsequent labor market participation of male and female migrants (Lesselier 2008). Men were the primary beneficiaries of labor-recruitment policies in both the United States and Western Europe through the 1960s and 1970s (Mahler and Pessar 2006; Lesselier 2008). Governments, especially those in Western Europe, severely restricted these legal channels of labor immigration after the mid-1970s but continued to allow migrants legally residing in destination countries to bring close family members to the host country under family reunification schemes.

Indeed, family reunification has become the main channel of legal entry into most Western European countries (Kofman 1999). In France, for example, 70 percent of entries in 2008 were for family reasons, and family reunification with long-term foreign residents has made up between 90,000 and 150,000 entries per year since 2000 (Lesselier 2008). Research has shown, though, that family reunification is highly gendered: women, mostly spouses, make up the majority of reunified family members (Kofman 1999). Fully 80 percent of annual entries for family reunification in France were women (Lesselier 2008). While not all women are reunified spouses—research has increasingly pointed to a growing "feminization" of autonomous migration (Kofman 2004b)—family reunification remains the dominant channel of entry for women into most destinations and structures their legal and economic incorporation into those destination countries.

Reunification and gendered dependency

Research has shown that family reunification policies create economic and administrative dependency for women and that these forms of dependency have implications for women's economic participation in destination-country labor markets (Boyd 1997; Lesselier 2008). Economic dependency among reunified spouses may arise from the legal requirements of demonstration of means of support by the sponsor. Family reunification policies often define male migrants as the primary breadwinners through the economic conditions imposed for reunification (Kofman 2004a; Mahler and Pessar 2006), creating economic dependency of women on their husband's income (Lesselier 2008). Reunified spouses may thus be less likely to work because of their sponsors' relatively high socioeconomic status (Toma 2012).

Economic dependency of reunified spouses may also arise because of legal barriers to their labor market participation. Legislation may impose waiting periods on the ability of reunified spouses to apply for and receive work permits, as is the case in Italy and Spain[2] (Kofman 1999). The separation of residence and work permits that is common in Europe thus means that the legal right to reunify is not always synonymous with the legal right of reunified spouses to enter the labor force (Boyd 1989). Indeed, research on the "admission category" of migrants has generally found that refugees and reunified family members have worse labor market outcomes than those of economic migrants (Constant and Zimmermann 2005). These findings demonstrate the barriers that admissions policies impose rather than the motivations or unobserved characteristics of the admitted migrants (González-Ferrer 2011a). Reunified women who are excluded from the labor force as a result of legal waiting periods are thus dependent on their spouses for economic support, or they are forced to work illegally. Indeed, women who have economic in addition to family motivations (i.e., to join a spouse) for migration may bypass the legal reunification channel because it imposes additional costs in terms of money and time but guarantees no better conditions in terms of accessing the labor market than irregular channels of reunification (González-Ferrer 2011a).

In addition to economic dependency as a result of family reunification, women are often subject to administrative dependency. Immigration legislation makes the possibility of reunification conditional on the sponsor's regular legal status (Lesselier 2008). A woman wishing to rejoin her husband legally is therefore dependent on his acquisition of regular legal status. In addition, the legal status of reunified spouses after arrival is dependent on the primary migrant's continued possession of regular legal status and the continuation of the marriage (Lesselier 2008).

Women's geographic mobility is thus subject to dependency both in relation to the state and within the household (Kofman 2004b). These asymmetric power relations may reduce women's autonomy in making decisions about labor market participation by tying them administratively to a husband's legal situation. This dependency can decrease women's bargaining power within the household, giving them less voice in their husbands' decisions in the allocation of their labor to either productive or reproductive efforts (Kofman 1999). In countries such as France where there is no waiting period to apply for a work permit, administrative dependency can still hamper reunified wives' labor participation by tying women's legal right to work to men's regular status (Lesselier 2008).

The administrative dependency fostered by family reunification also creates a gendered pathway into irregular status. Family reunification is not an automatic right conferred on migrants; on the contrary, states have imposed increasingly restrictive conditions that primary migrants have to meet before being allowed to bring family members to the destination country (Kofman 2004a). These conditions often require the sponsor to have a minimum period of prior residence, a stable income, and adequate housing in addition to regular legal status. The reunification of women whose husbands lack regular status or any of the other legal conditions must take place outside of the formal legal channel of reunification, for example, by overstaying an entry for tourism or other purposes (Lesselier 2008). Empirical research has shown that restrictive conditions do indeed lead to the incentivization of reunification outside or on the fringes of the legal system, especially among reunified wives who work upon arrival (González-Ferrer 2011b).

Family reunification and configurations of legal status

The specific legal rights granted to reunified migrants vary across destinations, giving rise to different legal statuses corresponding to different types of motivations for migration in different countries. For the purposes of this article, it is useful to examine the legal statuses granted to reunified spouses in France, Italy,

TABLE 1
Typology of Female Migrant Types by Legal Status and Country

	Legal Status		
Country	Regular	Mixed	Irregular
France	Reunified spouse	Student	Multiple
Spain	Worker	Reunified spouse	Multiple
Italy	Worker	Reunified spouse	Multiple

and Spain. In France, the legal reunification channel has consistently conferred the legal right to reside and work to reunified spouses (Lesselier 2008). Thus, women who follow the legal channel in France have legal authorization to work upon arrival. In Italy and Spain, however, immigration legislation has imposed a waiting period on reunified spouses' access to the labor markets; reunified spouses are thus likely to possess a residence permit but lack a work permit (Kofman 1999; González-Ferrer 2011b). The legal status granted to the category of "reunified spouses" and the concomitant legal access to the labor market thus varies across destinations. This variation is captured in the typology presented in Table 1.

Identical configurations of legal status can signal different types of (female) migrants under different legal regimes, as is evident in Table 1. For example, female migrants in France who lack a work permit—the legal status afforded to reunified spouses in Italy and Spain—are likely to be students. In contrast, female migrants in Spain and Italy with both a residence permit and a work permit—the legal status afforded to reunified spouses in France—are most likely labor migrants. There is thus substantial heterogeneity in the formal rights accorded to different admissions categories, making it imperative to examine both family context and legal status when considering the effect of family reunification on women's labor market participation.

Reunified women in the labor market

The economic and administrative dependency created by legal channels of family reunification may thus constrain women's legal participation in the labor force. Women have been marginalized in labor migration in part because many immigration policies implicitly assume that women are passive followers who do not seek employment (Kofman 2004a). Early research on the link between family ties and female migrants' economic participation tended to confirm this image. The "family migration model" (Sandell 1977) has traditionally seen migration as a disruptive event in women's work lives: because women are assumed to move as part of a family migration unit and the net benefit of a move for the family unit is positive, women will still migrate even if they are expected to have lower labor market participation rates after arrival (Sandell 1977; Mincer 1978).

Nonetheless, migrating for family reunification does not necessarily preclude participation in the labor force. Research has shown that family migration, far from hampering a tied mover's economic participation, can often lead to women's employment: the "family investment model" contends that women whose spouses have the highest expected earnings in a destination may actually be more likely to participate in the labor force and to be employed as a way of supporting their husbands' investments in destination-specific human capital (Duleep and Sanders 1993). Women's family context and the potential labor market success of a spouse thus emerge as important determinants of women's labor market performance.

Given that admission category/type of entry is not necessarily synonymous with the often multifaceted motivations for migration, it is also important to be attentive to transitions in both legal status and labor force participation after the year of arrival. Immigration policies with waiting periods built into their reunification regimes delay transitions from the initial status defined by this entry category: reunified spouses can eventually apply for formal permission to enter the labor force. Women's and households' preferences about the allocation of female labor may also shift over time, meaning that even reunified spouses who do not initially work despite a legal authorization to do so may eventually end up in the labor force. Indeed, women may have economic motivations for "associational" moves and may use family reunification strategically to enter labor markets while at the same time following socially sanctioned channels of mobility (Kanaiaupuni 2000).

When women do work, a gendered labor market funnels women into specific jobs, mostly in the informal sector (Lesselier 2008; Kofman 1999). For example, domestic work, especially in Southern Europe, draws women into low-skill, low-wage work (Kofman 1999, 2004b). Some countries, such as Italy and Spain, actively recruit female workers via employment quotas for low-skill domestic work (Kofman 2004b), while immigration legislation has also pursued high-skill migrants who tend to be male (Raghuram 2004; Lesselier 2008). Thus, immigration policies often actively channel women into specific low-wage sectors of the economy (with the exception of some female high-skill healthcare professionals; see Raghuram 2004). In countries such as France, where legal channels of labor immigration do not include such gendered occupations, women migrating autonomously for work are especially likely to do so irregularly (Lesselier 2008). Immigration policies thus conspire with gendered labor demand to create differential legal immigration channels and pathways of irregularity for men and women.

Limitations of Existing Research

It is clear that the labor market participation of female migrants is heterogeneous and is linked to their family context and the legal opportunities afforded by family-reunification policies, but much existing research on immigrant legal status and economic incorporation has been blind to the gendered nature of immigration policies and the legal statuses they create. Most studies of the United States, for example, do not examine the possibility that different legal statuses might have different effects for men and women; nor do they consider alternative measures of economic incorporation such as labor market participation or employment. Research in Europe has considered employment as an outcome with institutional variation in labor markets across multiple contexts of reception but has not been able to measure legal status or its differential effects for men and women.

Assuming participation: Undocumented status and wages in the United States

Most studies of the link between legal status and migrant economic incorporation in the United States find that undocumented status is associated with lower wages. Much of this research has used data from the Legalized Population Survey (LPS), conducted with a sample of undocumented migrants who were legalized by the 1986 Immigration Reform and Control Act (IRCA), to show that legalization was associated with an improvement in the economic opportunities among migrants whose status was adjusted (Rivera-Batiz 1999; Kossoudji and Cobb-Clark 2000, 2002); gaining regular legal status thus contributed positively to economic outcomes for migrants. At the same time, research has found that undocumented migrants faced additional deterioration in their earnings as a result of the stiffer penalties of this legislation, with employers passing on to them the costs and risks of unauthorized hiring (Donato and Massey 1993; Phillips and Massey 1999). Recent research, using longitudinal data with a larger comparison group and growth-curve modeling techniques, has continued to uncover disparities in earnings between documented and undocumented migrants (Hall, Greenman, and Farkas 2010).

Given the gendering of both migration policies and labor market participation, the negative effects of an undocumented status that research has put forth must be reexamined. Unfortunately, the studies cited above focus only on the United States and almost exclusively on Mexican men. While undoubtedly an important case to study given the high share of all immigrants in the United States that this group makes up, it is also a case with a distinct history and social and economic infrastructure (Massey, Durand, and Malone 2002), which, in some ways, might limit its generalizability. In looking almost exclusively at wages, these studies implicitly select only migrants who are both active in the labor market and employed. While some studies do attempt to model the effect of selection into the migrant labor force on wages (Massey 1987; Donato and Massey 1993), the issue of differential migrant participation in the labor market is not addressed as a main topic.

The assumption of both activity and employment might have held for earlier migration flows that were dominated by single, male workers (e.g., Piore's [1979] "birds of passage"); but most migration streams, even among Mexicans to the United States, have diversified in recent years. Women have made up larger shares of both documented and undocumented Mexican migrants since 1986 and accounted for 45 percent of all Mexican migrants in the United States in 2004 (Donato et al. 2008). Research has shown, though, that Mexican men and women in the United States have different motivations for migration: men tend to be motivated by employment and often move alone, while women almost always follow another family member and thus tend to have family motivations for their migration (Cerrutti and Massey 2001). The gendered nature of work means that these female migrants have different labor profiles than their male compatriots (Donato et al. 2008). Cultural understandings of women's role in the family have limited Mexican migrant women's ability to work: only 47 percent of Mexican-born adult women in the United States were in the labor force in 2006, compared to 88 percent of Mexican-born adult men (Donato et al. 2008). Motivations and value systems thus combine with reunification policies to limit women's participation in the labor market. Migrant women's labor market integration in destination countries therefore differs from that of men, and a focus on wages as the principal indicator of integration in the U.S. case excludes many women from the analyses.

Ethnic penalties on employment in Europe but no measures of legal status

The European research on immigrant economic incorporation helps to fill some of the blind spots in the American literature. Unlike in the United States, studies of immigrant labor market incorporation in Europe, where unemployment has historically been higher among both native-born and foreign workers, explain the likelihood of employment as a point of departure. This research has found, in general, that immigrants can often face an "ethnic penalty" (Heath and Ridge 1983) that translates into lower rates of employment compared to similar native-born workers (see Reyneri and Fullin [2011] for a review).

This general finding is tempered, however, by an insistence on cross-national variations in both the composition of migrant flows and institutional factors in the destination countries such as immigration policies, labor market structures, and welfare regimes. Kogan (2006) finds that male migrants from sub-Saharan Africa in fourteen European countries are substantially disadvantaged in their probability of employment compared to native workers, even after adjusting for human capital endowments, while migrants from Asia and Latin America have lower rates of unemployment than natives. This study also finds significant institutional variation across countries in the employment penalty: migrants face a lower penalty in countries with high demand for low-skilled labor, in countries with more flexible labor markets, and in countries with "liberal" welfare regimes, such as the UK and Ireland, which emphasize mobility and flexibility (Kogan 2006).

These cross-national institutional differences make a strong case for the importance of studying employment as an indicator of the labor market incorporation of migrants (González-Ferrer 2006). Earnings assimilation is a good measure of adaptation in countries with a flexible labor market and a low minimum wage, where immigrants can compensate for initial lower host country human capital by accepting lower pay (González-Ferrer 2006). Time spent in the destination can help immigrants to build human capital and "catch up" to natives in earnings, as has been found in the United States (Chiswick 1978; Borjas 1985, 1995). Institutional features such as labor market flexibility, however, vary cross-nationally; and in countries with less flexible labor markets there has been little evidence of earnings assimilation. These are the labor markets identified by the cross-national research as subjecting immigrants to an employment penalty, and additional years in the destination might reduce earnings because of a lack of initial attachment to the labor market (González-Ferrer 2006). Assimilation in the probability of employment is thus the process of primary concern in understanding the labor market performance of immigrants in highly regulated countries (González-Ferrer 2006).

Unfortunately, the European cross-national research is hampered by a number of issues that limit its applicability to the study of the impact of legal status on immigrant economic incorporation. The biggest limitation is the inability of most studies to include direct measures of migrants' legal statuses. Most studies simply compare legal immigrants to natives because data on legal status are not available: study designs either precluded sampling irregular migrants (Kogan 2006) or did not include questions on legal status (Bernardi, Garrido, and Miyar 2011). Even though studying the impact of legal status might not be the principal aim of these studies, they either acknowledge that the absence of unauthorized migrants in the sample may bias results (Kogan 2006) or point to the presence of unauthorized migrants as potential explanations for their findings (Bernardi, Garrido, and Miyar 2011). It is thus implicitly assumed that the legal limitations faced by migrants who lack regular status relegate them to temporary, low-skilled jobs in the informal sector that offer little opportunity for mobility, and that this unobserved heterogeneity contributes to the poor outcomes observed for all migrants (Bernardi, Garrido, and Miyar 2011).

The lack of direct measures of legal status also hamper European studies' ability to examine the interaction between gendered family reunification policies, the legal statuses they create, and the differential economic outcomes of men and women. Those studies that do include measures of legal status often do not consider the gendered family and legal contexts of women's work. Studies in Spain using the Encuesta Nacional de Inmigrantes (ENI) show that lack of regular status constitutes both a barrier to employment and a brake on earnings for immigrants in Spain (Bradatan and Sandu 2012; Amuedo-Dorantes, Malo, and Muñoz-Bullón 2013), but these studies do not consider how the effect of legal status might vary for men and women; nor do they differentiate between types of migrants based on family context.

The literature reviewed above demonstrates that gender is a crucial factor to take into account when studying migration. While men certainly display a wide variety of motivations for migration, women's migration is extremely heterogeneous. Women are overrepresented in legal family-reunification flows, indicating that they face legal and social constraints on their mobility arising from gendered migration policies. At the same time, women also migrate outside of legal reunification channels, either as informal reunifiers or as autonomous migrants, and with a wide variety of legal statuses. This diversity in types of female migration creates different labor market trajectories. The existing literature on migrant economic incorporation is largely unable to deal with this diversity, as it does not account for either differential labor force participation or the interaction between legal status and gender. This article adopts an approach that is sensitive to the diversity of female migration types while also comparing women to men.

The Case of Senegal

The sub-Saharan African immigrant population in Europe, even if not a large group overall, is particularly subjected to stereotypes and discrimination in the labor market (Agudelo-Suárez et al. 2009; Beauchemin et al. 2010). In addition, sub-Saharan immigrants tend to be a masculinized group in most cases, with family patterns that diverge from those of both natives of European countries and most other migrant groups, contributing to the emergence of gendered channels of migration (Beauchemin, Caarls, and Mazzucato 2013). Migration from Senegal constitutes a useful case in the study of the relationships among legal status, gender, and labor market integration because Senegalese have been present in multiple contexts of reception, introducing variation in both labor market conditions and immigration policies, and because Senegalese migration has increasingly undergone feminization through family reunification and autonomous female migration (Toma 2012; Beauchemin, Caarls, and Mazzucato 2013).

Migration of Senegalese men to France began during the colonial period as a result of military conscription and intensified as demand for unskilled foreign labor increased during the French economic boom of the 1950s and 1960s (Manchuelle 1997). Senegalese men were also commonly employed in low-skilled manual jobs in France, especially as garbage collectors in Paris (Barou 1993). France closed its borders to labor immigration in 1974 and renegotiated the bilateral accord regulating Senegalese immigration in the same year, subjecting Senegalese to the necessity of a residence permit for the first time (Vickstrom 2013). Some Senegalese men responded by reunifying their families in France starting in the 1970s (Timera 1997), and the Senegalese women who came to France eventually found work in unskilled service jobs (Barou 1993). In addition, high-skilled migrants and students from Senegal increasingly chose to go to France because of language ties and the similarities in the educational systems of the two countries (Toma 2012). These migrants often occupy white-collar jobs in public administration.

Senegalese migrants started to seek out new destinations in southern Europe during the 1980s (Riccio 2008) in response to the increasing difficulty in entering, working, and living in France, along with the demand for inexpensive and flexible workers in the secondary and informal labor markets of Spain and Italy (Pascual de Sans, Cardelús, and Solana Solana 2000). Senegalese migrants first started settling in Italy in the late 1980s and worked as informal street peddlers in Rome and on the beaches of Italy's tourist areas (Schmidt di Friedberg 1993). While such work is associated with irregular legal status and inability to find a better job in the Italian labor market (Schmidt di Friedberg 1993; Riccio 2001), other Senegalese migrants may embrace this occupation as a part of a "transnational livelihood" (Kaag 2008). After Italian regularization campaigns in the late 1980s and early 1990s, Senegalese moved to the north of Italy to work in manual jobs in small industry, construction, and food processing (Tall 2008; Riccio 2008). Senegalese in Spain, like other African migrants, are concentrated in unskilled jobs in agriculture, construction, and services (Pascual de Sans, Cardelús, and Solana Solana 2000). Jobs in Spanish agriculture tend to be seasonal and pay low wages; construction work tends to pay better but is also temporary (Toma 2012). In addition to these manual jobs, Senegalese work in street peddling in Spain (Toma 2012).

These descriptions indicate diversity in the contexts of reception, legal statuses, and sociodemographic characteristics among Senegalese migrants in Europe. While some research has suggested that sub-Saharan Africans living in Europe face difficulties in finding a job because of their low levels of qualifications (González-Enríquez 2009), other studies have found that work is relatively easy to come by, partly as a result of the rejection of manual labor among native-born workers, but the wages are low and the working conditions poor (Pascual de Sans, Cardelús, and Solana Solana 2000). This inconsistency likely reflects a difference in labor market regulations and the extent of informal economies, as Senegalese migrants tend to face higher unemployment in France (Tall 2008) but tend to have worse jobs when employed in Southern Europe. Indeed, quantitative research on Senegalese occupational trajectories has confirmed that Senegalese migrants experience a drop in occupational status after arrival in Europe (Obucina 2013).

These variations are also related to legal statuses. Senegalese migrants, for example, have benefited from multiple amnesty programs in Southern Europe that have allowed transitions between formal and informal work. However, they have been increasingly subject to restrictive immigration policies in France, which have likely made such mobility difficult. Finally, the characteristics of Senegalese migrants differ across these countries: Senegalese migrants in France tend to be more educated than those in Italy and Spain, where they may have the greatest ability to convert their human capital into employment (Castagnone et al. 2013). The variations in occupational and administrative statuses among Senegalese migrants across Europe make them a useful group to study.

Senegalese migration to Europe, in addition to demonstrating useful occupational and legal variation, also has gendered features that make it an instructive case: it has traditionally been heavily masculinized but has undergone increasing feminization since the 1980s. This evolution is evident in the gender imbalance of Senegalese migrants in France, Italy, and Spain: 45 percent of Senegalese migrants in France are women, compared to only 23 percent in Spain and 15 percent in Italy (Toma 2012). This imbalance partly reflects differential preferences for family reunification across countries, along with different lengths of settlement and maturity of Senegalese flows (Kaag 2008; Baizan, Beauchemin, and González Ferrer 2011), and thus has implications for both the legal statuses and the economic incorporation of Senegalese migrants.

The gendered nature of Senegalese migration to Europe is related to the stratification of Senegalese society along gender lines. This stratification has implications for Senegalese women's geographical mobility and subsequent labor market integration. Toma (2012) reviews the literature on gender norms in Senegal and argues that gender strongly determines life prospects there. The "traditional conjugal contract" subordinates women to the authority of a breadwinner husband within the household and, by assigning women to household tasks, places them outside of public life (Toma 2012). The Senegalese nuptial system is patrilocal, with women residing with husbands' parents after marriage and providing labor to that household. Polygamy is also widespread in Senegal, and women must often live in the same household as their cowives (Toma 2012). As a result of these gender norms, women's work outside the home is stigmatized. In addition, women tend to be less educated than men and thus less likely to participate in the labor force: according to Demographic and Health Survey (DHS) data, only 38 percent of Senegalese women were working in 2006, compared to 66 percent of men (Toma 2012).

Research on family reunification among Senegalese migrants in Europe has found that Senegalese are reluctant to reunify wives of male migrants and has linked relatively low levels of reunification to traditional gender norms. Multisited families and conjugal distance are common in Senegalese society, meaning that spouses are accustomed to physical separation (Beauchemin, Caarls, and Mazzucato 2013). While early Senegalese migration to France was based on a model of circular mobility, wherein male migrants could regularly travel home to visit family and wives, increased state regulation and an economic crisis in the mid-1970s (Vickstrom 2013) made this mobility more complicated. Some Senegalese migrants responded by reunifying their wives in France, but reunification was never a universal objective of Senegalese migrants, partly because of the difficulty of reunifying polygamous households (Beauchemin, Caarls, and Mazzucato 2013). In the new destinations of Italy and Spain, different social origins meant that Senegalese migrants were not subject to the same traditional authority as Senegalese migrants in France, but they also tended to be members of the Mouride Islamic brotherhood. Combined with economic considerations, this religious adherence has made Senegalese migrants in new destinations reluctant to bring their spouses from Senegal (Beauchemin, Caarls, and Mazzucato 2013). Evidence from the Migrations between Africa and Europe (MAFE) project indicates that only 13 percent of Senegalese migrants in Europe are a part of totally reunified families, while almost half live in a different country from their spouse(s) and child(ren) (Beauchemin, Caarls, and Mazzucato 2013).

Despite the reluctance of Senegalese migrants in Europe to reunify, research has also shown that family reunification remains an important channel for the migration of Senegalese women to Europe. Approximately 40 percent of women in the MAFE sample reunite with a partner at the destination country, and having a partner abroad is associated with substantially increased odds of migration among Senegalese women (Toma 2012). While female autonomy is low in Senegal and independent migration of Senegalese women is socially discouraged, there is some evidence of increasing migration in the last decade of single women from Senegal (Beauchemin, Caarls, and Mazzucato 2013). Nonetheless, even single Senegalese women are unlikely to migrate without having ties to close family members at the destination, indicating that even they face a degree of social control (Toma 2012).

Hypotheses

The legal rules governing family reunification and social parameters of the family context of individuals' migration are thus important determinants of both legal status of reunified spouses and their labor market integration at destination.

Given the gendered nature of family-reunification flows, these legal and social parameters are likely to be more important for women than for men. The economic and administrative dependency associated with family-reunification policies suggest that *Senegalese women migrating for family reasons in the context of legal family reunification will be less likely to work upon arrival than either women migrating autonomously or men with any legal status.*

Cross-national variation in the rights accorded to reunified migrants suggests that different configurations of legal status in different countries will be related to both family reunification and labor market participation (see Table 1). Regular status (having both a residence permit and a work permit) among Senegalese women in France is likely to indicate family reunification and thus be associated with lack of labor market participation upon arrival. In contrast, mixed status (possessing a residence permit but lacking a work permit) among Senegalese women in Italy and Spain is likely to indicate family reunification and thus be associated with lack of labor market participation upon arrival.

In contrast to Senegalese women who migrate for family reunification, *Senegalese women who migrate autonomously will be more likely to be employed upon arrival.* This category includes women with fully regular status in Italy and Spain. While women with mixed status in France are likely to be students, their relative autonomy may also make them more likely to seek work. Women with irregular status in all three countries may also seek to participate in the labor market; women with irregular status may be autonomous or nonformal family reunifiers, either of which could be consistent with economic motivations for migration.

Senegalese men's labor market participation at destination, in contrast to that of Senegalese women, will not be as closely linked to channels of family reunification. Men's employment upon arrival will be more closely associated with cross-national variation in labor market segmentation and demand for low-skilled labor as research has found that immigrants, even the undocumented, do not necessarily face an employment penalty in such economies. Thus, *Senegalese men in Italy and Spain, where there is higher demand for low-skilled labor and where the informal economy is larger, will be more likely to work than Senegalese men in France, where there is a more formally regulated labor market.* Given the size of the informal economy in Southern Europe, *irregular status may also be associated with increased employment among men in these countries.*

The empirical analysis also focuses on employment dynamics for both women and men. While family reunification may be related to inactivity among women during the year of arrival, it does not necessarily preclude eventual labor market participation. Women who lack the legal authorization to work upon arrival can eventually apply for such authorization, and those who possess work authorization from the beginning of their stay may also eventually work. Thus, *Senegalese women who possess both a residence and work permit after the year of arrival are likely to make a transition into employment.*

As Senegalese men are likely to be in the labor force from the beginning of their stay at a destination, the analysis focuses on transitions out of employment (or, equivalently, into unemployment). *Senegalese men with regular status are likely to be the least likely to transition into unemployment* because of provisions in immigration legislation that link continued possession of legal status to formal employment and vice versa, especially in Southern Europe (Vickstrom 2014). On the other hand, demand for low-skilled labor and the extent of the informal economy in Southern Europe also make informal employment easier to access and irregular status less burdensome, meaning that *irregular status may also be negatively associated with transitions to unemployment.*

Data and Methods

This article uses data from the MAFE-Senegal survey,[3] drawing on the retrospective biographical data on Senegalese migrants' economic activities, union formation, childbearing, and administrative history. It is useful to note for the purposes of this article that women were oversampled in all locations to ensure a sufficient number for separate gender analyses.

The study population

The sample for the analysis in this article includes individuals who have migrated at least once to Italy, France, or Spain while they were older than 18. Returned migrants interviewed in Senegal are included if they spent at least a year in at least one of the destination countries. Individuals can have multiple periods of residence in or "trips" to one or more of these destination countries. The analytic sample thus comprises 7,881 person-years and 727 trips: 3,548 person-years in France (287 individual trips), 2,258 person-years (221 individual trips) in Italy, and 2,075 person-years (219 individual trips) in Spain. Sixty-five percent of respondents had only one trip, and an additional 21 percent had two trips.

The MAFE-Senegal data are well suited to this investigation because the multisited nature of the data collection reduces potential biases stemming from selective emigration and return (Massey 1987) through the inclusion of current and returned migrants. The data, in addition to reconstructing migrants' family and labor market trajectories, also include extensive information on migrants' legal statuses during each year of residence abroad. Lack of such data on legal status has been a major impediment to investigations of the effect of legal status on labor market performance of immigrants in Europe (González-Ferrer 2011a; Amuedo-Dorantes, Malo, and Muñoz-Bullón 2013). The MAFE project also interviewed both women and men, allowing investigations of differential incorporation by gender. The sample includes 376 (57 percent) men and 286 (43 percent) women, although the weighted percentage of men is 70 percent. While the MAFE data offer advantages for our analysis, they also suffer from a lack of explicit information on whether people used legal family reunification channels. Accordingly, we had to make assumptions on how different legal status combinations are indicative of family reunification channels.

Outcome variables

We examine Senegalese migrants' labor market performance in France, Italy, and Spain by focusing on three different outcomes: economic activity status during the year of arrival, transitions into (for women) or out of (for men) employment, and occupational category conditional on being employed. The MAFE questionnaire asked respondents to identify their principal activity for each period of their lives. Respondents could answer that they were studying, economically active, unemployed, homemaking, retired, or otherwise inactive. We created a categorical variable to indicate whether migrants were working, unemployed, or economically inactive, with the last category including students, homemakers, retirees, and other inactive individuals. Table 2 presents weighted descriptive statistics for the sample and shows statistically significant bivariate gender disparities in economic activity during the year of arrival: 2.7 percent of women and 8.5 percent of men were unemployed ($p < .01$), 38 percent of women and 76 percent of men were employed ($p < .001$), and 59 percent of women and 15 percent of men were inactive ($p < .001$) during the first year in destination.

Although this last category is heterogeneous across the entire sample, it is strongly gendered: 85 percent of men who were inactive during the year of arrival were students, and 91 percent of all economically inactive person-years among men were spent studying; while 73 percent of women who were inactive during the year of arrival were homemakers, and 77 percent of all economically inactive person-years among women were spent homemaking. Men never declared being a homemaker and were retired or otherwise inactive during 9 percent of person-years. Twenty-three percent of inactive women were students during the year of arrival, but studying only made up 16 percent of all inactive person-years among women.

We created two additional variables based on the economic activity variable: a variable capturing transitions into unemployment, if the categorical employment variable equaled "unemployed" at time $t + 1$; and a variable capturing transitions into employment, if the categorical employment variable equaled "employed" at time $t + 1$. These indicators will serve as dependent variables in models for dynamic transitions into unemployment for men and into employment for women.

Predictor variables

The key predictors in each model are variables measuring legal status. We constructed a typology of legal status categories using indicators of entry visas, residence permits, and work permits. A dichotomous variable indicates if a migrant entered the destination country at the start of the current trip with or without a visa. Annual indicators of residence and work permits combine to form a categorical variable capturing both forms of authorization. This categorical variable takes the values of "NRP_NWP" for migrants who lack both a residence permit and a work permit ("fully irregular status"), and "RP_WP" for migrants who possess both a residence permit and a work permit ("fully regular status").

TABLE 2
Descriptive Statistics

Variable	Year of Arrival							All Person-Years						
	Women		Men		Total			Women		Men		Total		
	Mean	SD	Mean	SD	Mean	SD		Mean	SD	Mean	SD	Mean	SD	
Legal status: irregular (NRP_NWP)	0.39	0.49	0.53	0.5	0.49	0.5	**	0.18	0.38	0.18	0.38	0.18	0.38	****
Legal status: mixed (RP_NWP)	0.15	0.35	0.13	0.33	0.13	0.34	****	0.12	0.33	0.09	0.29	0.1	0.3	**
Legal status: regular (RP_WP)	0.47	0.5	0.35	0.48	0.38	0.49	**	0.7	0.46	0.73	0.44	0.72	0.45	****
Entry without visa	0.35	0.48	0.4	0.49	0.38	0.49		0.36	0.48	0.45	0.5	0.43	0.49	****
Destination: France	0.76	0.43	0.43	0.5	0.53	0.5	****	0.83	0.37	0.52	0.5	0.61	0.49	****
Destination: Italy	0.11	0.31	0.32	0.47	0.26	0.44	***	0.073	0.26	0.31	0.46	0.24	0.43	****
Destination: Spain	0.13	0.34	0.25	0.44	0.22	0.41	****	0.092	0.29	0.17	0.38	0.15	0.36	****
Occupation: agriculture	0.04	0.20	0.13	0.34	0.11	0.32	****	0.014	0.12	0.056	0.23	0.046	0.21	****
Occupation: self-employment	0.15	0.36	0.34	0.47	0.30	0.46	****	0.09	0.29	0.17	0.37	0.15	0.35	****
Occupation: service	0.61	0.49	0.16	0.36	0.24	0.43	****	0.48	0.5	0.17	0.37	0.24	0.43	****
Occupation: manual	0.12	0.33	0.33	0.47	0.30	0.46	****	0.19	0.39	0.49	0.5	0.42	0.49	****
Occupation: white-collar	0.08	0.27	0.04	0.20	0.05	0.21	***	0.22	0.42	0.12	0.33	0.15	0.35	***
Unemployed	0.027	0.16	0.085	0.28	0.068	0.25	***	0.02	0.14	0.032	0.18	0.029	0.17	
Employed	0.38	0.49	0.76	0.43	0.65	0.48	****	0.65	0.48	0.88	0.32	0.81	0.39	***
Inactive	0.59	0.49	0.15	0.36	0.28	0.45	****	0.33	0.47	0.083	0.28	0.16	0.37	***
Years in destination	1	0	1	0	1	0		10.2	8.98	9.34	7.77	9.61	8.17	****
Arrival after 1990	0.8	0.4	0.7	0.46	0.73	0.44	****	0.54	0.5	0.51	0.5	0.52	0.5	****
Age at migration	28.7	7.72	28	7.13	28.2	7.31		27.2	7.96	26.8	6.56	26.9	7.02	****
Gender: male	0	0	1	0	0.71	0.45		0	0	1	0	0.7	0.46	
Years of education	10.1	5.47	9.74	6.22	9.85	6.01		8.78	6.2	9.56	6.24	9.33	6.24	****
Destination-specific education, years	—	—	—	—	—	—		0.89	1.93	0.73	1.9	0.78	1.91	****
Ethnicity: Wolof	0.35	0.48	0.58	0.49	0.51	0.5	***	0.28	0.45	0.52	0.5	0.45	0.5	****

(continued)

TABLE 2 (CONTINUED)

Variable	Year of Arrival							All Person-Years						
	Women		Men		Total			Women		Men		Total		
	Mean	SD	Mean	SD	Mean	SD		Mean	SD	Mean	SD	Mean	SD	
Religion: Mouride	0.33	0.47	0.42	0.49	0.39	0.49	°	0.21	0.41	0.38	0.49	0.33	0.47	°°°°
Economic status before trip	0.12	0.32	0.08	0.27	0.091	0.29		—	—	—	—	—	—	°°°°
Number of contacts at destination	2.56	2.00	1.69	2.00	1.94	2.04	°°°°	4.21	2.57	2.94	2.68	3.32	2.71	°°°°
Number of trips	1.35	0.72	1.70	1.18	1.60	1.08	°°°	1.23	0.58	1.63	1.26	1.51	1.12	°°°°
Does not speak destination language	0.17	0.38	0.36	0.48	0.31	0.46		0.17	0.38	0.32	0.47	0.28	0.45	°
Spouse or children at destination	0.64	0.48	0.099	0.3	0.26	0.44	°°°°	0.85	0.36	0.34	0.47	0.49	0.5	°°°°
Spouse or children in Senegal	0.42	0.49	0.47	0.5	0.46	0.5	°°°°	0.21	0.41	0.5	0.5	0.41	0.49	°°°°
Geographic origin: Dakar	0.35	0.48	0.29	0.45	0.3	0.46	°°°°	0.29	0.45	0.28	0.45	0.28	0.45	°°°°
Father's education: less than secondary	0.6	0.49	0.69	0.46	0.66	0.47	°°°	0.58	0.49	0.72	0.45	0.68	0.47	°°°°
Trip paid for by family	0.73	0.45	0.25	0.44	0.39	0.49	°°°°	0.67	0.47	0.29	0.45	0.4	0.49	°°°°
Definitive plans to stay	0.48	0.5	0.47	0.5	0.47	0.5	°°°°	0.4	0.49	0.48	0.5	0.46	0.5	°°°°
Trip motivation: work	0.24	0.43	0.65	0.48	0.53	0.5	°°°°	0.27	0.44	0.68	0.47	0.56	0.5	°°°°
One or more parent alive	0.93	0.26	0.89	0.31	0.9	0.3	°°°°	0.84	0.36	0.78	0.42	0.8	0.4	°°°°
Work experience in Senegal, years	5.02	8.25	10	9.27	8.58	9.27		5.37	6.84	7.42	7.67	6.8	7.49	°°°°
Work experience in destination, years	—		—		—			—		—		—		
N	300		427		727			3,315		4,566		7,881		

SOURCE: MAFE-Senegal. NRP_NWP = no residence permit and no work permit; RP_NWP = residence permit but no work permit; RP_WP = residence permit and work permit.

NOTE: Weighted statistics.

°p < .10. °°p < .05. °°°p < .01. °°°°p < .001.

"RP_NWP" indicates that migrants have a residence permit but lack a work permit ("mixed status"), a situation common among students and reunified family members in France, Italy, and Spain (Mezger and González-Ferrer 2013).

While the combination of lacking a residence permit and possessing a work permit is theoretically possible and is declared in 4 percent of person-years by Senegalese migrants, the immigration policies of the receiving countries have almost always made work permits conditional on possessing a permit to reside lawfully or possession of work permits have automatically made such residence lawful, and migrants may have declared this status because of recall bias or incomplete understanding of their statuses. We have thus chosen to exclude person-years in which migrants declared "NRP_WP" status from the analytic sample for this investigation.

Table 2 indicates that, during the first year in destination, Senegalese women are more likely to have fully regular status than men, while men are more likely to have fully irregular status; the proportions of women and men with mixed status during the first year are not statistically different. Approximately 17 percent of all person-years among both men and women display fully irregular status, with no significant gender difference. Women are significantly more likely to spend time in mixed status, accounting for 12 percent of their person-years compared to slightly more than 9 percent of men's. Women spend a slightly higher proportion of person-years in fully regular status. The fully regular category serves as the reference category in regression models. Regarding visa status, there was no statistically significant difference in the proportion of men and women arriving without visas.

The other key predictor variable is the context of reception, as captured by indicators for country of residence. Table 2 shows that women tend to be concentrated in France during the year of arrival: 76 percent of Senegalese women migrants live in France, compared to 11 percent in Italy and 13 percent in Spain. Only 43 percent of trips for men start in France, with 26 percent starting in Italy and 22 percent starting in Spain. A similar pattern for women holds across all person-years: they are overwhelmingly concentrated in France (83 percent of person-years). Men also tend to spend more time overall in France across all person-years (52 percent), while they spend 31 percent of person-years in Italy and 17 percent in Spain.

A dichotomous variable indicates whether the migrant has a spouse and/or children living in the same destination. According to Table 2, 64 percent of Senegalese women declared having a spouse and/or a child in the same destination at the year of arrival, while only 10 percent of men declared the same. A similar variable indicates whether the migrant has a spouse and/or children residing in Senegal: 42 percent of women and 47 percent of men declared having these family members at origin. An additional dichotomous variable indicates whether the migrant has at least one parent still alive in Senegal. All of the family variables are time-varying.

Variables indicating human capital during the year of arrival include years of education, ability to speak the language of the destination country (does not speak vs. speaks well or gets by), age at the time of the start of the trip, and years of work experience in Senegal prior to migration. Time-varying human capital indicators include the number of years spent in the destination, the cumulative years of education acquired in the destination, and the cumulative years of work experience acquired in the destination. Language ability can also vary over time. A variable measuring the number of family members and other close members of the migrant's personal network who live in the same destination country captures social capital and can vary over time. The number of trips a migrant has made indicates migration-specific capital. Other variables capture migrants' motivations: a dichotomous variable indicates whether work was the main motivation for migration, and another dichotomous variable indicates whether the migrant plans to stay definitively in the current destination.

Variables indicating the migrant's social and cultural context of exit include ethnicity (Wolof vs. other), religion (Mouride vs. other), and geographic origin (Dakar vs. other). Variables indicating the migrant's economic context of exit include self-reported economic status prior to migration (more than sufficient for daily needs and better than others in the same place vs. other), father's educational level (less than secondary school vs. secondary school or more, which is a proxy for social class), and financial participation of family members in the financing of the current trip (yes vs. no).

Models

We estimate separate models for men and women for the outcomes of economic activity status and transitions to and from employment. Due to sample size restrictions, separate models by gender for the occupational status outcome are not estimable; this model thus includes interactions between gender and other key predictors.

First-year economic activity. We estimate multinomial logistic regression models predicting economic activity status during the first year of residence in France, Italy, or Spain as specified by the following equation:

$$ln\left(\frac{\Pr\left(Activity_{it1} = i\right)}{\Pr\left(Activity_{t1} = Unemployed\right)}\right) = \alpha + X_1\beta_1 + X_2\beta_2 + (X_1 \times X_2)\beta_3 \\ + X_4\beta_4 + X_5\beta_5 + X_6\beta_6, \tag{1}$$

where i indexes activity states unemployed, employed, and inactive at time $t = 1$; X_1 is a vector of indicators of legal status (visa and residence/work authorization); X_2 is a vector of indicators of country of residence; $X_1 \times X_2$ represents the interaction between legal status and country of residence; X_4 is a vector of variables indicating human, social, and migration-specific capital; X_5 is a vector of variables indicating family links; and X_6 is a vector of variables capturing the migrant's context of exit. All variables in this model are measured at time $t = 1$, the year in which the migrant arrives at the destination. We estimate separate models for men and women.

We use discrete-time survival models to estimate the risk of transitions either into or out of employment. We select men for studying the first transition out of employment and estimate the following model:

$$ln\left(\frac{Pr\left(Unemployed_{t+1}\right)}{1-Pr\left(Unemployed_{t+1}\right)}\right) = \alpha + X_{1t}\beta_1 + X_{2t}\beta_2 + (X_{1t} \times X_{1t})\beta_3$$
$$+ X_{4t}\beta_4 + X_{5t}\beta_5 + X_{6t}\beta_6 + X_{7t}\beta_7, \tag{2}$$

where the outcome variable is a dichotomous indicator of unemployment at time $t + 1$. All of the predictor vectors are as in the first model, except that some can vary over time; these are thus measured at time t. X_4 additionally includes the number of years spent at the destination, the cumulative time spent in employment or in formal studies at the destination, the prestige score of the migrant's current job, and a dichotomous variable indicating the activity status of the migrant in year t (inactive vs. employed). X_7 is a vector of time-counting variables indicating the duration at risk for falling into unemployment (number of years) and the number of activity spells. Only men who are employed or inactive are subject to the risk of falling into unemployment, and exit the risk set either through censoring or becoming unemployed.

We select women for studying the first transition into employment and estimate the following model:

$$ln\left(\frac{Pr\left(Employed_{t+1}\right)}{1-Pr\left(Employed_{t+1}\right)}\right) = \alpha + X_{1t}\beta_1 + X_{2t}\beta_2 + (X_{1t} \times X_{2t})\beta_3$$
$$+ X_{4t}\beta_4 + X_{5t}\beta_5 + X_{6t}\beta_6, \tag{3}$$

where the outcome variable is a dichotomous indicator of employment at time $t + 1$. The predictors are identical to those in equation 2, with the exception of the employment-related variables, which are unmeasured for women because this model examines the risk of first entry into employment; the model for women does, however, include a variable indicating cumulative work experience in Senegal. Only women who are inactive or unemployed are subject to the risk of becoming employed, and exit the risk set either through censoring or becoming employed.

We present results from multivariate models in the form of average marginal effects (AMEs). AMEs are calculated by computing a marginal effect for each case and averaging the value over all cases. If predictors are categorical, the AME represents the expected change in the outcome with a discrete change in the value of the categorical variable. AMEs are useful for interpretation of results of nonlinear models, as they display the change in the outcome variable on its original scale with a one-unit change for a given predictor variable. Standard errors for AMEs are calculated using the delta method.

Gender, Partner Location, and Legal Status

The MAFE data show a clear connection between partner location and the vary-ing legal status configurations outlined in Table 1, which are indicative of family reunification for women in different destinations. Figure 1 shows the legal status of Senegalese men and women during the year of their arrival in Europe, by their destination and the location of their partners. Women who rejoin a partner in France are overwhelmingly likely to have fully regular legal status during their year of arrival: 63 percent of women with a partner in France possess this status, compared to only 33 percent of women in France without a partner in that loca-tion. Senegalese women with fully regular status in France and a spouse in that destination are thus likely to have accessed this status through legal channels of family reunification, as France's immigration policies allow both residence and work authorizations for reunified spouses.

In contrast, Senegalese women going to Spain or Italy to rejoin a partner are not likely to have fully regular status, and results are indicative of the operation of both legal and irregular channels of reunification. Mixed status—possessing a residence permit but lacking a work permit—is the most common for Senegalese women with a partner in Italy, indicative of family reunification in a legal context that imposes a waiting period on employment. Irregular status is also common among women joining a partner in Italy, which suggests the operation of an irregular-reunification pathway. In Spain, more than half of Senegalese women rejoining a partner report having either mixed or fully irregular status upon arrival, indicating the prevalence of both the legal channel of family reunification that imposes a work-authorization waiting period (giving rise to mixed status) and an irregular pathway to reunification. Figure 1 suggests that the distribution of legal statuses during the year of arrival among Senegalese men conditional on partner location does not vary as much as for women.

Examination of women's motivations for migration along with the location of their partner elucidates the link between family-reunification policies and women's first-year legal status. Figure 2 shows that women who migrate for family reasons and join a partner at destination are likely to have the configurations of legal status indicative of family reunification (fully regular status in France and mixed status in Italy and, to a slightly lesser extent, Spain). In contrast, women with a partner at their destination who migrate for work reasons are far more likely to have fully irregular status in all destinations, indicating a willingness to circumvent legal chan-nels of family reunification that may inhibit their ability to work upon arrival. These descriptive findings are suggestive of the link between women's legal status during the year of arrival and the gendered channel of family reunification.

First-Year Economic Activity

Legal status was hypothesized to have different effects for Senegalese men's and women's economic status during the year of arrival at destination. Descriptive

FIGURE 1
Legal Status at Arrival by Gender, Destination, and Location of Spouse

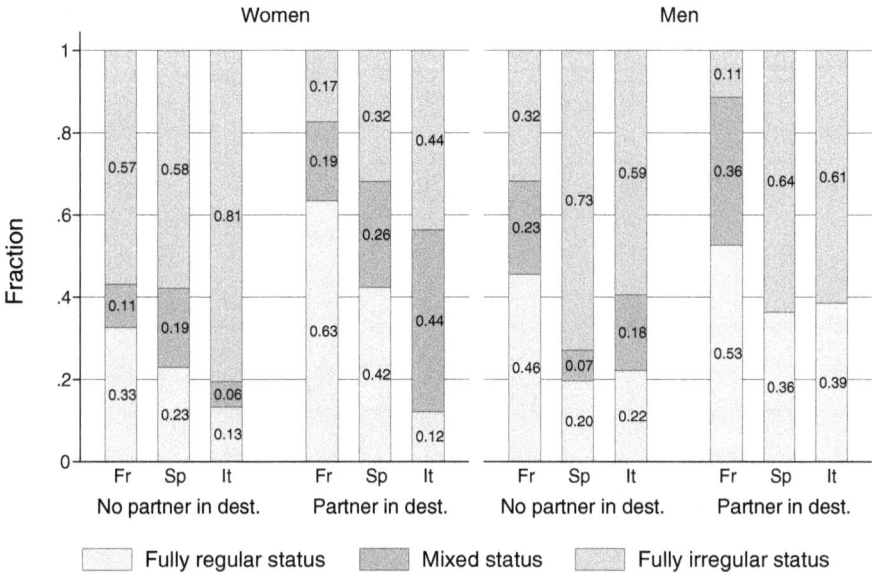

SOURCE: MAFE-Senegal.
NOTE: Weighted data.

statistics largely support this view, with much greater variation in economic activity across women's legal statuses than men's.

The descriptive statistics in Table 2 demonstrate differences in Senegalese men's and women's labor force participation during their year of arrival at destination: women are more likely to be inactive, and among those in the labor force, men are more likely to be unemployed. Figures 3 and 4 show additional variation in labor force participation and employment among both men and women by their legal status upon arrival and their destination country. Figure 3 shows that Senegalese men in France across all legal statuses tend to be inactive more frequently than Senegalese men in Italy or Spain, reflecting the fact that there is a significant flow of Senegalese students to France given the colonial and linguistic links between the two countries. Male migrants also tend to have a higher rate of inactivity in Spain and Italy when they have a mixed status upon arrival. A very small proportion of Senegalese men with fully regular status are inactive in Italy or Spain. Unemployment rates among men are quite low across countries and legal statuses. Having fully irregular legal status is positively associated with unemployment in Italy during the year of arrival, while a higher risk of unemployment is associated with having a mixed status in Spain.

Figure 4 shows a different pattern for women: rates of labor force participation and employment vary strongly by country of residence and legal status. Senegalese women with mixed status (RP_NWP) have the highest rates of

FIGURE 2

Legal Status among Senegalese Women during Year of Arrival, by Destination, Partner
Location, and Migration Motivation

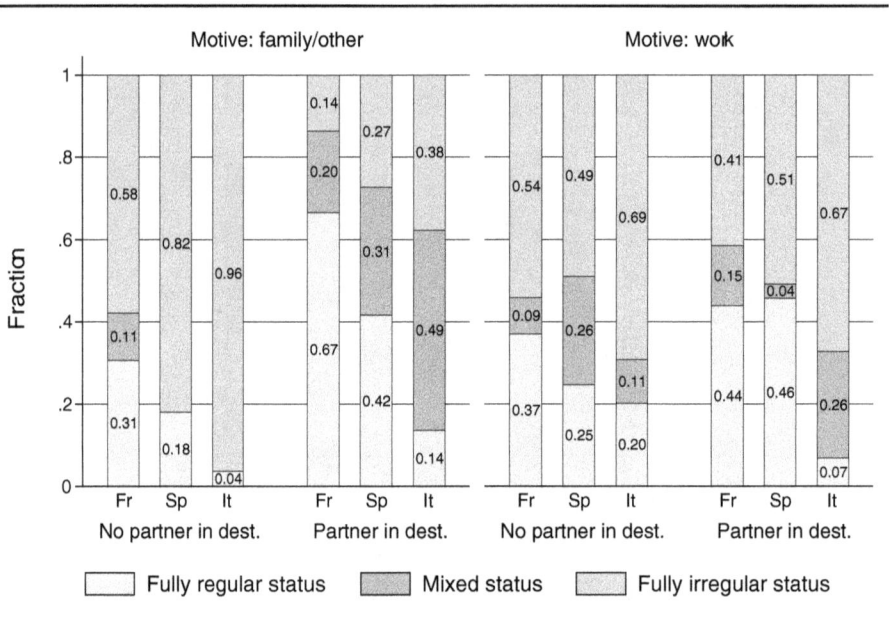

SOURCE: MAFE-Senegal.
NOTE: Weighted data.

inactivity, and these rates are higher in Spain and Italy than in France. Among
Senegalese women in France, those with fully irregular status have the lowest
rate of inactivity, while those with fully regular status have the highest rates of
inactivity. The pattern for Italy and Spain is reversed: female migrants with fully
irregular or fully regular statuses, respectively, have the lowest rates of inactivity.
As with male Senegalese migrants, having fully irregular status in Italy during the
year of arrival seems to increase the risk of unemployment for those women in
the labor market, especially compared to female migrants with fully regular status in Italy, who experience little unemployment during the year of arrival.
Female migrants in Spain and France seem to face low levels of unemployment
across legal statuses.

Results from the multinomial regression models for men and women also suggest that the effect of legal status on first-year economic activity is gendered.
Table 3 displays results from the separate multinomial logistic regressions of first-
year activity status for Senegalese men and women. For Senegalese men, having
mixed legal status (RP_NWP) is positively associated with being inactive: compared to male migrants with fully regular status, male migrants who lack only a
work permit are 6 percentage points more likely to be inactive. Conversely, legal
status does not have a statistically significant association with probabilities of
working or being unemployed during the year of arrival for men.

FIGURE 3

First-Year Activity Status by Legal Status and Country of Residence, Senegalese Men

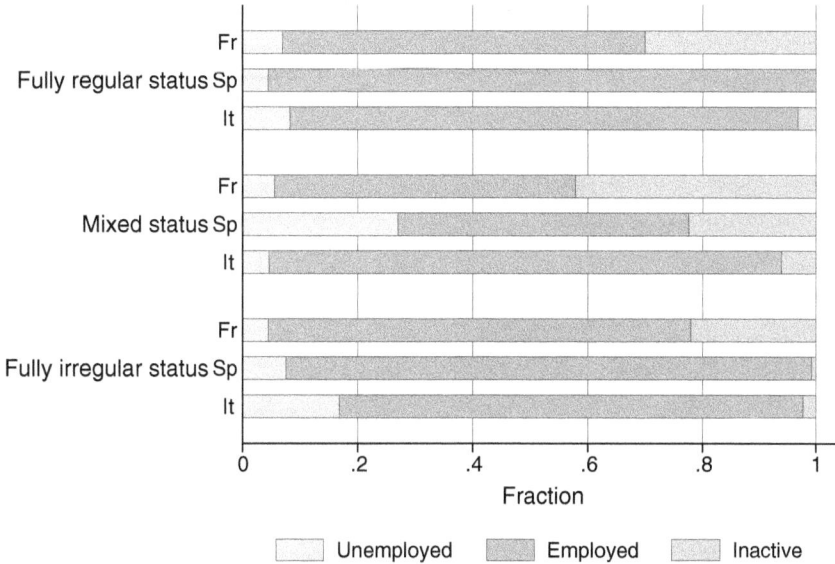

SOURCE: MAFE-Senegal.
NOTE: Weighted data.

While the effect of legal status on men's first-year activity is limited, legal status is more consistently associated with first-year activity for Senegalese women. Having mixed (RP_NWP) status is positively associated with being inactive compared to having fully regular status (RP_WP), although only at $p < .10$. Women with fully irregular (NRP_NWP) status face a higher risk of unemployment compared to women with fully regular status (RP_WP): lacking both residence and work authorization is associated with a 5-percentage-point increase in the probability of being unemployed compared to being inactive or employed. Entering the country without a visa has no effect on any of the outcomes for either men or women. The effect of legal status thus varies by gender. Lacking only a work permit increases the probability of being inactive for both men and women, indicating the role of student migration for men and family reunification for women. Other predictors in this model lend credence to this interpretation. Years of education is significantly positively related to inactivity and negatively related to employment for men, while years of work experience in Senegal is associated with increased likelihood of employment and decreased likelihood of inactivity. Acquired human capital thus has opposite effects: those male Senegalese migrants who are more highly educated tend to be economically inactive students during their year of arrival, while those with acquired employment experience tend be economically active and working.

Other predictors in the model are also suggestive of distinctive profiles of labor market participation in keeping with family reunification for women. Among

FIGURE 4
First-Year Activity Status by Legal Status and Country of Residence, Senegalese Women

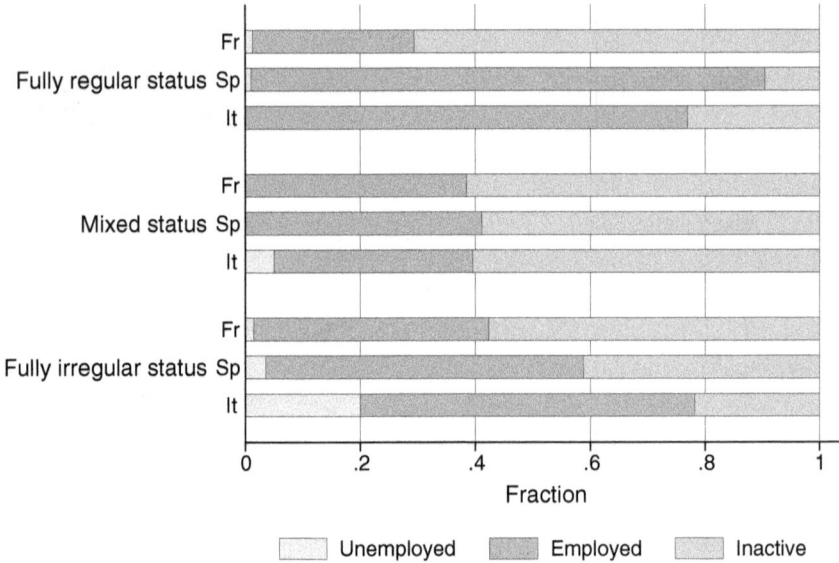

SOURCE: MAFE-Senegal.
NOTE: Weighted data.

women, those who indicated work as the primary motivation for their migration are 17 percentage points less likely to be inactive than those women who indicated family as the primary motivation. In addition, women who intend to stay definitively at the destination and those whose families contributed financially to the trip[4] are more likely to be inactive and less likely to be working. These associations among motivations, intentions, family financial participation, and likelihood of inactivity are indicative of family reunification. Interestingly, having a spouse and/ or children at the destination had no direct effect on women's first-year economic activity net of legal status and other predictors, suggesting that direct measures of women's legal status and motivations are more important predictors of economic participation than measures of family structure.

Other predictors were indicative of autonomous-migration profiles among both women and men. Those women with a spouse or children in Senegal are less likely to be inactive and more likely to be working, indicating that they are probably independent pioneer migrants who migrated, in part, to support family in Senegal through working in Europe. For men, having a spouse or child in the same destination is positively predictive of employment and negatively predictive of both inactivity and unemployment. While legal status and other predictors define distinctive profiles for inactive migrants among both men and women, legal status is not related to employment for active men. It does seem, however, to structure women's employment chances: female migrants with fully irregular status are more likely to be unemployed.

TABLE 3

Multinomial Logistic Regression of First-Year Activity Status by Gender, Average Marginal Effects

	Men						Women					
	Unemployed		Employed		Inactive		Unemployed		Employed		Inactive	
Predictor	AME	SE	AME	SE	AME	SE	AME	SE	AME	SE	AME	SE
Legal status: (ref: fully regular)												
Fully irregular (NRP_NWP)	.026	.030	-.042	.040	.016	.029	.047**	.023	-.049	.065	.0020	.062
Mixed (RP_NWP)	-.0042	.039	-.056	.046	.060**	.029	-.0086	.019	-.13*	.071	.13*	.069
Destination (ref.: France)												
Spain	-.0039	.035	.17***	.059	-.17***	.056	-.037	.043	.20**	.081	-.16**	.081
Italy	.045	.039	.13**	.056	-.17****	.044	.011	.049	.25***	.088	-.26***	.085
Entry status: no visa	.014	.031	-.015	.039	.00086	.026	.022	.066	-.0064	.063	-.016	.067
Period of arrival: post-1990	.0039	.036	.017	.044	-.020	.028	.0015	.059	.0030	.078	-.0045	.068
Age at start of current trip	.00030	.0031	-.0019	.0039	.0016	.003	-.0013	.003	.0023	.0039	-.00099	.0034
Years of education	.00028	.0025	-.01****	.0037	.013****	.003	.0028	.004	-.0049	.006	.0021	.005
Ethnicity: Wolof	-.050*	.028	.055	.035	-.0050	.020	-.032	.037	.00060	.056	.032	.050
Religion: Mouride	-.032	.028	.046	.036	-.015	.023	-.021	.036	.043	.062	-.022	.056
Number of contacts at destination	.0023	.0061	-.0048	.0079	.0025	.0056	-.012**	.0060	.0048	.013	.0070	.013
Number of trips	-.0039	.011	.017	.016	-.013	.014	-.085**	.042	.0098	.049	.075*	.041
Does not speak lang. of destination	.017	.033	-.018	.054	.0011	.050	.044	.029	-.13**	.067	.090	.066
Self-reported economic status: good	.0018	.053	-.035	.060	.033	.032	-.050***	.018	.17**	.084	-.12	.083

(continued)

189

TABLE 3 (CONTINUED)

| | Men | | | | | | Women | | | | | |
| | Unemployed | | Employed | | Inactive | | Unemployed | | Employed | | Inactive | |
Predictor	AME	SE	AME	SE	AME	SE	AME	SE	AME	SE	AME	SE
Spouse or children at destination	−.062***	.024	.15****	.034	−.08****	.025	.013	.024	−.074	.065	.061	.062
Spouse or children in Senegal	.026	.027	−.027	.038	.00077	.028	.012	.027	.15***	.058	−.16***	.055
Geographic origin: from Dakar	−.0006	.030	−.045	.034	.045**	.021	.076***	.029	−.057	.049	−.019	.047
Father's education: < secondary school	−.0023	.030	.013	.037	−.011	.022	−.041	.033	.067	.052	−.026	.046
Trip paid by family	.041	.035	.024	.038	−.07****	.018	−.0053	.023	−.12**	.058	.13**	.054
Plan to stay: definitive	−.012	.027	.0033	.033	.0087	.021	.056**	.026	−.17****	.050	.12**	.047
Motive for migration: work	.018	.026	−.17****	.047	−.17***	.065	−.050	.12	.098	.13	−.048	.050
At least one parent alive in Senegal	.076****	.023	−.056	.062	−.020	.058	.06****	.013	−.14**	.071	.081	.071
Employed before trip	−.072	.062	.061	.071	.011	.046	−.14*	.072	.066	.12	.071	.098
Inactive before trip	−.12	.070	−.095	.093	.21***	.075	−.13*	.080	−.27**	.13	.40****	.11
Years of work exp. (Senegal)	−.0019	.0018	.0044**	.0023	−.003*	.0015	.0042	.0028	−.0035	.0044	−.00073	.0039
N	454						309					
Log likelihood	−177.34						−161					
Pseudo R²	.44						.39					

SOURCE: MAFE-Senegal. NRP_NWP = no residence permit and no work permit; RP_NWP = residence permit but no work permit.
NOTE: Models include interaction between legal status and destination.
*p < .10. **p < .05. ***p < .01. ****p < .001.

The effects of legal statuses vary across destinations, but more so for women than for men. Table 3 also shows significant variation in the probabilities of first-year activity status between contexts of reception. For both men and women, compared to their compatriots in France, Senegalese in Italy and Spain are less likely to be inactive and more likely to be employed during their first year of residence. Country of residence does not have a significant relationship with unemployment for either men or women. Given the variation in first-year activity status by both legal status and country of residence, the model includes an interaction between these predictors that can help us to examine how the effect of legal status might vary by country of residence. Table 4 displays the average marginal effects of legal status derived from the coefficients in Table 3 by country of residence for both men and women. The top panel of the table shows that this interaction does not produce statistically significant variation in the effects of legal status for men.

On the other hand, variation in the effect of legal statuses on first-year economic activity across destinations is consistent with different configurations of legal status for reunified Senegalese female migrants in different countries. The bottom panel of Table 4 shows that the effects of legal status do vary by destination for women. For women in France, not having fully regular legal status is associated with a decrease in the probability of being inactive: women with mixed (RP_NWP) status are 21 percentage points less likely to be inactive than women with fully regular status, and women with fully irregular status are 24 percentage points less likely to be inactive than women with fully regular status. These lower inactivity rates for women without fully regular status in France are offset by a relative increase in the probability of employment: women with mixed or fully irregular status have employment probability roughly 22 percentage points higher than fully regular women in France, while legal status has no effect on unemployment for women in France. These findings are indicative of their migration via the legal reunification channel, which confers fully regular legal status. The lower activity rate of these likely reunified spouses supports previous findings that reunified women are less likely to participate in the labor force because of administrative and economic dependency.

The association between legal status and inactivity among Senegalese women in Italy and Spain is also consistent with legal channels of family reunification. Women with mixed legal status in Italy and Spain are more likely to be inactive than women in those countries with fully regular status. These higher inactivity rates translate into a negative effect of mixed legal status on employment in both of these countries. As in the case of France, these results are consistent with the channel of family reunification in these countries. Italy and Spain differ from France in the specific configuration of legal status associated with the family-reunification channel: both Italy and Spain impose a waiting period on the reunified spouses' applications for a work permit. The lack of a work permit among otherwise legal migrants is a sign of reunification and limited rights of formal participation, which result in lower participation in the labor force for reunified Senegalese women in Southern Europe.

TABLE 4
Average Marginal Effects (AME) of Legal Status on First-Year Activity Status, by
Country of Residence and Gender

	Outcome					
	Unemployed		Employed		Inactive	
	Irregular Status	Mixed Status	Irregular Status	Mixed Status	Irregular Status	Mixed Status
	AME	SE	AME	SE	AME	SE	AME	SE	AME	SE	AME	SE
Men												
France	−.03	.04	−.02	.05	.017	.07	−.034	.07	.01	.07	.049	.05
Spain	.041	.04	.077	.11	−.061	.05	−.14	.13	.02	.02	.065	.09
Italy	.083	.06	−.05	.06	−.098	.07	−.020	.07	.02	.03	.071	.04
Women												
France	.025	.04	−.018	.02	.22°°	.10	.2°°°°	.07	−.2°°	.10	−.2°°°	.07
Spain	−.02	.05	−.05	.04	−.090	.12	−.30°	.16	.11	.11	.34°°	.15
Italy	.2°°°	.05	.058	.05	−.4°°°°	.09	−.4°°°°	.11	.2°°	.09	.4°°°°	.10

SOURCE: MAFE-Senegal.
°$p < .10$. °°$p < .05$. °°°$p < .01$. °°°°$p < .001$.

Senegalese women with legal statuses upon arrival that are indicative of non-reunification pathways are more likely to attempt to work. Mixed or irregular statuses are associated with employment among Senegalese women in France, indicating that students (who generally lack a work permit) and migrants with irregular status are more likely to work than reunified spouses, and this is true despite their lack of formal authorization to do so. In contrast, having fully regular status is predictive of employment in both Italy and Spain. Unlike in France, where this status is associated with family reunification, this association suggests that Senegalese women might be able to access formal channels of labor recruitment, perhaps through quotas for domestic workers.

These results show a fairly simple pattern: Senegalese women who have legal statuses consistent with family reunification (fully regular in France and mixed in Spain and Italy) tend to have higher rates of inactivity than Senegalese women with other legal statuses. The specific configuration of legal statuses associated with reunification varies across destinations, though, giving rise to different associations between particular statuses and the probability of inactivity in different countries. These results also strongly suggest the heterogeneity of Senegalese women's legal statuses and a systematic association between nonreunification statuses—even those that do not include formal residence and/or work authorization—and the propensity to be employed upon arrival. In contrast, the labor force participation and employment of Senegalese men are not as sensitive to variation across legal statuses or destinations, indicative of a near-universal motivation to work (with the possible exception of male students in France).

Transitions out of Employment for Men

The dynamic model of transitions into unemployment for Senegalese men shows that lack of fully regular legal status does not increase the likelihood of losing a job; nor does possessing fully regular status increase the likelihood of keeping a job. Table 5 presents results for the discrete-time survival analysis of transitions into unemployment for men. These results show that mixed or fully irregular legal status is not associated with a statistically significantly different risk of falling into unemployment compared to fully regular status, nor is having entered without a visa predictive of this transition. Senegalese men in Spain face a 2.3-percentage-point higher risk of falling into unemployment than Senegalese men in France. Interactions between legal status and country of residence do not show any significant effects. Formal, legal barriers to transitions out of employment thus seem to be limited for Senegalese men.

Indeed, few predictors in this model have a significant association with the risk of falling into unemployment, which is due in part to the rarity of the transition: only 8 percent of subjects eventually fail, and the survivor function after seven years—the median duration at risk for unemployment—is 95 percent. The risk of transitioning to unemployment is marginally higher for more recent arrivals, perhaps suggesting secular declines in labor market conditions. The risk of unemployment also increases with the number of activity spells and the prestige score of jobs, indicating that frequent change of jobs and having a "better" job increase the likelihood of becoming unemployed. This pattern may indicate that Senegalese men indeed experience a trade-off between employment and job quality: bad jobs are easier to get and to hold on to than good jobs (Fullin and Reyneri 2011). Conversely, male migrants whose families participated in financing their trip are less likely to become unemployed, indicating that such migrants may be more likely to keep jobs because, in part, they face pressure to "pay off" this investment through remittances (Chort, Gubert, and Senne 2012).

Transitions into Employment for Women

Transitions to employment for women are suggestive of the eventual transformation of reunified spouses into labor migrants. The probability of a transition into employment among women is much higher than the transition examined for men: after the median duration of time at risk for becoming employed (four years), the survivor function is only 62 percent; the figure falls to 30 percent after 10 years. The baseline risk for women is thus quite high, indicating that the majority eventually experience a transition into economic activity.

The dynamic model of women's transitions into employment indicates that secure legal status is a strong predictor of eventual work. Table 5 presents average marginal effects for the discrete-time survival analysis of transitions into employment for women, and shows significant effects of legal status. Compared to fully regular status, mixed (RP_NWP) status is associated with a 10-percentage-point decline in the risk of becoming employed, while there is no average

TABLE 5
Discrete-Time Survival Analysis of Transitions into and out of Employment
by Gender, Average Marginal Effects

Predictor	Men		Women	
	Unemployment		Employment	
	AME	SE	AME	SE
Legal status (ref.: fully regular)				
Fully irregular (NRP_NWP)	−.0039	.0073	−.043	.044
Mixed (RP_NWP)	−.0085	.0091	−.10°°°°	.031
Destination (ref.: France)				
Spain	.023°°	.0089	.0097	.053
Italy	.011	.0089	−.072	.047
Entry status: no visa	−.00031	.0037	.093°°	.038
Years in destination	−.0079	.0068	.0050	.0097
Duration at risk	.00049	.0027	.0076	.0095
Period of arrival: post-1990	.0092°	.0049	.10°°°°	.027
Number of activity spells	.022°°°°	.0036	.064°°°°	.015
Age at start of current migration spell	−.00060	.00040	−.0014	.0018
Years of education	−.00024	.00056	.0072°°°	.0027
Ethnicity: Wolof	.0033	.0064	−.034°	.021
Religion: Mouride	−.0078	.0060	−.026	.042
Years of education in destination	.0070	.0070	−.0037	.0073
Number of contacts at destination	−.0019°	.0011	.0095°°	.0047
Number of trips	−.00016	.00100	.043	.027
Does not speak language of destination	−.0068	.0053	−.0078	.047
Work experience at destination	.0086	.0080	—	—
Unemployed	—	—	ref.	
Employed	ref.		—	—
Inactive	−.0031	.0089	−.093	.067
Manual occupation	.0030	.0045	—	—
International Socioeconomic Index of Occupational Status (ISEI)	.00028°°	.00013	—	—
Spouse or children at destination	.0019	.0037	.0063	.036
Spouse or children in Senegal	−.0047	.0046	.038	.044
Geographic origin: from Dakar	−.00082	.0044	.023	.031
Father's education: < secondary school	−.0044	.0036	.0096	.027
Trip paid by family	−.013°°°	.0049	.0012	.028
Plan to stay: definitive	.0035	.0040	.055°	.029
Motive: work/better life	−.0052	.0038	.045	.034
Work experience in Senegal (years)	—	—	.0055°°°	.0017
Self-reported economic status: good	—	—	−.018	.051
N (person-years)	4,010		819	
Events	36		90	
Log likelihood	−131.21		−231.49	
Pseudo R^2	.36		.18	

SOURCE: MAFE-Senegal. NRP_NWP = no residence permit and no work permit; RP_NWP = residence permit but no work permit.
NOTE: Models include interaction between legal status and destination.
°p < .10. °°p < .05. °°°p < .01. °°°°p < .001.

statistically significant difference between fully irregular and fully regular status. Additional statistical tests indicate that the difference in AMEs between fully irregular and mixed statuses is significant at $p < .10$. While mixed status is associated with family reunification and thus inactivity during the year of arrival in Italy and Spain, most (95 percent)[5] women with mixed status eventually transition into fully regular status and thus gain access to the labor market. Reunified Senegalese women in France have this status from the start of their stay and thus face no legal barriers to eventual employment, even if their economic and administrative dependence constrains their work initially. These results indicate that Senegalese women who possess or access fully regular status in the process of family reunification are likely to make an eventual transition to employment.

Irregular entry status, on the other hand, is also significantly predictive of the risk of becoming employed: having entered without a visa is associated with an increase of 9.3 percentage points in the hazard of becoming employed. Thus, women who entered without a visa are likely to become employed. While seemingly at odds with the finding that current fully regular status is associated with employment, the relationship between irregular entry and eventual employment may be indicative of interlinked regularization and employment strategies: women who enter outside of legal channels may pursue regular status as part of an employment-focused trajectory.

Variation in the effects of legal statuses for women across destinations supports the interpretation that reunified wives are likely to make a transition into employment, especially in France. Table 6 displays the substantial variation in the effects of legal status categories in different destinations. Having mixed status in France is associated with a lower risk of becoming employed than having fully regular status, as is having fully irregular status. Women with fully regular status in France—who are likely to have entered through the channel of legal reunification and were the most likely to be inactive during the year of arrival—are thus the most likely to undergo a transition to employment.

The results for the Southern European destinations are more complicated. Mixed status is significantly negatively related to the transition to employment in Spain, while there is no association in Italy. In contrast, there is no statistically significant effect of fully irregular status in Spain, while fully irregular status in Italy is associated with an increase in the risk of employment by 20 percentage points. Senegalese women in Spain with regular status are thus the most likely to make a transition to employment, and this group is likely to include both reunified spouses who gained work authorization after arrival and labor migrants with regular status—the most likely to work upon arrival in Spain. The latter group is excluded from the model's risk set if they are already employed, meaning that the women with regular status making transitions to employment are likely to be reunified wives.

Other results may be indicative of autonomous migration strategies. The positive association between fully irregular status and transitions to employment in Italy means that migrants with fully irregular status in the first year—who are the most likely to be both in the labor force and unemployed—tend both to stay in this status and to find work. The effect of entry status is concentrated in France,

TABLE 6
Average Marginal Effects (AME) of Legal Status on Risk of Employment for Women, by
Country of Residence

	Legal Status					
	Irregular Status		Mixed Status		No Visa	
Destination	AME	SE	AME	SE	AME	SE
France	−.099*	.058	−.12***	.037	.21***	.071
Spain	−.13	.085	−.15**	.077	−.058	.048
Italy	.20**	.10	−.015	.052	.060	.042

SOURCE: MAFE-Senegal.
*$p < .10$. **$p < .05$. ***$p < .01$.

where Senegalese women who enter without a visa have an employment transition probability 21 percentage points higher than women who entered with a
visa; these results may indicate an autonomous strategy where irregular entry is
associated with eventual transitions to regular status and employment.

These results confirm the importance of including both entry status and time-
varying legal status in models of employment for women (González-Ferrer
2011a) and suggest that women who enter through family-reunification mechanisms, who often have a mixed legal status that precludes work, are less likely to
become employed than women who may circumvent such mechanisms.

Other predictors in the model are suggestive of a positive selection of
employed Senegalese women: years of education, number of contacts at destination, and work experience in Senegal are all positively associated with becoming
employed, suggesting that human and social capital play a role in this transition.
In addition, planning to stay definitively in the destination is positively associated
with becoming employed, while there is no association with having family either
at destination or in Senegal.

Discussion

This article's main hypothesis is that the effect of legal status on Senegalese
migrants' labor market participation—as measured by first-year economic activity and employment dynamics—varies systematically by gender as a result of
family reunification policies that produce different constraints and opportunities
for men and women. The results for Senegalese women are largely consistent
with such a gendered migration system—one that is constructed both by constraints on female autonomy and mobility present in a patriarchal Senegal and by
the legal channels open to women as they are received in new host countries.
Across all three destination countries, women with a legal status indicating the
primacy of family reunification in their migration were more likely to be

economically inactive during the year of arrival: women with fully regular status in France were less likely to work than women with mixed or irregular statuses, while women with mixed status in Italy or Spain were less likely to work than women with fully regular statuses. These findings indicate the operation of administrative dependency (Boyd 1997; Kofman 1999; Lesselier 2008) and a concomitant decrease in the ability of women to enter the labor market. This is especially true in Spain and Italy, where legally mandated waiting periods for work permits erect a formal barrier to reunified spouses' participation.

Other variables associated with family reunification were also strongly predictive of first-year inactivity among women, including plans to stay definitively in the destination country, family financial participation in the trip, and having family motivations for the trip. The financial participation of women's families is overwhelmingly provided by reunifying husbands, and the association between this variable and women's inactivity suggests that men who can demonstrate the legally required financial means to bring a spouse can prevent reunified wives from working, both by removing the economic necessity for the women to work and potentially by making women economically dependent. Reunification and its associated economic dependency is thus a way to reproduce gendered hierarchies in a context where women's migration, even for reunification purposes, is strongly discouraged because of the fear of the loss of social control (Beauchemin, Caarls, and Mazzucato 2013).

Family reunification is often associated with dependency for women and at least an initial exclusion from labor market participation, but research has also shown that reunified women may eventually work either as part of a family investment strategy (Duleep and Sanders 1993) or because of camouflaging of economic motivations in an "associational" move (Kanaiaupuni 2000). The results from this article support the contention that family reunification is not necessarily exclusive of eventual work. Discrete-time survival analysis shows that some of the legal status configurations that were indicative of family reunification and first-year inactivity also predict transitions into employment for women. This was directly evident for France, where women with fully regular status were more likely to make the transition to work than women with mixed or irregular status. In Spain, women with mixed status were less likely than women with regular status to make the transition; while reunified women have mixed status in Spain upon arrival, they are also able to access work authorization after a waiting period, and those who do so are likely to find work. In these two countries, Kofman's (1999) observation that family reunification is liable to transform into another form of labor migration is accurate. These findings also make a strong case for taking a longitudinal approach to the study of the effects of admission category on labor market integration of reunified migrants.

Despite the predominance of family reunification as a legal migration channel for Senegalese women, the results here also point to the existence of autonomous migration among Senegalese women who largely have economic motives for their mobility. Senegalese women in France with mixed or irregular status during the year of arrival were likely not to be joining a partner and have economic motivations for their migration and were thus more likely to be employed during the year of arrival than women with fully regular status. These legal status configurations indicate the predominance of semiregular (in the case of students) and irregular work strategies among autonomous Senegalese women in France. In contrast, Senegalese women with fully regular status in Italy and Spain were more likely to work during the year of arrival than women with other statuses, indicating that these women are able to access legal channels of labor migration.

In contrast to the labor trajectories of Senegalese women, Senegalese men's labor market participation showed little association with different configurations of legal status. Mixed status (lacking a work permit) was associated with inactivity, which is indicative of flows of students to Europe, especially France. Contrary to the hypotheses, irregular status was not predictive of employment during the year of arrival, and regular status was not associated with transitions into unemployment. Senegalese men in Italy and Spain did exhibit significantly higher probabilities of employment during the year of arrival, however, which lends support to the hypothesis that cross-national variation in labor markets would be associated with labor market participation. It thus seems that Senegalese men are able to access employment in Southern Europe regardless of their legal status, perhaps due to the high demand for low-skilled labor in these countries' robust informal economies, while Senegalese students in France are the only male migrants who face legal barriers to their employment.

These findings for Senegalese men are in keeping with literature that shows that migrants in such countries do not face an "ethnic penalty" in the probability of employment, but may face challenges in occupational mobility (Fullin and Reyneri 2011). Research with the MAFE data is indicative of the relatively low occupational attainment of Senegalese migrants in Europe (Obucina 2013), but additional research will be necessary to examine the link between legal status and occupational types. At the same time, Senegalese men in Spain face a higher risk of falling into unemployment than Senegalese men in France, indicating that employment, while perhaps easy to obtain, is somewhat precarious.

Conclusion

The relationship between legal status and immigrant labor market participation is a major concern of both policymakers and scholars, but studies generally do not examine how the family context of migration influences both women's legal statuses and their participation in the labor market at destination. Legal status may matter more for women's labor market participation because of the gendered immigration policies that produce them. While female migrants' experiences are growing more heterogeneous, many of them have entered destinations via the legal channel of family reunification. Their legal status is thus subject to their family situations.

Family-reunification legislation strongly structures entry channels for Senegalese women and produces legal statuses that either directly preclude their labor market participation (as in Italy and Spain) or create other forms of economic and administrative dependency that may make them less likely to work even if they have the legal authorization to do so (as in France).

Drawing on longitudinal data on legal status but not on the admission category of family reunification, this article found that Senegalese women with configurations of legal status indicative of family reunification were more likely than women with other legal statuses to be economically inactive upon arrival, while there is little association between Senegalese men's legal status and their participation in the labor market. This finding held across destination countries despite the differing configurations of legal status granted to reunified spouses: while mixed status among women was associated with higher inactivity in Spain and Italy, so was fully regular status in France.

This is consonant with research that finds that reunified spouses tend to be less likely to be economically active (Kofman 1999). In the case of Spain and Italy, these women face legal barriers to their participation as a result of waiting periods (Kofman 2004a). Women in France, however, do not face such barriers, meaning that their legal situation is also indicative of economic dependency (Lesselier 2008).

The results also show, however, that family reunification does not preclude labor market participation, as many of the women with family-reunification profiles eventually transitioned into economic activity. This finding echoes the observation that family migration may transform into a form of labor migration (Kofman 1999). It also supports the view that female migrants have a diversity of motivations for their migration, and may often strategically participate in an "associational" move for economic reasons (Kanaiaupuni 2000).

In contrast to Senegalese women, male migrants with fully irregular status (NRP_NWP) did not face any penalty in labor market participation, employment, or the risk of transition to unemployment compared to migrants with fully regular status. The legal constraint of irregularity of legal status on economic activity for Senegalese migrants in Europe thus seems to be weak, supporting views that immigrants to countries with labor market structures that favor low-skilled labor and informality reduce the immigrant "employment penalty" (Kogan 2006), perhaps at the risk of funneling them into "bad jobs" (Fullin and Reyneri 2011).

Notes

1. "Irregular" is often used interchangeably with "undocumented," "unauthorized," "clandestine," or "illegal" to describe both an aggregate process of migration and an individual attribute of migrants (Donato and Armenta 2011). "Irregular" is often used in the European context and has broad connotations that can refer to both flows and stocks of migrants and can encompass a variety of legal arrangements (Triandafyllidou 2010). This article thus uses the term "irregular" to describe legal statuses that arise from migration that occurs outside of the legally defined framework for entry, residence, or work of foreigners in a destination country and, by extension, migrants who have engaged in such entry, residence, or work.

2. Spanish legislation in this regard was changed in 2009.

3. The MAFE project is coordinated by INED (C. Beauchemin) in partnership with the Université catholique de Louvain (B. Schoumaker), Maastricht University (V. Mazzucato), the Université Cheikh Anta Diop (P. Sakho), the Université de Kinshasa (J. Mangalu), the University of Ghana (P. Quartey), the Universitat Pompeu Fabra (P. Baizan), the Consejo Superior de Investigaciones Científicas (A. González-Ferrer), the Forum Internazionale ed Europeo di Ricerche sull'Immigrazione (E. Castagnone), and the University of Sussex (R. Black). The MAFE project has received funding from the European Community's

Seventh Framework Programme under grant agreement 217206. The MAFE-Senegal survey was conducted with the financial support of INED, the Agence Nationale de la Recherche (France), the Région Ile de France and the FSP program International Migrations, territorial reorganizations and development of the countries of the South.

4. Previous empirical research with the MAFE data has shown that husbands overwhelmingly participate in the decision-making for their wives' migration (Toma 2012). Family financial contributions to women's migration also come mostly from husbands: 74 percent of Senegalese women who reported such financial contributions received them from their partners.

5. Tabulation available upon request.

References

Agudelo-Suárez, Andrés, Diana Gil-González, Elena Ronda-Pérez, Victoria Porthé, Gema Paramio-Pérez, Ana M. García, and Aitana Garí. 2009. Discrimination, work and health in immigrant populations in Spain. *Social Science & Medicine* 68 (10): 1866–74.

Amuedo-Dorantes, Catalina, Miguel A. Malo, and Fernando Muñoz-Bullón. 2013. New evidence on the impact of legal status on immigrant labor market performance: The Spanish case. *Labour* 27 (1): 93–113.

Baizan, Pau, Cris Beauchemin, and Amparo González Ferrer. 2011. *A reassessment of family reunification in Europe: The case of Senegalese couples.* Paris: Institut National d'Etudes Démographiques.

Barou, Jacques. 1993. Les immigrations africaines en France: des "navigateurs" au "regroupement familial." *Revue française des affaires sociales* 47 (1): 193–205.

Beauchemin, Cris, Kim Caarls, and Valentina Mazzucato. 2013. *Senegalese migrants between here and there: An overview of family patterns.* Paris: Institut National d'Etudes Démographiques.

Beauchemin, Cris, Christelle Hamel, Maud Lesné, and Patrick Simon. 2010. Discrimination: A question of visible minorities. *Population & Societies* (466): 1–4.

Bernardi, Fabrizio, Luis Garrido, and Maria Miyar. 2011. The recent fast upsurge of immigrants in Spain and their employment patterns and occupational attainment. *International Migration* 49 (1): 148–87.

Borjas, George J. 1985. Assimilation, changes in cohort quality, and the earnings of immigrants. *Journal of Labor Economics* 3 (4): 463–89.

Borjas, George J. 1995. Assimilation and changes in cohort quality revisited: What happened to immigrant earnings in the 1980s? *Journal of Labor Economics* 13 (2): 201–45.

Boyd, Monica. 1989. Family and personal networks in international migration: Recent developments and new agendas. *International Migration Review* 23 (3): 638–70.

Boyd, Monica. 1997. Migration policy, female dependency, and family membership: Canada and Germany. In *Women and the Canadian welfare state: Challenges and change,* eds. Patricia Marie Evans and Gerda R. Wekerle, 142–69. Toronto: University of Toronto Press.

Bradatan, Cristina E, and Dumitru Sandu. 2012. Before crisis: Gender and economic outcomes of the two largest immigrant communities in Spain. *International Migration Review* 46 (1): 221–43.

Castagnone, Eleonora, Papa Sakho, Tiziana Nazio, Bruno Schoumaker, and Nirina Rakotonarivo. 2013. *African migrants at work. Patterns of labour market integration in Europe, transnational economic participation and economic re-integration of migrants in origin countries: The case of Senegal.* Paris: Institut National d'Etudes Démographiques.

Cerrutti, Marcela, and Douglas S. Massey. 2001. On the auspices of female migration from Mexico to the United States. *Demography* 38 (2): 187–200.

Chiswick, Barry R. 1978. The effect of Americanization on the earnings of foreign-born men. *Journal of Political Economy* 86 (5): 897–921.

Chort, Isabelle, Flore Gubert, and Jean-Noël Senne. 2012. Migrant networks as a basis for social control: Remittance incentives among Senegalese in France and Italy. *Regional Science and Urban Economics* 42 (5): 858–74.

Constant, Amelie, and Klaus F. Zimmermann. 2005. Immigrant performance and selective immigration policy: A European perspective. *National Institute Economic Review* 194 (1): 94–105.

Donato, Katharine M., and Amada Armenta. 2011. What we know about unauthorized migration. *Annual Review of Sociology* 37:529–43.

Donato, Katharine M., and Douglas S. Massey. 1993. Effect of the Immigration Reform and Control Act on the wages of Mexican migrants. *Social Science Quarterly* 74 (3): 523–41.

Donato, Katharine M., Chizuko Wakabayashi, Shirin Hakimzadeh, and Amada Armenta. 2008. Shifts in the employment conditions of Mexican migrant men and women the effect of U.S. immigration policy. *Work and Occupations* 35 (4): 462–95.

Duleep, Harriet Orcutt, and Seth Sanders. 1993. The decision to work by married immigrant women. *Industrial and Labor Relations Review* 46 (4): 677–90.

Fullin, Giovanna, and Emilio Reyneri. 2011. Low unemployment and bad jobs for new immigrants in Italy. *International Migration* 49 (1): 118–47.

González-Enríquez, Carmen. 2009. Spain, the cheap model: Irregularity and regularisation as immigration management policies. *European Journal of Migration and Law* 11 (2): 139–57.

González-Ferrer, Amparo. 2006. Family and labor strategies in migration: Family reunification, marital choices and labor participation of immigrants in the host country. PhD diss., Universidad Autónoma de Madrid.

González-Ferrer, Amparo. 2011a. Explaining the labour performance of immigrant women in Spain: The interplay between family, migration and legal trajectories. *International Journal of Comparative Sociology* 52 (1–2): 63–78.

González-Ferrer, Amparo. 2011b. The reunification of the spouse among recent immigrants in Spain. Links with undocumented migration and the labour market. In *Gender, generations and the family in international migration*, eds. Albert Kraler, Eleonore Kofman, Martin Kohli, and Camille Schmoll, 143–66. Amsterdam: Amsterdam University Press.

Hall, Matthew, Emily Greenman, and George Farkas. 2010. Legal status and wage disparities for Mexican immigrants. *Social Forces* 89 (2): 491–513.

Heath, Anthony, and John Ridge. 1983. Social mobility of ethnic minorities. *Journal of Biosocial Science* 15 (S8): 169–84.

Kaag, Mayke. 2008. Mouride transnational livelihoods at the margins of a European society: The case of Residence Prealpino, Brescia, Italy. *Journal of Ethnic & Migration Studies* 34 (2): 271–85.

Kanaiaupuni, Shawn Malia. 2000. Reframing the migration question: An analysis of men, women, and gender in Mexico. *Social Forces* 78 (4): 1311–47.

Kofman, Eleonore. 1999. Female "birds of passage" a decade later: Gender and immigration in the European Union. *International Migration Review* 33 (2): 269–99.

Kofman, Eleonore. 2004a. Family-related migration: A critical review of European studies. *Journal of Ethnic and Migration Studies* 30 (2): 243–62.

Kofman, Eleonore. 2004b. Gendered global migrations. *International Feminist Journal of Politics* 6 (4): 643–65.

Kogan, Irena. 2006. Labor markets and economic incorporation among recent immigrants in Europe. *Social Forces* 85 (2): 697–721.

Kossoudji, Sherrie A., and Deborah A. Cobb-Clark. 2000. IRCA's impact on the occupational concentration and mobility of newly-legalized Mexican men. *Journal of Population Economics* 13 (1): 81–98.

Kossoudji, Sherrie A., and Deborah A. Cobb-Clark. 2002. Coming out of the shadows: Learning about legal status and wages from the legalized population. *Journal of Labor Economics* 20 (3): 598–628.

Lesselier, Claudie. 2008. Politiques d'immigration en France: appréhender la dimension de genre. *Les cahiers du CEDREF. Centre d'enseignement, d'études et de recherches pour les études féministes* 16:189–208.

Mahler, Sarah J., and Patricia R. Pessar. 2006. Gender matters: Ethnographers bring gender from the periphery toward the core of migration studies. *International Migration Review* 40 (1): 27–63.

Manchuelle, François. 1997. *Willing migrants: Soninke labor diasporas, 1848–1960*. Athens, OH: Ohio University Press.

Massey, Douglas S. 1987. Do undocumented migrants earn lower wages than legal immigrants? New evidence from Mexico. *International Migration Review* 21 (2): 236–74.

Massey, Douglas S., Jorge Durand, and Nolan J. Malone. 2002. *Beyond smoke and mirrors: Mexican immigration in an era of economic integration*. New York, NY: Russell Sage Foundation.

Mezger, Cora, and Amparo González-Ferrer. 2013. *The ImPol database: A new tool to measure immigra-tion policies in France, Italy and Spain since the 1960s.* Paris: Institut National d'Etudes Démographiques.

Mincer, Jacob. 1978. Family migration decisions. *Journal of Political Economy* 86 (5): 749–73.

Obucina, Ognjen. 2013. Occupational trajectories and occupational cost among Senegalese immigrants in Europe. *Demographic Research* 28:547–80.

Pascual de Sans, Angels, Jordi Cardelús, and Miguel Solana Solana. 2000. Recent immigration to Catalonia: Economic character and responses. In *Eldorado or fortress? Migration in Southern Europe,* eds. Russell King, Gabriella Lazaridis, and Charalampos Tsardanidis, 104–24. New York, NY: St. Martin's Press.

Phillips, Julie A., and Douglas S. Massey. 1999. The new labor market: Immigrants and wages after IRCA. *Demography* 36 (2): 233–46.

Piore, Michael J. 1979. *Birds of passage: Migrant labor and industrial societies.* Cambridge: Cambridge University Press.

Portes, Alejandro. 1978. Introduction: Toward a structural analysis of illegal (undocumented) immigration. *International Migration Review* 12 (4): 469–84.

Raghuram, Parvati. 2004. The difference that skills make: Gender, family migration strategies and regu-lated labour markets. *Journal of Ethnic and Migration Studies* 30 (2): 303–21.

Reyneri, Emilio, and Giovanna Fullin. 2011. Labour market penalties of new immigrants in new and old receiving West European countries. *International Migration* 49 (1): 31–57.

Riccio, Bruno. 2001. From "ethnic group" to "transnational community"? Senegalese migrants' ambivalent experiences and multiple trajectories. *Journal of Ethnic and Migration Studies* 27 (4): 583–99.

Riccio, Bruno. 2008. West African transnationalisms compared: Ghanaians and Senegalese in Italy. *Journal of Ethnic & Migration Studies* 34 (2): 217–34.

Rivera-Batiz, Francisco L. 1999. Undocumented workers in the labor market: An analysis of the earnings of legal and illegal Mexican immigrants in the United States. *Journal of Population Economics* 12 (1): 91–116.

Sandell, Steven H. 1977. Women and the economics of family migration. *Review of Economics and Statistics* 59 (4): 406–14.

Schmidt di Friedberg, Ottavia. 1993. L'immigration africaine en Italie: Le cas Sénégalais. *Études interna-tionales* 24 (1): 125–40.

Tall, Serigne Mansour. 2008. Les émigrés sénégalais en Italie: Transferts financiers et potentiel de dével-oppement de l'habitat au Sénégal. In *Le Sénégal des migrations: Mobilités, identités et sociétés, hommes et sociétés,* ed. Momar-Coumba Diop, 37–67. Paris: Karthala.

Timera, Mahamet. 1997. L'immigration Africaine en France: Regards des autres et repli sur soi: La France et les migrants africains. *Politique africaine* 67:41–47.

Toma, Sorana. 2012. Ties that bind? Networks and gender in international migration. D.Phil. diss., University of Oxford.

Triandafyllidou, Anna. 2010. Irregular migration in Europe in the 21st century. In *Irregular migration in Europe: Myths and realities,* ed. Anna Triandafyllidou, 1–21. Surrey: Ashgate Publishing.

Vickstrom, Erik. 2013. The production and consequences of migrant irregularity: Senegalese in France, Italy, and Spain. PhD diss., Princeton University, Princeton, NJ.

Vickstrom, Erik. 2014. Pathways into irregular status among Senegalese migrants in Europe. *International Migration Review* 48 (4): 1062–99.

Different but the Same: How Legal Status Affects International Migration from Bangladesh

KATHARINE M. DONATO,
AMANDA R. CARRICO,
BLAKE SISK,
and
BHUMIKA PIYA

This article builds on prior studies that document how legal status stratifies society, specifically in outcomes related to international migration. Here, we study such outcomes in Bangladesh, a low-lying nation that has experienced dramatic environmental changes in recent decades and high rates of out-migration. We do event history analyses of a new and unique dataset that includes information from approximately eighteen hundred households in nine villages to investigate whether and how legal status differentiates out-migration from Bangladesh. We find substantial variation in legal status among the women and men who make an initial international trip and that unauthorized migration affects other labor market and economic outcomes: it reduces the number of hours that migrants work in destination countries, lowers the odds that migrants pay taxes or open a bank account, and increases the odds that migrants use social contacts to find jobs.

Keywords: international migration; Bangladesh; environment; out-migration

In March 2014, the *New York Times* named Bangladesh as the poster child for understanding the effects of climate change (Harris 2014). Sea-level rise, land erosion, and growth in the intensity of weather patterns in this low-lying nation have led to nonsustainable land loss. Its many cyclones have led to thousands of

Katharine M. Donato is a professor of sociology at Vanderbilt University. She writes extensively about international migration, and its causes and consequences. Her recent work examines the effects of environmental stress on out-migration from villages in southwestern Bangladesh. In 2015, she published (with Donna Gabaccia) Gender and International Migration: From the Slavery Era to the Global Age (Russell Sage Foundation).

Amanda R. Carrico is an assistant professor of environmental studies at the University of Colorado. Her work examines processes of household and community adaptation to environmental stress, environmental influences on migration, and public perceptions of environmental risk.

Correspondence: Katharine.donato@vanderbilt.edu

DOI: 10.1177/0002716216650843

deaths, widespread infrastructural damage, and have left millions homeless. Other changes, such as the shift from rice cultivation to shrimp production, have also degraded the environment. For example, salinity from shrimp ponds is associated with very high salt levels in drinking water, and shrimp aquaculture also damages forest cover and threatens biodiversity in the region (Agrawala et al. 2003; Datta, Roy, and Hassan 2010; Rogers et al. 2013). Although nationwide improvements in water quality have recently occurred, the World Health Organization (WHO) and UNICEF (United Nations Children's Emergency Fund) described Bangladesh's progress toward improved sanitation as "not on track" in 2014 (WHO and UNICEF 2014, Annex 3).

Given these challenging conditions, it is easy to imagine that climate change may represent the biggest push behind international migration in the near future. Yet we know very little about migration from nations such as Bangladesh. The objective of this article is to examine international migration from Bangladesh and consider whether and how legal status matters. We examine the likelihood of making a first international trip from Bangladesh and the extent to which illegality, migrant social capital, and the timing of migrant trips influence out-migration. Given that prior studies document legal status as having a substantial effect on the labor market outcomes of immigrants in many destinations, we also ask how legal status affects a set of labor market outcomes reported by Bangladeshi international migrants. Thus, we examine whether and how legal status stratifies the labor market experiences of immigrants from Bangladesh.

Below we set the context for our analysis by reviewing prior studies that examine the effect of legal status on immigrant outcomes and international migration from Bangladesh. We then describe a new dataset that relies on ethnosurvey methods initially employed by the Mexican Migration Project. Using data from the Bangladesh Environment and Migration Survey (BEMS), we calculate the cumulative probabilities that Bangladeshis will make a first international trip by age 44 and investigate whether and how legal status stratifies these chances. We also examine legal status variation in four outcomes related to Bangladeshi international migrants' labor market conditions: hours worked per week and whether immigrants used social contacts to obtain a job, pay taxes, or open a bank account. Generally speaking, comparable to the experiences of immigrants in a variety of global contexts, our findings reveal that illegality is a salient marker of disadvantage for Bangladeshi immigrants.

Blake Sisk received a PhD in sociology from Vanderbilt University in 2014. His research investigates the intersection of international migration and social stratification.

Bhumika Piya is a PhD student in sociology at Vanderbilt University. Her research interests include international migration, environmental demography, and global health policy. Her dissertation examines environmental stress, out-migration, and the health of women and children in Bangladesh.

NOTE: This article was presented at the 2016 annual meeting of the Population Association of America. We are grateful to the U.S. Office of Naval Research's Multidisciplinary University Research Initiative and Vanderbilt University's College of Arts and Science for their generous support of this project.

The Power of Legal Status and Its Effects

In the United States and other nations that have received a large number of immigrants in the twentieth century, legal status has become a robust and salient predictor of inequality and stratification (Massey 2007). Worldwide, countries now view border enforcement as an essential function of the state linked to national security, as illustrated by the more than forty nations that have built physical barriers on national borders since the 1990s (*The Economist* 2016). Nations have built these fences, whether physical or virtual, to prevent illegal migration and reduce the smuggling of goods. Growth in their construction signals less about their success, and more about how migrants, especially those without legal documents, are now embedded in a powerful institutionalized politic unlikely to quickly or easily change.

As a consequence, legal status has become an attribute that stratifies many immigrant experiences and outcomes. Menjívar (2006) described how many Salvadoran and Guatemalan immigrants live in a state of liminal legality, or an "in-between status," that affects all aspects of life in the United States. Since then, many others have used the term to describe how nation-states interfere in the everyday lives of immigrants and the consequences of such interference (e.g., Abrego 2008; Gonzales 2008; Chacón, forthcoming).

One life domain that many social scientists have studied is the labor market, especially whether and how legal status affects the conditions that immigrants experience in the labor market. After the implementation of the 1986 Immigration Reform and Control Act (IRCA) and subsequent polices designed to restrict the entry of the unauthorized, studies show that the wages and other labor market conditions of unauthorized Mexican immigrants have worsened (Donato, Durand, and Massey 1992; Donato and Massey 1993; Phillips and Massey 1999; Massey, Durand, and Malone 2002; Massey 2007; Donato and Sisk 2012). As Durand, Massey, and Pren (this volume) demonstrate, Mexican immigrants to the United States receive lower wages, work longer hours, and are more likely to work in the informal economy than their legal counterparts. Other studies also show large legal status disparities in the wages of U.S. Mexican immigrant men and women (Hall, Greenman, and Farkas 2010), that undocumented Mexican women experience more wage deterioration than men (Donato et al. 2008), and that the wage losses of unauthorized men from the Dominican Republic and Nicaragua are similar to those for Mexicans (Donato, Aguilera, and Wakabayashi 2005). As Massey and Gentsch (2014) show, this disadvantage occurred after 1986, when the hiring of undocumented migrants was criminalized.

International Migration from Bangladesh

Since the 1980s, Bangladesh's manpower agency has sent more than 5 million persons to other countries for work. Although initially almost all contract laborers went to Gulf States, other countries are now popular destinations, including Malaysia, South Korea, Japan, and Singapore. In 2014 alone, more than 400,000 Bangladeshis were processed by their government for foreign employment (Bureau of Manpower, Employment and Training 2015), and in the same year, the World Bank (n.d.) estimates that Bangladesh received approximately $15 billion in remittances. Until recently, almost all labor migrants were men. In 2005, women became eligible for foreign employment after Bangladesh abolished its ban on the export of low-skilled women's labor (Siddiqui 2005; Oishi 2005); women now represent approximately 5 percent of Bangladesh's contract laborers.

As government-sponsored out-migration has grown, reports suggest that unauthorized migration from Bangladesh has also grown. There is no estimate of the prevalence of this type of out-migration, but recently concerns have loomed large, especially near or at the western Bengali border of Bangladesh-India, where incidents of violence and conflict have been common. For example, allegations of rising illegal migration since the 1990s led to the construction of a border fence by India's Border Security Force. The fence now covers approximately 1,500 miles of the 2,500-mile border between the two nations. Moreover, at times border conditions have been very tense; in 2010, Human Rights Watch described the Indian Border Security Force as having a shoot-on-site policy (Adams 2011; Human Rights Watch 2011). Other signs of migration exist throughout the country—among them are the trains on which migrants are perched, traveling with small bags of personal items.

Studies suggest that migration in Bangladesh is one of several different adaptation strategies employed by its residents to confront the effects of climate change.[1] Migration is recognized as a way to disperse risks and diversify economic livelihoods. For example, Kartiki (2011) describes how many people migrated in the wake of Cyclone Aila, which occurred in 2009, just two years after Cyclone Sidr, a category 5 storm, killed thousands. Kartiki points out that although migration related to employment was commonplace, especially in the coastal areas of Bangladesh, the large-scale and sudden migration that occurred after Aila worsened, rather than improved, the situations of migrants.

Gray and Mueller (2012) examined impacts of natural disasters—flooding and crop failure unrelated to flooding—on long-term local and long-distance migration in rural Bangladesh. Using data from a longitudinal survey covering a 15-year period, they find that a community's exposure to flooding had a significant nonlinear effect on mobility net of household and other characteristics. Moderate levels of flooding increased the odds of local moves by 28 percent, but low and high levels of flooding lowered these odds. Compared to periods of no crop failure, severe crop failure increased the odds of migration by 138 percent, but the odds of migrating locally were 197 percent higher and of migrating long-distance were 82 percent higher. These effects varied by gender and socioeconomic status. Compared to nonflood years, women and the poor had higher odds of migrating in moderate flood years but not in severe flood years. In addition, the effects of crop failure on mobility at the community level were substantial, with women's odds of mobility increasing by 178 percent and men's increasing 91 percent.

Donato et al. (2016) use data from the Bangladesh Environment and Migration Survey to examine whether and how meteorological conditions are associated with making a first international or internal migration trip. Among rainfall and temperature, only the latter has a significant effect; that is, periods of unusually cool temperatures lowered the risk of making a first internal trip. The effect of rainfall on internal and international migration trips was not significant. Interestingly, effects for social capital were more powerful. Those who had migrant parents and/or siblings had higher risks of making a first internal or international migration trip than those without such connections.

In 2011, the UK government's Foresight Project commissioned a review on environmental change and migration in Bangladesh (Government Office of Science 2011). The assessment focused on population movement in hazard-prone environments, especially coastal and deltaic floodplains. Findings suggest that while the loss of life due to climatic hazards has declined substantially in the last two to three decades, damages to homes, farmland, and assets have not declined. In addition, although men often migrated outside their village to secure livelihoods after experiencing an adverse environmental event, the rest of the family stayed behind. Consistent with previous research, the report also indicates that migration was mainly short-term and temporary, except when total losses of homesteads and land occurred. In these extreme cases, people migrated permanently. The Sussex Center for Migration Research and Refugee and Migratory Movements Research Unit Bangladesh (2013) projects future long-term migration of Bangladeshi residents as a consequence of environmental conditions there. Derived from spatial differences in population growth rates, it estimates that approximately 9.5 million people will migrate between 2011 and 2050 from various subdistricts in Bangladesh.[2]

Therefore, although legal status differentiates out-migration in other areas of the world, and it has consequences for the economic assimilation of migrants in many host societies, little is known about whether the likelihood of making a first international trip from Bangladesh varies by legal status (authorized or not) and, if so, what are its consequences. The studies reviewed above suggest that international migration from Bangladesh is on the rise, that climate change appears linked to migratory behavior and that the Indian government—which shares the largest border with Bangladesh—has increased enforcement activity that includes, but is not limited to, constructing a fence on more than half of the border. Thus, we expect that legal status will have appreciable effects on the labor market conditions of Bangladeshi international migrants, and it will stratify the likelihood of making a first international trip.

Data and Methods

In this article, we use new data collected in the southwestern region of Bangladesh. The Bangladesh Environment and Migration Survey (BEMS) contains retrospective migration and employment histories from more than three thousand people in nine villages. After completing a census of households in each village in 2014, we randomly sampled approximately eighteen hundred households in nine sites in this low-lying region of Bangladesh.

To collect these data, we used the same ethnosurvey methodology developed by the Mexican Migration Project. It relies on a set of tables into which data are added from open-ended and flexible interviews with household members. It is unobtrusive and nonthreatening in part because question wording and ordering are field-tested but not fixed. As such, specific phrasing and timing for each query are left to the interviewer's discretion, which is especially important for the collection of sensitive data, such as legal status. Following these field procedures, the BEMS collected detailed migration and economic livelihood histories, as well as migration intentions, health, household assets, and access to water and other natural resources.

In this analysis, we distinguish between the odds of making a first international trip for those with and those without legal documents. We focus on men and women who were household heads, spouses, and other adults in households, and use their year-by-year life histories up to the date of the first international trip. The resulting discrete-time person-year files follow each subject from birth to survey year, or the year of the first international trip, whichever came first. If someone reported a first international trip, then migration equals 1; if not, it equals 0.

We then use logistic regression to estimate the chance of migrating with or without authorization, versus not migrating at all. Among the covariates are two types of migrant social capital. Prior to the year of a respondent's first trip, we measure whether he or she had a parent or sibling who made an international trip. If so, then the dummy variable for having a parent or sibling migrate equals 1; 0 otherwise. We also control for gender (female = 1); headship status measured with three dummy variables with household head (reference category), spouse, and other adult; and age in five-year categories relative to younger than 15 years of age (reference category) up to 50 years and older. Year of first trip is also a set of dummy variables that represents categories with the reference of 1973 to 1979. Upazila, a geographic unit equivalent to a U.S. county, is a set of nine dummy variables; Sharsha, a small agricultural area, is the reference category.

We estimate age-specific models separately by legal status and from them calculate the conditional likelihood that male and female household members of a given age migrate with or without documents on a first international trip. Using these probabilities, we then generate life tables to estimate the cumulative chances that they make a legal or undocumented international trip by age 44, assuming the probabilities of out-migration that prevailed up to 2013. They illustrate what would happen if someone were to go through life subject to the age-specific probabilities of out-migration estimated from the multivariate models. We thus present the cumulative probabilities below to describe legal status differences in migration over the life course.

In the second part of the analysis, we use data from 271 international migrants in the BEMS and create four dependent variables related to labor market conditions in the host society. These are total number of hours worked per week, whether migrants obtained jobs through social networks (yes = 1; 0 otherwise), whether migrants paid taxes (yes = 1; 0 otherwise), and if migrants had a bank account (yes = 1; 0 otherwise). We estimate ordinary least squares and logistic regression models to understand whether and how demographic and migration attributes explain variation in these outcomes. The demographic variables include age at migration (in years), and whether respondents were household heads (= 1; 0 = other), and female (= 1; 0 = otherwise). Migration-related characteristics include legal status (unauthorized = 1; 0 = otherwise), and period of entry (2005–2012 = 1; 1973–2004 = 0). Two other migration characteristics are included: the number of migration trips is a dummy variable (more than one trip = 1; one trip only = 0), and purpose of trip is a dummy variable (to earn money = 1; 0 = other reason). In these models, we focus on whether and how legal status predicts the four labor market outcomes.

Findings

Below we describe findings from discrete-time event history models that predict making a first authorized or unauthorized international trip, using person-years as the unit of analysis. (Table A1 in the appendix presents means and standard deviations for the variables in these models.) Table 1 presents coefficients from two models that predict making a first authorized and unauthorized international trip from Bangladesh. The coefficients reveal that migrant social capital positively affects the likelihood of making a first unauthorized trip, but it has no effect on making a first authorized trip. Thus, having a parent or sibling with international migration experience significantly increases the likelihood of making a first unauthorized trip. In contrast, gender displays robust effects in both models. Being female depresses the likelihood of making a first authorized or unauthorized international trip.

In addition to migrant social capital, household status also operates differently across the two models. Spouses are much more likely to make an authorized trip, but persons other than spouses are less likely than household heads to make an unauthorized trip. What is interesting is that age profiles for those making an authorized or unauthorized trip differ, too. That is, those making a first authorized trip are older than those making a first unauthorized trip. Relative to those 15 years old or younger, those who are older are significantly more likely to make a first authorized trip. By contrast, compared to the reference category, only those who are 15–19 years of age up through the age group 30–34 are more likely to make a first unauthorized trip. Among those older than 35 years, however, there are no age differences in making a first unauthorized trip.

Year of first trip also documents different effects across the two models. Relative to those making a first trip before 1980, the likelihood of making an initial authorized trip is significantly different (and positive) in 2005–2009 and in 2010–2012. However, the chance of making a first unauthorized trip is considerably greater in every period since 1980, compared to 1973–1979. We also see substantial spatial variability in the upazila coefficients, and there are differences across the two models. For example, people from Morrelganj and Kalia—two very poor areas that differ in terms of water quality and access to other resources—are much more likely to have made a first unauthorized trip; but

TABLE 1
Logistic Regression Model Predicting First International Migration Trip:
Legal and Unauthorized Trips

	Legal Migration		Unauthorized Migration	
	B	SE[a]	B	SE[a]
Migrant social capital				
International migrant parent (ref = none)	0.709	0.447	0.995***	0.258
International migrant sibling (ref = none)	0.406	0.284	0.955***	0.174
Gender (ref = male)				
Female	−3.945***	0.389	−1.093***	0.147
Household status (ref = head)				
Spouse	2.249***	0.244	0.182	0.181
Other	0.260	0.213	−0.649***	0.146
Age (ref = <15)				
15–19	1.385*	0.540	0.539**	0.187
20–24	2.299***	0.491	0.809***	0.178
25–29	2.165***	0.499	0.626**	0.199
30–34	2.277***	0.506	0.515*	0.222
35–39	1.625**	0.537	0.289	0.256
40–44	1.319*	0.603	0.311	0.286
45–49	1.273*	0.648	0.021	0.355
50+	−1.03	1.111	−0.442	0.339
Year (ref = 1973–1979)				
1980–1984	−0.844	1.230	1.288*	0.508
1985–1989	0.261	0.880	1.414**	0.492
1990–1994	1.084	0.779	1.857***	0.473
1995–1999	0.902	0.780	1.624***	0.479
2000–2004	0.931	0.774	1.968***	0.476
2005–2009	1.801*	0.752	1.802***	0.484
2010–2012	2.320**	0.753	2.172***	0.489
Upazila (ref = Sharsha)				
Mongla	−2.769***	0.730	−2.143**	0.750
Keshabpur	−2.578***	0.720	−1.804**	0.630
Narail Sadar	−0.182	0.251	−1.426*	0.558
Phultala	−2.428***	0.596	−1.465**	0.561
Satkhira Sadar	−1.290***	0.374	0.261	0.323
Tala	−1.036**	0.334	−0.227	0.360
Morrelganj	−1.281**	0.418	2.036***	0.269
Kalia	0.149	0.217	2.111***	0.263
Constant	−9.30***		−8.74***	
Chi-square	351.31***		237.00***	
Pseudo R-squared	.225		.164	
Person-years	209,350		209,350	

a. Robust standard errors that adjust for within-individual cluster correlation.
*p < .05. **p < .01. ***p < .001.

FIGURE 1

Cumulative Probability of First International Migration Trip by Age 44 by Migrant Social Capital Type and Legal Status

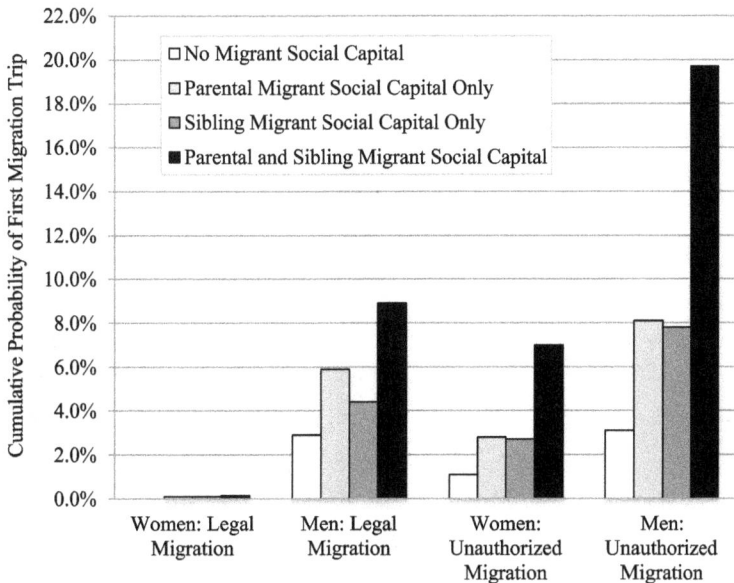

NOTE: Cumulative probabilities generated from logistic regression models presented in Table 1.

those from areas with higher literacy and education levels, such as Keshabpur and Phultala, were significantly less likely to make a first unauthorized (or authorized) trip.

To visualize these effects, we calculate cumulative probabilities of making a first authorized and unauthorized international trip by age 44, from the models in Table 1. Figure 1 presents these cumulative risks for women and men by type of migrant social capital and legal status. It shows that having two forms of migrant social capital increases respondents' lifetime chances of making a first trip. Among men, the chance of making a first unauthorized trip by age 44 is highest, at approximately 20 percent, if they have both a sibling and parent with migrant experience. Having just one form of social capital is associated with an 8 percent chance of making a first unauthorized trip; whereas the cumulative risk, by age 44, for men having no social capital is just 3 percent.

Among women, the lifetime risk of making a first unauthorized trip is also highest for those with both forms of migrant social capital, although their overall risk is much lower than that for men. The chances that women, by age 44, make a first illegal trip with access to one form of social capital is smaller, and having no social capital yields a lifetime risk of just 1 percent. Correspondingly, the chances that men, by age 44, make a first authorized trip are highest for those

FIGURE 2

Cumulative Probability of First International Migration Trip by Age 44 by Period and Legal Status

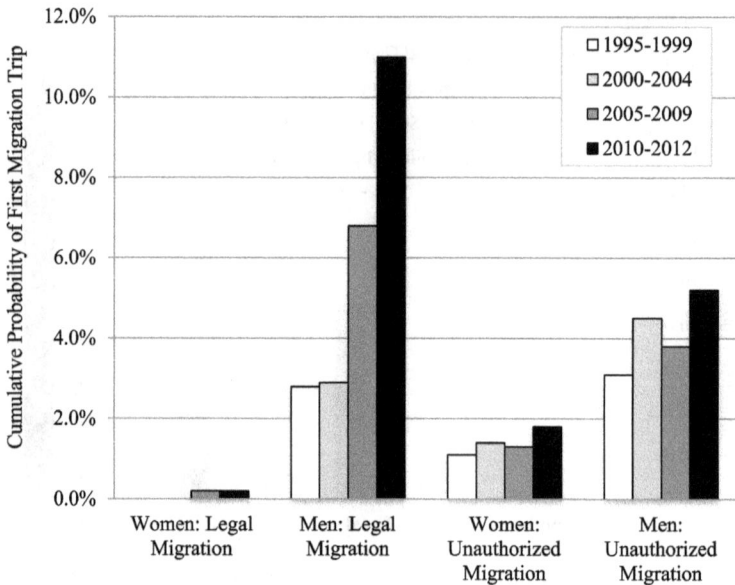

NOTE: Cumulative probabilities generated from logistic regression models presented in Table 2.

with access to both forms of social capital and lowest for those without migrant social capital. Among women, migrant social capital does not differentiate their cumulative chances, which are close to zero.

Figure 2 offers a different view of the cumulative risks of making first international trips by period of first trip and legal status. These probabilities dramatically illustrate growth in men's cumulative chances over time. For example, the chance of men making a first authorized trip, by age 44, was highest in 2010–2012. Compared to a cumulative risk of just 3 percent in 1995–1999 and in 2000–2004, the chance that men make a first authorized trip jumps to approximately 7 percent in 2005–2009, and then rises again to 11 percent in 2010–2012. Although period of entry differentiates the lifetime chances that men migrate without legal documents, it does so to a much lesser extent. In 1995–1999, the risk is just 3 percent; and by 2010–2012, it increases to 5 percent. Among women, period of entry has little effect on their chances of making a first unauthorized trip and no effect on making a first documented trip.

We now shift gears to examine the effects of legal status in regression models that predict four labor market outcomes of Bangladeshi international migrants. Table 2 presents models that predict hours worked per week, whether migrants obtained their jobs through social contacts, whether they paid taxes, and whether

TABLE 2
Results for Regression Models Predicting Economic Outcomes on Most Recent International Migration Trip (Individual-Level Analysis)

	1. Hours Worked		2. Social Contacts for Job		3. Paid Taxes		4. Bank Account	
	B	SE[a]	B	SE[a]	B	SE[a]	B	SE[a]
Demographic characteristics								
Age at migration (years)	-0.136	0.109	-0.001	0.013	0.003	0.021	0.007	0.021
Household head (ref = other)	6.209*	2.887	0.227	0.350	-0.761	0.512	-0.409	0.506
Female (ref = male)	3.688	4.833	0.353	0.626	-1.032	1.145	0.135	0.869
Migration characteristics								
Unauthorized trip (ref = legal)	-8.815***	2.471	0.937**	0.294	-1.919***	0.457	-2.705***	0.525
Years 2005–2012 (ref = 1973–2004)	6.862*	2.662	0.609	0.329	-1.156*	0.515	-0.391	0.512
More than one migration trip (ref = one trip)	-0.73	3.145	-0.159	0.375	1.010*	0.491	0.364	0.520
Purpose of trip to earn money (ref = other)	19.599*	7.657	0.097	1.054	-0.197	0.891	0.918	1.139
Constant	37.295***		-0.595		-0.08		-1.485	
Pseudo R-squared/R-squared	.088		.046		.158		.214	
N	271		270		285		287	

NOTE: Model 1 is an OLS regression model, and models 2–4 are logistic regression models.
$^*p < .05.$ $^{**}p < .01.$ $^{***}p < .001.$

they opened a bank account while on their international trip. (Table A2 in the appendix presents means and standard deviations for the variables in these models.) Using ordinary least squares (OLS) and logistic regression, we examine the effects of demographic and migration characteristics, including legal status. Coefficients in model 1 reveal an especially strong effect for legal status: unauthorized migrants worked fewer hours per week than authorized migrants. Being a household head, migrating in 2005–2012, and reporting that the purpose of the trip was to earn money increased the numbers of hours international migrants worked.

Table 2 also shows that, for the remaining three outcomes, unauthorized status is a key predictor. Being on an international trip without legal documents increases the likelihood of using social contacts to find a job, and it reduces the odds of paying taxes or opening a bank account, net of other relevant variables. In addition, only when predicting taxpaying among international migrants do two other significant effects appear. Compared to migrating between 1973 and 2004, migrating between 2005 and 2012 lowers the chance of paying taxes. However, having migration experience beyond a first trip raises that chance.

Summary and Conclusion

Using a new data source that contains migration histories of residents in southwestern Bangladesh, we examine whether and how legal status affects international migration. Our findings suggest that legal status is a powerful attribute that stratifies the process of international migration from Bangladesh in ways that are similar to those reported in other global migration circuits. The process of making a first international trip varies considerably by legal status. For example, the chances of making a first unauthorized trip are substantially greater for those who have access to migrant social capital, and for those making a first trip after 1979. In addition, being unauthorized reduces the number of hours that migrants work. It also lowers their odds of paying taxes or opening a bank account but increases the odds that they use social contacts to find jobs in their international destinations.

These findings, taken together, suggest that even among international migrants from Bangladesh, a nation that faces large-scale environmental challenges from climate change and other forms of anthropogenic degradation, legal status operates in salient ways to stratify and differentiate migration. Similar to the disadvantages extensively documented in prior studies about Mexican migrants in the United States, being unauthorized structures the daily experiences and social relationships of Bangladeshi migrants in ways that are different from their authorized counterparts. These findings, together with those from other articles in this volume, suggest that the laws, political narratives, and institutional social structures that exist around global migration in the early-twenty-first century similarly affect the lives of international migrants.

Appendix

TABLE A1

Means and Standard Deviations of Variables Used in Analysis (Person-Year Analysis)

	Mean	SD
Dependent variables		
Legal international migration in PY	0.001	0.025
Unauthorized international migration in PY	0.002	0.040
Independent variables		
Migrant social capital		
International migrant parent (ref = none)	0.014	0.116
International migrant sibling (ref = none)	0.044	0.206
Gender (ref = male)		
Female	0.521	0.500
Household status (ref = head)		
Spouse	0.252	0.434
Other	0.461	0.498
Age (ref = <15)		
15–19	0.134	0.341
20–24	0.119	0.323
25–29	0.099	0.299
30–34	0.079	0.269
35–39	0.060	0.237
40–44	0.046	0.209
45–49	0.032	0.176
50+	0.062	0.240
Year (ref = 1973–1979)		
1980–1984	0.084	0.278
1985–1989	0.106	0.308
1990–1994	0.129	0.335
1995–1999	0.147	0.354
2000–2004	0.151	0.358
2005–2009	0.149	0.356
2010–2012	0.147	0.355
Upazila (ref = Sharsha)		
Mongla	0.107	0.309
Keshabpur	0.119	0.324
Narail Sadar	0.111	0.314
Phultala	0.108	0.310
Satkhira Sadar	0.122	0.327
Tala	0.112	0.315
Morrelganj	0.097	0.296
Kalia	0.125	0.331
Person-years	209,350	

TABLE A2
Means of Variables Used in Analysis by Legal Status of Most Recent International
Migration Trip (Individual-Level Analysis)

	Total	Legal	Unauthorized
Dependent variables			
Hours worked per week	55.00	59.34	52.25
Obtained job through social networks	0.63	0.50	0.71
Paid taxes	0.13	0.26	0.05
Had a bank account	0.15	0.32	0.03
Independent variables			
Demographic characteristics			
Age at migration (years)	29.52	29.97	29.22
Household head (ref = other)	0.60	0.37	0.76
Female (ref = male)	0.06	0.04	0.07
Migration characteristics			
Unauthorized trip (ref = legal)	0.60	—	—
Years 2005–2012 (ref = 1973–2004)	0.59	0.70	0.51
More than one migration trip (ref = one trip)	0.15	0.17	0.14
Purpose of trip to earn money (ref = other)	0.97	0.95	0.98
N	287	172	115

Notes

1. Nonmigration adaptation strategies include growing saline resistant crops (Rabbani, Rahman, and Mainuddin 2013), using agricultural calendars to sync with the changing weather patterns (Meze-Hausken 2004), and shifting economic livelihoods to shrimp farms (Islam 2008; Azad, Jensen, and Lin 2009).

2. Other studies examine the effects of migration in Bangladesh on health. Kuhn (2005) focuses on the relationship between adult children's migration and the health of their parents in Matlab, a rural area in Bangladesh. He finds that son's migration is positively and significantly associated with parents' survival and physical functioning, but daughter's migration had no health effects.

References

Abrego, Leisy. 2008. Legitimacy, social identity, and the mobilization of low: The effects of Assembly Bill 540 on undocumented students in California. *Law and Social Inquiry* 33 (3): 709–34.
Adams, Brad. 23 January 2011. India's shoot-to-kill policy on the Bangladesh border. *The Guardian*.
Agrawala, Shardul, Tomoko Ota, Ahsan Uddin Ahmed, Joel Smith, and Maarten van Aalst. 2003. *Development and climate change in Bangladesh: Focus on coastal flooding and the Sundarbans*. Paris: Organisation for Economic Co-operation and Development.
Azad, Abul Kalam, Kathe R. Jensen, and C. Kwei Lin. 2009. Coastal aquaculture development in Bangladesh: Unsustainable and sustainable experiences. *Environmental Management* 44 (4): 800–809.
Bureau of Manpower, Employment and Training (BMET). 2015. *Overseas employment and remittances from 1976-2015 (up to September)*. Dhaka: BMET. Available from http://www.bmet.org.bd/BMET/stattisticalDataAction# (accessed 17 October 2015).
Chacón, Jennifer M. Forthcoming. Producing liminal legality. *Denver University Law Review*.

Datta, Dilip Kumar, Kushal Roy, and Nazia Hassan. 2010. Shrimp culture: Trend, consequences, and sustainability in the south-western coastal region of Bangladesh. In *Management and sustainable development of coastal zone environments*, eds. Alagappan Ramanathan, Piyal Bhattacharya, Thorsten Dittmar, Mathukumalli Bala Kriishna Prasad, and Ramji Prasad Neupane, 227–44. Dordrecht: Springer.

Donato, Katharine M., Michael Aguilera, and Chizuko Wakabayashi. 2005. Immigration policy and employment conditions of U.S. immigrants from Mexico, Nicaragua, and the Dominican Republic. *International Migration* 43 (5): 5–29.

Donato, Katharine M., Amanda Carrico, Blake Sisk, and Bhumika Piya. 2016. Social capital, environmental conditions, and out-migration from Bangladesh. Paper presented at the annual meeting of the Population Association of America, Washington, DC.

Donato, Katharine M., Jorge Durand, and Douglas S. Massey. 1992. Changing conditions in the U.S. labor market. *Population Research and Policy Review* 11 (2): 93–115.

Donato, Katharine M., and Douglas S. Massey. 1993. Effect of the Immigration Reform and Control Act on the wages of Mexican migrants. *Social Science Quarterly* 74 (3): 523–41.

Donato, Katharine M., and Blake Sisk. 2012. Shifts in the employment outcomes among Mexican migrants to the United States, 1976–2009. *Research in Social Stratification and Mobility* 30 (1): 63–77.

Donato, Katharine M., Chizuko Wakabayashi, Shirin Hakimzadeh, and Amada Armenta. 2008. Shifts in the employment conditions of Mexican migrant men and women. *Work and Occupations* 35 (4): 462–95.

Durand, Jorge, Douglas S. Massey, and Karen A. Pren. 2016. Double disadvantage: Unauthorized Mexicans the U.S. labor market. *The ANNALS of the American Academy of Political and Social Science* (this volume).

The Economist. 7 January 2016. More neighbours make more fences. Available from http://www.economist.com.

Gonzales, Roberto G. 2008. Left out but not shut down: Political activism and the undocumented Latino student movement. *Northwestern Journal of Law and Social Policy* 3 (2): 219–39.

Government Office for Science. 2011. *Foresight: Migration and global environmental change*. London: The Government Office of Science. Available from https://www.gov.uk/government/organisations/government-office-for-science.

Gray, Clark L., and Valerie Mueller. 2012. Natural disasters and population mobility in Bangladesh. *Proceedings of the National Academy of Sciences* 109 (16): 6000–6005.

Hall, Matthew, Emily Greenman, and George Farkas. 2010. Legal status and wage disparities for Mexican immigrants. *Social Forces* 89 (2): 491–513.

Harris, Gardiner. 28 March 2014. Borrowed time on disappearing land: Facing rising seas, Bangladesh confronts the consequences of climate change. *New York Times*.

Human Rights Watch. 24 July 2011. India: New killings, torture at Bangladeshi border. Available from https://www.hrw.org/news/2011/07/24/india-new-killings-torture-bangladeshi-border.

Islam, Muhammad. 2008. *Toward certification and ecolabelling: A compliance study of Bangladesh shrimp aquaculture*. Tokyo: United Nations University, Fisheries Training Program. Available from http://www.unuftp.is/static/fellows/document/seraj08prfa.pdf.

Kartiki, Katha. 2011. Climate change and migration: A case study from rural Bangladesh. *Gender and Development* 19 (1): 23–38.

Kuhn, Randall S. 2005. The determinants of family and individual migration: A case-study of rural Bangladesh. Working Paper, Institute of Behavioral Science, Research Program on Population Processes, University of Colorado at Boulder.

Massey, Douglas S. 2007. *Categorically unequal: The American stratification system*. New York, NY: Russell Sage Foundation.

Massey, Douglas S., Jorge Durand, and Nolan J. Malone. 2002. *Beyond smoke and mirrors: Mexican immigration in an age of economic integration*. New York, NY: Russell Sage Foundation.

Massey, Douglas S., and Kerstin Gentsch. 2014. Undocumented migration and the wages of Mexican immigrants in the United States. *International Migration Review* 48 (2): 482–99.

Menjívar, Cecilia. 2006. Liminal legality: Salvadoran and Guatemalan immigrants' lives in the United States. *American Journal of Sociology* 111 (4): 999–1037.

Meze-Hausken, Elisabeth. 2004. Contrasting climate variability and meteorological drought with perceived drought and climate change in northern Ethiopia. *Climate Research* 27:19–31.

Oishi, Nana. 2005. *Women in motion: Globalization, state policies, and labor migration in Asia*. Stanford, CA: Stanford University Press.

Phillips, Julie A., and Douglas S. Massey. 1999. The new labor market: Immigrants and wages after IRCA. *Demography* 36 (2): 233–46.

Rabbani, Golam, Atiq Rahman, and Khandaker Mainuddin. 2013. Salinity-induced loss and damage to farming households in coastal Bangladesh. *International Journal of Global Warming* 5 (4): 400–415.

Rogers, Kimberly G., James P. M. Syvitski, Irina Overeem, Stephanie Higgins, and Jonathan M. Gilligan. 2013. Farming practices and anthropogenic delta dynamics. *Proceedings of HP1, IAHS-IAPSO-IASPEI Assembly* 358:133–42.

Siddiqui, Tasneem. 2005. *International labour migration from Bangladesh: A decent work perspective*. Geneva, Switzerland: Policy Integration Department, National Policy Group, International Labour Office.

Sussex Center for Migration Research and Refugee and Migratory Movements Research Unit. 2013. *Making migration decisions amid climate change in Bangladesh*. Sussex and Dhaka: Sussex Center for Migration Research and Refugee and Migration Movements Research Unit.

World Bank. n.d. *World databank: World development indicators*. Washington, DC: World Bank. Available from http://databank.worldbank.org/data/home.aspx (accessed 7 October 2015).

World Health Organization (WHO) and UNICEF (United Nations Children's Emergency Fund). 2014. *Progress on drinking water and sanitation*. Geneva, Switzerland: WHO. Available from http://www.unicef.org/gambia/Progress_on_drinking_water_and_sanitation_2014_update.pdf (accessed 16 January 2016).

SAGE Deep Backfile Package

Content ownership is becoming increasingly important in hard budgetary times. Investing in the SAGE Deep Backfile Package means owning access to over 400 SAGE journal backfiles.

5 good reasons to own the deep archive from SAGE...

1. Breadth

SAGE has collected over 400 journal backfiles, including over 500,000 articles of historical content covering interdisciplinary subjects in business, humanities, socials science, and science, technology and medicine.

2. Depth

SAGE's deep backfile coverage goes to volume 1, issue 1; through the last issue of 1998 (content from January 1999 to the present is included in the current subscription). You will own content spanning over a century of research. Our oldest article is from 1879 in **Perspectives in Public Health** (formerly *The Journal of the Royal Society for the Promotion of Health*).

3. Quality

We pride ourselves on high-quality content, meeting our markets' need for interdisciplinary, peer-reviewed, journal backfiles to provide your library. Close to 50% of the journals in the entire **SAGE Deep Backfile Package** are ranked in the Thomson Reuters Journal Citation Reports®.

4. Award-winning *SAGE Journals* online delivery platform

Materials are easy to find on *SAGE Journals* (SJ), hosted on the prestigious HighWire Press platform.

5. Pricing

We offer **flexible backfile purchase and lease options** to accommodate library budgets of all sizes. This package option offers the most value for your money, including great savings off list price for individual journal backfile purchases.

In compliance with GPSR, should you have any concerns about the safety of this
product, please advise: International Associates Auditing & Certification
Limited The Black Church, St Mary's Place, Dublin 7, D07 P4AX Ireland
EUAR@ie.ia-net.com

www.ingramcontent.com/pod-product-compliance
Lightning Source LLC
Chambersburg PA
CBHW072121020426
42334CB00018B/1677